RETURN OF THE OSPREY

RETURN OF THE

Osprey

A Season of Flight and Wonder

by David Gessner

ALGONQUIN BOOKS OF CHAPEL HILL

2001

Published by
Algonquin Books of Chapel Hill
Post Office Box 2225
Chapel Hill, North Carolina 27515-2225

a division of
Workman Publishing
708 Broadway
New York, New York 10003

Library of Congress Cataloging-in-Publication Data
Gessner, David, 1961–
    Return of the osprey : a season of flight and wonder /
by David Gessner.
        p. cm.
    Includes bibliographical references.
    ISBN 1-56512-254-2 (hardcover)
    1. Osprey—Massachusetts—Cape Cod.   I. Title.
QL696.F36 G48 2001
598.9'3'0974492—dc21   00-068230

10 9 8 7 6 5 4 3 2 1
First Edition

To my mother,
Barbara Gessner,
and
to John Hay,
who journeyed here
and called it home

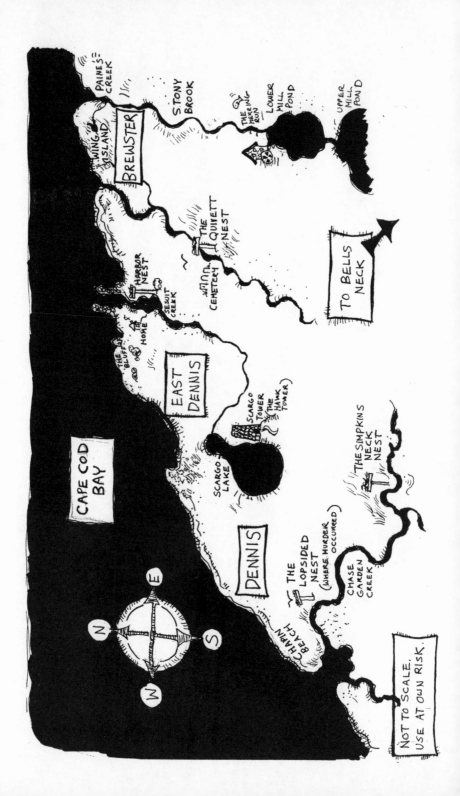

CONTENTS

As a group, with their masterly powers of flight and their swashbuckling mode of life, the birds of prey are by far the most exciting and romantic of all our breeding species. . . . The "King of the Birds," the eagle is recognized the world over as a symbol of power and flight; but surely Nature in the course of evolution has not fashioned anything quite so superb in every way as the osprey.

—*George Waterson*

Every man is followed by a shadow which is his death—dark, featureless, and mute. And for every man there is a place where his shadow is clarified and is made his reflection, where his face is mirrored in the ground. He sees his source and his destiny, and they are acceptable to him. He becomes the follower of what pursued him. What hounded his tracks becomes his companion.

That is the myth of my search and my return.

—*Wendell Berry*

RETURN OF THE OSPREY

Openings

M arch is the waiting time. Everything poised, ready to become something else, a world in need of a nudge. The buds on the old post oak bulge hard as knuckles, the first blades of grass cut through the dark purple rim of the cranberry bog, and the willow branches yearn toward yellow. Almost every morning I watch the sun edge its way up over the harbor, and the world it lights grows steadily greener and warmer. While the season itself may waver uncertainly, the birds insist on spring. As I head out for my morning walk, all of Sesuit Neck seems caught in the upward twirl of birdsong. Cardinals whistle their upward whistle, mourning doves coo, and the brambles fill with the chittering of finches and chickadees.

Down at the beach two hundred sanderlings cover the end of the jetty, and when I walk toward them they take off as one, veering east, showing their white bellies, skimming over the water before banking and heading right back toward me. Just when it looks like I'll die a silly death—pierced by the beaks of a hundred small birds—they split like a curtain around my body. Then the split groups split, heading off in seemingly random directions before joining up, reshuffling, and then—*one* again—banking, their white bellies flicking to blackish backs like a magic trick. They put on their show for some time before tiring of it, and I watch, half stunned, thinking how this sight has come like a sign of early spring or the definition of grace, an undeserved gift.

Is it my imagination or do all of us—animal, plant, and human
—take a raw, near-doltish pleasure in the coming season? This,
more than January, seems the time of year for resolutions, and I
have already made mine. I have vowed to spend more time outside. It's true I've lived a fairly pastoral life over the past two years,
walking the beach daily, but this year I want to live more out than
in, to break away from desk and computer, and see if I can fully
immerse myself in the life of Sesuit Neck, the life outside of me.
"Explore the mystery" was the advice the Cape Cod writer Robert
Finch gave me long ago. That is what I'll do. Specifically, I have
vowed to spend more time with my neighbors; more specifically,
with those neighbors who nest nearby: the ospreys. Also known
as fish hawks, these birds, with their magnificent, nearly six-foot
wingspans, will soon return to Cape Cod from their wintering
grounds in South America. One man-made osprey platform, which
will hopefully be the site for a nest, stands directly across the harbor from me, the pole on which it rests bisecting the March sunrise. In anticipation of the opsreys' arrival I, like a Peeping Tom,
aim my binoculars directly from my living room into theirs. Other
nearby pairs have nested out at Quivett Creek, on the end of the
western jetty, on Simpkins Neck, and on the marsh by Chapin
Beach, and so I set out every day on my rounds, wanting to be
there to greet them, hoping to catch the return of these great birds
on the wing. So far there's been no sign, and I fear I'm being stood
up. But that just adds to the building anticipation of this indeci-
sive month, and soon enough they'll fill the air with their high-
pitched calls, strong eagle flapping, and fierce dives.

THESE WERE SIGHTS I never saw growing up in the 1960s
and '70s. Not a single osprey pair nested on Sesuit Neck when
I spent summers here as a child. For me these sights were as
mythic and distant as those described by early pioneers heading
west: migrations of thousands—*millions*—of birds, when the

sun would be blotted out and the whole sky darkened for an hour.

Of course, the ospreys weren't that chronologically distant. Only thirty years earlier, in the 1930s, they had dotted the New England shore, nesting on every high perch they could find. In the late 1940s Roger Tory Peterson wrote of how the abundant osprey "symbolized the New England Coast more than any other bird," and when Peterson moved to Old Lyme, Connecticut, in 1954, he found, within a ten-mile radius of his home, "approximately 150 occupied Osprey nests." But soon after this the decline of the ospreys began, a decline caused directly by residual DDT in the fish that made up their entire diet. The birds were nearly killed off in New England, pesticides contaminating their eggs and preventing them from hatching, wiping out 90 percent of the osprey population between 1950 and 1975.

The situation on Cape Cod was even more complicated. Here the birds had been dealt a double blow. This land is a recovering one, coming back from earlier environmental devastation. By the mid-1800s there was hardly a tree left on the Cape, all viable lumber having been cut down for the building of ships. Without their primary nesting requirement—trees—few ospreys nested here. A century later, DDT did in those few. The writer John Hay, our most penetrating local observer, has little memory of ospreys on Cape Cod in the years after World War II. Twice within two hundred years, in ways characteristic of each century, we found ways to expel birds that had likely bred here since the Ice Age.

Now the birds are back. It has been a gradual comeback, a refilling of old niches. By the late 1970s a few birds had returned, by the '80s many more, and now a sudden rush. Only recently, in the mid-'90s, have the ospreys begun to reinhabit my town, East Dennis.

The story of the ospreys is a hopeful one in many ways, a rare example of humans reversing our tendency to try to control nature, of recognizing that we have done wrong and then correcting it. It's also the story of the possibility of cohabitation. Who could imagine a more wild sight than an osprey spotting a mere shadow of a fish from a hundred feet above the sea and diving into the water headlong, emerging with the fish in its talons? And yet this wild creature next turns the fish straight ahead for better aerodynamics, carrying it like a purse, flapping home to a nest that sits directly above a car-littered parking lot. Ospreys aren't picky about their homesites. In addition to trees, they commonly nest on utility and telephone poles, above highways, and atop buoys near constant boat traffic. Osprey expert and author Alan Poole sees this as a sign of their remarkable adaptability. Thanks in large part to this adaptability, the birds give us the gift of the wild in the midst of the civilized. I understand that it's a fallacy to see nature as a kind of self-help guide for humans, but there may be a lesson here. Perhaps we, too, can retain some of our wildness while living in this increasingly cluttered, concrete world.

WHILE I'VE VOWED to spend more time with the birds this spring, I will try not to draw too many lessons from them. That is, I'll try to resist the temptations of my own hyperactive imagination. It isn't easy. A few years back, during a year spent on Cape Cod, I saw my first osprey, and couldn't help but also see my own life mirrored in the phoenixlike rise of the bird. I was thirty going on eighteen, and my world spun in tight solipsistic circles. Perhaps I made too much of the fact that DDT and its residues had also been found to lead to an increase in the rate of testicular cancer. Having suffered from that disease and survived, I felt even more connected to the fish hawks, and even more joyous about their comeback and return to the Cape. Connections crackled; their fierce revival boded well for my own. The interconnectedness of our worlds excited me.

Two springs ago, in 1997, I returned to live on Cape Cod

again, but there were many differences from my earlier year. The first time I'd wintered alone on the Cape, looking to Thoreau as my guide, but this time I brought Nina with me. It was Walden with a wife, and I worried about having dragged my mate away from her beloved western mountains, back to a cold lair of a house where ocean winds buffeted the uninsulated walls. "There's no such thing as spring on Cape Cod," said our neighbor Heidi Schadt, and we tended to agree. The meteorologists called it spring, of course, though they also called it the coldest on record; it didn't get up to seventy through the first week of June. "It's like living on a ship," Nina said (happily at first). And it was. The creaking beams were the ship's belly, the dinging flagpole our mast, the back porch our poop deck, the surrounding vegetation waves and the gulls a hopeful sign of land. But when landfall didn't come we got stir-crazy, feared scurvy, and dreamed of the true spring we were missing back in Colorado. I tried to stay upbeat, since moving had been my idea, and pointed out to my wife that the birds and buds were carrying on *as if* it were spring: the post oak exploding dully and drooping with leaves like dud bottle rockets, the honeysuckle blooming, and the bushes around the house filling in daily like a beard. But Nina didn't seem entirely convinced.

Why had we come back?

Besides more practical reasons, I'd had a hunch that we might be able to live cheaply and spend an off-season of fires, beach walks, baths, naps, and writing. "The world is sick for lack of elemental things," wrote Henry Beston in *The Outermost House,* and it was elemental things we were after. Spring thoughts raced ahead to the next fall: to getting a cord of wood (or three) and living, writing, and chopping wood and walking the beach every day. There were worse ways to watch a year go round.

But, while we had tentatively begun to answer "writers" when people asked us what we did, the truth was that our profession had yet to yield up much cash. While we were essentially squatting in my family home, the house, if a boat, was a leaky one, and the oil and electricity bills rivaled what we had paid for rent back in Colorado. *Back in Colorado,* of course, was where our thoughts often strayed: to a front range filled with friends and belongings and joint memories that became more paradisical with each passing second.

But if I had doubts, they were eased with my first walk out the jetty. It was a walk I'd walked a thousand times before, as comfortable as the old sweats I'd taken to wearing day and night, and, despite the novelty of being back, I didn't expect to see anything new. And not expecting to see the new, I didn't, not even the huge, tattered nest that drooped over the small warning light at jetty's end. It was *my* beach, after all—tame and known despite the wildness I purported to celebrate.

Surprise came in size and movement. The flash of wings and a high-pitched warning cry, as loud and unmistakable as a car alarm. It was too big to be a bird, but a bird it was, dropping off the nest and lifting skyward with strong eagle flaps. The shine of white and chocolate brown—a white, proud chest and black-brown wings and bandit eye-band—against a green sea that heaved up as if trying to knock me into it. For almost as long as I could walk I'd come out to the end of these rocks and never seen a sight like that. For the first time since I was born, a pair of ospreys were nesting at the end of the western jetty of Sesuit Harbor.

Soon the drama of the ospreys became the drama of our year, easing the gloom of that first rainy spring. Each day I would stake out a spot at a respectful distance behind the last jutting rock, a distance that wouldn't provoke the car alarm or the protective circling of whichever bird wasn't tending the nest. I found I could tell them apart: the larger female wore a dark speckled necklace on her white throat, the smaller male more purely white. I spent hours on the jetty, and while it's true I was a voyeur, I tried to be a quiet one. For a few weeks I watched. Watched as they flew over to collect sticks—and sometimes full branches—from the bluff to repair the nest each morning after another stormy night; watched as they carried fish home, turned straight in their torpedo-like fashion; watched as the male perched on the small reflector next to the nest and tore off chunks of fish until, apparently sated, he switched positions with his mate, handing off what was left of the meal.

For all the movement and effort that spring, the birds' main activity was a sedentary one: the dull and vital job of nesting, of staking out a place for oneself and one's family. Most of the nesting was done by the female, the male occasionally relieving her. "We are all precarious nesters," I scribbled in my journal. As fascinated as I was by the birds' behavior, I was equally fascinated by the nest itself. "An osprey's work is never done," said Nina, and that seemed so. As important as eating obviously was, during early spring nest repair was the top priority, at least in terms of time allotment. This required constant circling trips from the jetty's end over to the bluff, picking up, say, a clump of seaweed, flapping back into the gusts, hovering above the nest, balancing in the wind, and finally dropping off that trip's deposit before landing to pack it down. Then another trip for a branch or a sheet of plastic or some boat line from over by Northside Marina. That was the thing about the nest: unlike environmentalists, the birds didn't bother with the niceties of organic materials—anything would do. And, for all the work they put into it, there was something essentially unkempt, even sloppy, about the nest's appearance. Sticks jutted out like bowsprits, plastic sheets flapped in the wind, strands of line hung down like floss.

Of course, while neatness may count, a certain battered look could be forgiven when you factored in the nightly beating the nest was taking. As windy as it was in the day—and I often had trouble walking out to the end of the jetty if it was blowing from the north—at night it began to sound as if someone were slamming a sledge against the seaside wall of our house. Nina and I built fires and huddled close, and we took to going to bed early with the cats and pulling up the covers to block out the howling and shrill whistling as the wind streamed through the harbor masts. If there was something romantic about this, there was also something cold. What would it be like to spend a night out at the end of the jetty, exposed to a wind that built up speed across the bay, as well as to the nearly nightly rains? Perhaps the birds could be forgiven if they looked a little harried in the morning, and if their home was less than meticulous.

It was during that cold spring of 1997 that I finally started to become more curious about my neighbors' affairs. I drove over to the Cape Cod Museum of Natural History and took out Alan Poole's comprehensive book on ospreys. I read about how the birds are "mostly" monogamous, though there are exceptions, and about how the nests have to be open from above because, while great fliers, ospreys don't maneuver well in closed spaces. I also read about their majestic "fish dance" or "sky dance" and copied down a traditional song of the West African Senegalese fisherman:

> Osprey, the special one
> Fisherman of the sea,
> He does not have nets,
> He does not beg for fish,
> And he eats only fat fish,
> The fisherman and his boat,
> The Osprey and his skills,
> There will be no lack of fish.

SOMETIMES, FOR ALL our efforts, nesting doesn't take. To work hard, obsessively hard—dawn-to-dusk hard—and to get nothing in return is common enough in the animal world. Once the weather finally broke that spring there came a terrible day when the human fisherman began to crowd the end of the jetty near the osprey nest. The first time it happened my face went flush. I felt angry, panicked. A half dozen men and women stood right below the nest, oblivious to the agitated bird flapping and screeching above them. I walked out to my spot by the rock and watched as one man (wearing appropriate plunderer's garb: an Oakland Raiders sweatshirt and a leather jacket) leaned his back against the structure that supported the nest itself. Only the female was home, and she flapped around nervously for ten minutes before flying off. I weighed the effectiveness of delivering the lecture I could feel building inside me but, deciding it would do no good, swallowed my rage and retreated to the beach. Before heading home, I took one last look back through my binoculars and saw an astounding sight. Dusk had begun to drive most of the people away, but one teenage girl remained and, before leaving, she decided a final indignity was in order. As I watched, she walked up to the warning light, climbed the supporting structure, and peered right into the nest.

Hoping she wouldn't yell for the police when she saw the man charging out the jetty toward her, I calmed myself so that I could politely explain the situation: these birds had been trying to nest here since March and they deserved some degree of privacy and respect. I lied and told her that I was with the Wellfleet Audubon Society and that we'd soon be erecting a barrier at the second rock. She was friendly enough, nodding and saying "uh-huh" to my explanation, but when I asked her not to disturb the nest again, she replied casually: "Oh, it's no problem. I didn't even see any eggs in there."

After she left I stayed out at my rock for another hour. But the ospreys did not return.

. . .

THE NEXT MORNING the world was back in place, at least temporarily. The female was nesting again, and the male was going about the morning chore of nest repairs. She sat hook-nosed, looking satisfied, while he worked around the house. When I got home I called the town environmental office, told them the situation (which they already knew about), and asked if a barrier was going to be erected. They told me that, yes, it would be, and within a week the barrier was up, despite the grumbling of the fishermen. From well behind the barrier I watched as the ospreys again hunkered down low, riding out the end of a cold, windy May.

But they'd begun to spend more and more time away from the nest. By Memorial Day, when the white apple blossoms bloomed, it was still cold, and by early June the nest was sagging down like Rasta dreadlocks. The female remained deeply intent on nesting, or what I thought was nesting, her proud bandit-masked head down low, just above the nest's rim; only, according to the books I'd taken out of the library, the young should have hatched by then, and there was no sign of them. Despite this the male continued to play along, going about his work of gathering and fishing, the wind ruffling his feathers as he returned to the nest. Then on June 10 the real change finally came to the Cape, velvety summer breezes and summer sun. As Heidi Schadt had predicted, we'd had no spring, just a straight drop-off from winter to summer. Suddenly I could barbecue in shorts at six at night, and the mourning doves sounded slightly different, cooing with a still hollow but happier melancholy. The ocean grew tame, a gentle green pool that lapped at the harbor's edge. The next morning the nest was deserted. I saw the two ospreys fishing and circling together. And then a third! At the time I didn't know what to make of this. Was this one of the "mostly" monogamous situations I'd read about, the occasional threesome? Had the nest failed?

On the morning of the summer solstice the nest was again deserted, looking even more tattered and windblown than it had during the worst of the winter weather. I watched awhile, and sure enough the male and female, without the mysterious third, appeared. She swooped in from below and glided up above the nest before landing, while he, with a fish in his talons, had a harder time maneuvering into it. They rested for a while before flying off, the fish still intact. The nest, it seemed, had become no more than a pit stop.

In fact, that was the last time I saw them in the nest. Later, in mid-July, hiking in the marsh behind the graveyard where my father is buried, I saw three ospreys and thought they might have been the jetty birds, but from the distance I couldn't be sure. My books informed me that ospreys fly south in September, but ours were gone by August.

As I SAY, sometimes nesting doesn't take. A depressing story perhaps, and one without a warm and fuzzy moral for Nina and me. But during the next winter another osprey platform was erected across the harbor, and by March 1998 I began taking frequent walks, filled with the excitement of anticipation. It wasn't until mid-April that I noticed the ospreys taking up residence. Drinking my tea each morning during our second spring back, I would stand on our back deck and watch as they flew off to search for branches, observing their nest from mine. They had gotten a late start, and, like the last pair, were immature, and it would come to pass that they would produce no young. But they often flew right over the house, emitting their by then familiar cries, and with neighbors like that, we decided we'd have to stay for another year. Though no birds were brave enough to try to nest again at the jetty's end, the platform at Chapin Beach and the one behind my father's gravesite were both occupied. "Don't worry about them," my neighbor Tommy Olsen, a boatbuilder, said to me. "They're like pigeons down south." Indeed, if my books were right, we might soon be approaching the number of birds that had nested here in the early nineteenth century.

By watching the pair across the harbor, I learned that I had perhaps been overprotective of the jetty ospreys the year before. Compared to other raptors, ospreys are not particularly shy or private. For instance, the harbor pair carried on their daily affairs thirty feet above a busy parking lot in the midst of summer. It is, I understand now, more likely that weather and inexperience, and not human interference, were what did in the first pair's chances of reproducing. And while I still resent that people didn't respect them enough to leave them alone, I'm glad the birds at least tried to make their desperate stand at rocks' end. Long after they'd left, in late summer and early fall, their disheveled nest still flew like a flag of wildness over our increasingly suburban neighborhood. And, thinking of it now, I see it not just as a flag of wildness but one of resilience and of hope.

NOW OUR THIRD spring is trying to eke its way out of winter. Pussy willows sprout silky goat hooves, an early herald of the time to come, but ice still flakes on the harbor banks. There is no sign of the birds this morning, but I'm content to wait, readying myself. While I look forward to their return, I also see it as something of a challenge. Having spent two years getting to know the ospreys, I now want more. I want to see things my binoculars can't help me with; in fact, adding another lens between myself and them is the opposite of what I hope for this season. Instead I'd like to remove a layer that exists between me and the birds. Perhaps what I want is the direct experience of something wild, something other than myself.

I've had hints of what I'm after. One day during Nina's and my first summer back, I stumbled through the phragmites at Quivett Creek at dusk, crashing over the crackling reeds with all the subtlety of an elephant. When I emerged from the grasses into the

marsh I found a nearly full orange moon shining with cartoon
clarity. I also found myself close, too close, to an enormous nest.
The nest was the result of a strange union, equal parts Commonwealth Electric and osprey; the birds had built their home on top
of a pole and platform that the electric company provided. But if
the nest was only half wild, I felt wholly so standing there, my feet
encased in marsh muck, with the daylight fading. From my angle,
looking almost straight up, I could see no sign of the young that
rested in the nest, but soon enough one of the parents—the
mother, I suspected—was floating nearly on top of me, less than
twenty feet away, blowing sideways and swooping back and forth
in the wind as if swaying on a giant puppet string. Her urgent cries
came faster and faster, calling out, "Don't come closer" and "Don't
hurt my babies" and, finally, urgently, *"Back off or I will hurt you!"*
For a second I didn't back off, euphoria rooting me in place, staring up at the nearly eagle-sized bird that was clearly and urgently
speaking to me. But even if I wanted desperately to stay there, to
draw that moment out as long as I could, I had to acknowledge
just what the bird was saying. And so, after a minute or two of
rudeness, I finally listened and, minding my manners, retreated
through the reeds. It only seemed fair that I give way, after all,
since I was there as a mere watcher, a collector of moments, while
she was living a life.

Now, in this new season of expectation, winter unlocking
into spring, I want to become more than a watcher. I want immersion as well as contact. I want to learn everything I can about
these wild birds, and not just by the book. So far my attempts to
know my winged neighbors have been halting and half-baked, but
it's a deeper, truer intimacy I'm after, an attempt, perhaps doomed
to failure, to see the ospreys not as a reflection of myself, but for
themselves.

I no sooner finish resolving this than my mind turns again.
While I want to greet the ospreys on their own terms, I'm not en-

tirely opposed to learning a thing or two from the birds. We hope to learn from our neighbors, after all, and I secretly hope they can teach me a little of what it means to reinhabit a place, to make a place home.

But more than lessons I simply want to be close. If these birds were once so common, why does it feel like a miracle that they have come back now? Perhaps it's because even the plain facts of the coming spring are miraculous. Almost gone from these parts forever, the osprey has rejoined life's circle. They will be arriving any day now, and I feel poised, ready. Excited by sights I'll soon see, I let the coming season infect me. I share the world's anticipation. Eager to begin.

Coming Back

I bundle in my coat, down on the marsh off Quivett Creek behind my father's grave, still waiting for the birds. The tea I bought at the corner store quickly loses its heat, my hood flaps wildly, and ducks shoot through the low, crazed morning light. After the early surge of spring, winter has reclaimed the marsh, ringing it with ice—a color scheme of deep blue and dead yellow-brown, all fringed with white. Only a week ago grainy snow echoed off the house like thrown pebbles. Now this late March has brought a string of gray days that might as well be December.

Except for the persistent hints. While the buds haven't opened yet, they are meatier, fatter, quivering with this morning's gel-like dew. And while ice still edges the marsh, the Canada geese have noisily set up shop, and the chickadees and sparrows, anticipating the warmth, have begun the frenetic scurrying activities of nest building and wooing. A red-winged blackbird sings a garbled love song on the black oak above the reeds, and this morning when I walked down the path a red-tailed hawk lifted off its roost and let out a noise part shriek, part whistle. There are human hints, too, like my neighbor Todd stacking lobster pots on the bed of his pickup.

Staring out at the platform that the ospreys will hopefully return to, I see that last year's nest has weathered the winter storms pretty well, that there will be a good base for the birds to build from. Looking at the lifeless platform through my binoculars, as if willing the ospreys to appear, I soon feel bored and cold. I gulp down the last sip of icy tea and question whether I have the necessary patience for this sort of daily discipline. The furthest thing from a scientist, I've set myself a scientist's task of observation, hoping to watch the birds at their homes throughout the season. The truth is I'm every inch an amateur. As evidence I need look no further than my footwear—running sneakers soaked through with cold, briny water—or at my enormous binoculars, circa World War II. My field guide is equally outdated, insisting that, among other things, a green heron is in fact a green-*backed* heron. But it isn't so much the equipment that's faulty. While I've been living here, on and off, all my life, I'm still ignorant of the names of most of the sedges and grasses and trees around me. Spending time in nature produces, among other results, a general feeling of stupidity, constantly reminding you of the thousands of obvious facts you don't know. I never hunted as a kid, never tramped around swamps searching for salamanders or toads. Now I worry that there's a bit of the drawing-room nature lover in me, more familiar with Thoreau than tree frogs. Sometimes I suspect that, at my worst, I like reading about nature more than nature itself.

But this season will be different. It's time to go out into it and get my hands dirty. In my favor is the simple fact of curiosity. I want to learn, want to know more. My daily walks remind me that I'm perhaps less of a phony than I imagine in more self-accusatory moods. Each afternoon I head up the beach to gather driftwood, while staring out at the harbor seals that cover Tautog rock. Some flop and lounge over the rock like mink coats on the bed at a rich lady's party, while others balance on the middle of their stomachs, bending upward like bananas at both ends, occasionally moving along in this way, a strange sort of inverse sit-up. In front of the seals, eiders coo; when I get closer, they emit warning cries like muted bomb signals rising up in their throats. While I come to the beach for fuel, more than driftwood has been thrown up on shore this past winter: horsewhips of brown-green kelp, a seal carcass that I've watched sink into the sand over the past months (bringing its skull home in February, so that it now rests on the desk in front of me like Yorick as I type), and, most recently, a harbor porpoise, black and four feet long. The porpoise's eyes had been picked out by gulls and the black flesh ripped back, revealing a shining jawbone and tiny even white teeth. Each day, my arms full of wood, I check in on the progress of decay.

Words and books have little to do with the elation I feel when I climb up from the beach and see a doe and her three young giving back some of its former wildness to the suburbia of Old Town Lane. The summer people who own the houses are nowhere in sight as the deer browse lazily across their lawns. In Colorado we had to shoo deer out of our driveway, but here this rare sighting speaks of nature insisting on wildness despite our worst efforts. Having come back to my home place, I feel that I'm becoming a small part of this resurgence. Over the last two years, since we returned to Cape Cod, my learning about my neighborhood has been fragmented—"incremental," as my friend Reg Saner points out all nature-learning is—but I've stumbled forward, if forward is the direction I've indeed been going in. Downward sometimes seems more accurate.

Now, at home on these still-wintery nights, I ready myself for the ospreys, sitting close to the woodstove in the rocking chair, reading ornithology texts and rereading Alan Poole's book, filling my journal with facts about the birds. The books stacked around me, I alternate between taking notes and getting down on my knees to feed gathered wood into the stove's maw. My reading tells me that by early March the ospreys have left their wintering grounds in South America and are well on their way up here, traveling between one and two hundred miles per day. They have already flown over the Caribbean in one great effort, and, after that daring crossing, they'll move a bit more slowly, stopping and fishing and resting as they go. Their annual journey is not as streamlined as that of some other birds—sandpipers and orioles, for instance —but they are still compelled by urgency. "Pressures to breed early are obviously great," Poole writes; "early nesting Ospreys produce the most surviving young." I imagine our local birds to be in the mid-Atlantic by now, along the coast of Delaware, maybe, moving closer to the Cape with each passing day. In Audubon's account of ospreys I read that fishermen in the mid-Atlantic states, upon seeing the first osprey return, "would hail its appearance with joy," as a harbinger of the fish, and the spring, to come.

Ospreys are specialists, eating only fish that they dive for and snare in their talons. Like swallows keying on the return of insects, ospreys follow fish. Soon our local flounder and bass and, most spectacularly, our mobs of herring will begin to swim back into the shallow warming coastal waters. As spring surges northward, life following life, the birds will return to feed. It won't be long before the season gets down to it, and just as the herring will surely return, the ospreys will be there to feast: peering down at the dark fish with their yellow eyes, hovering above, wings beating, treading air, then plunging with the fierce sureness of a shot arrow.

ONE OF THE things I do during these cold nights, as the woodstove ticks and the wind bullies the walls, is educate myself about the time when the ospreys did not return. That was from the late '50s through the '70s, and DDT—dichloro-diphenyl-trichloroethane—was the culprit. Invented in 1874, DDT had already been around for over sixty years or so before the Swiss scientist Paul Müller figured out that one of the things it did well was kill bugs. For this he won a Nobel Prize. In the years following World War II, drunk on the notion of a wonderful antiseptic, insectless world, American chemists, farmers, and administrators sprayed the insecticide liberally over thousands of acres of fields and woods and marshes. This, as Rachel Carson would soon point out, had a few unfortunate side effects. Here is how she put it in *Silent Spring* in 1962: "Chemicals sprayed on croplands or forests or gardens lie long in the soil, entering into living organisms, passing from one to another in a chain of poisoning and death. Or they pass mysteriously by underground streams until they emerge and, through the alchemy of air and sunlight, combine into new forms that kill vegetation, sicken cattle, and work unknown harm on those who drink from once pure wells."

Looking back, it's easy to wonder how we could have so profoundly underestimated the interconnectedness of the world. As Carson had predicted, DDT, and its organochloride compound cousins, seeped into everything. Blown by wind, sliding off soil, carried by water, they quickly found their way into many so-called nontarget life forms. One of the problems was that DDT was a stable—that is, long-lasting—compound. Worse, it was fat-soluble and therefore became trapped in the fatty lymph tissues of animals. This last fact led to a process called biomagnification, whereby the concentration of the chemicals becomes greater and greater as they climb the food chain. The concept took me a while to grasp, but it really isn't that complicated. Consider the case of the ospreys. First humans spray DDT over a marsh in hopes of killing off the mosquitoes. Naturally enough, the DDT finds its way into the water and into plankton, where it concentrates in fairly minuscule amounts. The problem is that small fish eat large amounts of plankton and have no way to rid themselves of the chemicals, which lodge in their fatty tissues. Then, as any first grader knows, big fish eat little fish—the big fish again unable to expel the DDT. Finally, ospreys eat the big fish and, with each fish devoured, the concentration of DDT builds up in their lymphatic system. After a few hundred fish or so, the concentration in their bodies is a million times more than it had been in the plankton.

While this is still only a minuscule amount of the chemical—a few parts per million—it has tragic results for the ospreys.

Here is what DDT, or rather DDE, the insecticide's main metabolic breakdown component, does to the birds. It interferes with their ability to reproduce in the most insidious way, impeding the female's ability to produce enough calcium for her eggshells. This leads to thin eggshells, which leads to death for the unborn chicks. Maternal instinct compels the mother osprey to incubate her brood, but when she climbs on top she commits unintentional infanticide, cracking her own thin-shelled eggs, destroying her own offspring.

ON MY THIRD morning at the Quivett marsh I watch from a world barely waking, holding out my hands toward the rising sun as if it were a just-built fire. The seesaw struggle between winter and spring continues, and while the hints of what will come are here, I can't bring myself to trust them. But I remind myself that despite appearances, spring is coming. The world *will* warm.

The foundation of sticks from last year's nest sits atop the nesting platform, a foundation that the returning birds will, hopefully, add to. Though I check in with all the other neighborhood nests, including the one that I can see from the back deck of my house, I find I'm coming here, to the Quivett marsh, most often. I'm already establishing a routine, parking directly across from my father's gray slate gravestone—DAVID MARSHALL GESSNER, BELOVED OF FAMILY AND FRIENDS, it reads—and walking down the path in the cemetery's northeast corner. Throughout these first days (and throughout the spring it will turn out), the red-tail's shriek-whistle serves as my greeting when I enter the short path. The path weaves down through the catbrier and then through the fifteen-foot-tall phragmites that are my gateway to the marsh itself. I spread the phragmites like beads hanging over a hippie doorway and, once through, walk along the marsh edge. I tote lawn chair, binoculars, bird books, and journal, plopping all down when I get to my spot below the black oak where deer have flattened a circled mat of grass for their beds. A small brown bird's nest from last year is interwoven into blades of spartina grass, and a row of elder bushes guard the marsh. I set up my chair, take out my binoculars, and watch and wait.

To say there is something a little like prayer in this routine is not going too far, particularly with the cemetery so near. I scribble all the sights in my journal, composing while my elders decompose nearby, turning the marsh into a map, recording the location of the heron's nest and the Canada geese's. My prayer is active, but today the weather won't let me worship long. While the calendar has announced the first day of spring, the wind violently disagrees. Rain flies sideways, and the marsh leans with the wind: spartina grass, trees, even, it appears, the unoccupied osprey nest bend with the gusts. I've barely unpacked all my equipment and begun to take notes about an empty nest when it's time to pack up again. Driven off the marsh, I run for my car. Rain like pencil points drums the roof. Back home I watch the ocean swell, white froth almost covering the jetties. No sign of ospreys across the harbor, but a brave kingfisher rattles low over the water, landing on a rotted old piling. Its Mohawk crown looks ragged, water-sprayed. I imagine it taking shelter in its ten-foot-long tunnel that twists into the muck bank, the tunnel floor littered with the bones of fish.

The ospreys have no such protection. Their homes jut right up into the wind like flagpoles. Alan Poole wrote of watching ospreys return near his home, where they were blasted by an early spring snowstorm and took refuge down low in the marsh until the storm abated. Are the birds already here, huddled down out of all this cold and wind? I worry for them. What if they can't complete their annual journey? Weather is just one variable; there are so many other threats. How can they hope to survive and breed?

• • •

As the rains usher in spring, my nightly reading picks up momentum. Nina makes fun of my reading style, since I need to be involved with at least three or four books at once. She prefers the old-fashioned technique of starting a book at the beginning and reading it straight through before heading on to the next one. By contrast, I read "by inclination," as Samuel Johnson put it, which is a fancy way of saying I go where I please. At its worse this leads to a lazy dawdling and lots of unfinished books, but at its best a kind of electric cross-pollination occurs. That is what happens now. Every sentence I stumble on seems relevant. Alan Poole's book, *Ospreys: A Natural and Unnatural History,* remains my central text, and I return to it again and again, taking Talmudic care to learn the details of the birds' behavior. But there is also Rachel Carson's *Silent Spring,* which I've somehow managed to live thirty-eight years without reading. If in its time the book served as a clarion call and an antidote to a glossy vision of chemically aided Progress, it now, for me, acts also as an antidote to the fear of impotence. Here are words that actually made a difference, that had an effect on the world. This fact is almost as exciting as the fact of the osprey's return. It also leads me to Linda Lear's biography of Rachel Carson, where, in the undisciplined style that irritates my wife, I skip right to the parts about the composition of *Silent Spring.* By that point cancer had spread through Carson—news her doctor at first refused to tell her because she was a woman—and she finished her brave book about unseen poisons while being bombarded with chemotherapy.

This nudges me in a less sanguine direction. Though my own cancer is in the past, there are times when worry seeps in. A hypochondriac at heart, I can't read long about DDT without taking it personally, imagining the chemical disseminating into the clear, yellowish lemonade that is my lymph. Now I put aside the Carson biography and track down the article in *Nature* magazine that proposed the link between testicular cancer and DDT or, more accurately, the metabolite DDE. DDE has, as it turns out, potent "oestrogenic ('feminizing') and anti-androgenic ('demasculinzing')" capabilities. The article is careful to only suggest the link between testicular cancer and DDT, and its main conclusion is that more research is needed. But it does point to the rise in the incidence of testicular cancer that coincided with the use of the pesticides, and to the astounding fact that most of us had our first encounters with DDT in utero, and that we all still store the chemical in our fat. Finally, lest we think this a problem of the past, the author, Richard Sharpe, mentions that DDT use in developing countries "probably exceeds the level of its use historically." Though not a scientist, I doubt that DDT respects national borders.

Connections again. Over and over, I'm impressed by how intertangled the world is. As I read more I'm particularly impressed by the strange marriage of ospreys and DDT. Not only in the ugly death dance that occurred at the nests, but as emblems, symbols, and indicators of the environmental movement. While there were chemicals a hundred times more harmful, DDT, largely through Rachel Carson's work, got star billing, becoming the villainous symbol that the nascent environmental movement rallied against. In a similar way, ospreys became emblematic, acting in many cases as an indicator of environmental health. This was due in part to the simple fact that they, like peregrine falcons and bald eagles, were big. You couldn't miss them, and when you did miss them you knew something was wrong. And soon enough ospreys were missed, which would yield surprising results.

ONE OF THE first to miss the ospreys was a gentle man named Dennis Puleston. Near the end of her life one of Rachel Carson's concerns was about who would continue her life's work, but soon after she died it was clear that others were rushing in to take up the fight. Puleston was one of those others. Since 1948 he had been carefully observing and sketching the resident ospreys on Gardiners Island, off the eastern end of Long Island, a small hump of land suspended within the island's forked tail. Puleston, later considered the "gray eminence" of the Environmental Defense Fund, was well on his way to becoming an environmental legend. While growing up in England, Puleston had never seen an osprey in the wild, the birds having been wiped out there. Moving to Long Island after World War II, Puleston looked forward to living close to what he considered a "somewhat mythical bird." Not long after his move he began his studies at Gardiners Island. When he first observed the ospreys, there were hundreds of active nests, but over the years he noticed great changes. "I began keeping records of each nest and its reproductive history. In 1948, an average of more than two chicks fledged from each nest. . . . By 1966, active nests on Gardiners Island had dwindled from over 300 in 1948 to under 50, and in these we could find only four chicks. Ornithologists predicted the end of the osprey as a breeding bird in the Northeast."

Puleston had great respect for Rachel Carson, whom he called "that splendid woman": "Knowing of her work, we collected overdue osprey eggs and took them to the laboratory for analysis by gas chromatography. As we anticipated, residues of DDT were present." Puleston wasn't the first to tie the osprey's decline to the use of pesticides, but his observations would help convert this conclusion into political action. At the time Puleston was a member of a central Long Island conservation group called the Brookhaven Town Natural Resources Committee, or BTNRC. The BTRNC fought local environmental battles, its members comparing notes on, among other issues, the disastrous effects of DDT. At first they operated within more or less conventional means: letter writing, phone calls, and one-person campaigns. But all that changed one day in April 1966. That was when Charles Wurster, the chemist who had run the tests on Puleston's osprey eggs, left a BTRNC meeting and went home to write a letter to local newspapers criticizing the Long Island Mosquito Control Commission's use of DDT.

The letter set off a rapid chain of events. It was promptly read by a flamboyant local lawyer named Victor Yannacone. Yannacone was not shy about suing and was already in the midst of a suit against the mosquito commission, claiming that DDT had led to a large fish kill. Victor Yannacone's concerns were not specifically environmental, but Wurster's letter sparked his interest. In his recollections of the time, Wurster remembers Yannacone asking him if he "had specific evidence of damaging effects of DDT" and "whether I would help him in his lawsuit." "I said 'yes' to both questions," Wurster recalled, "adding that others on Long Island might want to help."

Those others included a hearty local biology teacher and birdwatcher, Art Cooley, the BTRNC's founder and unofficial chair, and Dennis Puleston, with his mounting evidence of the ospreys' decline. The atmosphere during those early meetings must have been charged and, though they didn't know it at the time, the BTRNC was about to undergo a dramatic metamorphosis. Less than a week after that meeting, Yannacone presented an affidavit to the New York Supreme Court, requesting an injunction against the mosquito commission's use of DDT. To the surprise of the BTRNC members, that injunction, bolstered by their scientific evidence, worked. DDT use was blocked until the case went to trial in November 1966.

If DDT, through Carson's crusades, could be said to have led to the beginning of the modern environmental movement, then both DDT and the ospreys would be responsible for the birth of what is now known as environmental law. Ospreys, it would turn out, were central to the first DDT trial. Since they were at the top of the food chain, where the chemical concentrated, they provided the most dramatic evidence. By then Dennis Puleston had brought

more damaged eggshells of the Gardiners Island ospreys to
Charles Wurster at the Brookhaven National Laboratory, and
Wurster's tests had determined that the DDT levels were danger-
ously high. Against this the commission had no defense. Despite
the fact that the presiding judge had to look up the word *ecology*, it
was soon obvious that he was impressed with the mounting evidence. Though the same judge would finally rule that the court
had no jurisdiction over the mosquito commission, by then two
summers had passed without spraying. In that time the public had
been made aware of the problem, and the Suffolk County legisla-
ture had forbidden the commission from ever using DDT.

For the first time science was wed to law to gain environmental results, giving legal muscle to Rachel Carson's concerns. And
the team of BTRNC scientists wasn't done. Inspired by their success, they launched a national campaign to, as they privately put it,
"sue the bastards." In 1967 they incorporated as the Environmental Defense Fund, with Puleston, Wurster, and Cooley among the
founding trustees. Their lawsuits would lead directly to the banning of DDT not only on Long Island but, soon after, in Wiscon-
sin and, then, throughout the country. Of course, it wasn't easy.
Like Carson before them, they were accused of being Communists
and, inevitably, perverts, for their attacks on the all-American
chemical. But despite the industry's attempts to smear their names,
they kept on pushing the DDT suits right up through June 14,
1972. On that day—a happy one for both the original BTRNC
members and the ospreys—EPA administrator William Ruckelhaus
permanently banned DDT use in the United States.

BY NIGHT I read about one comeback, by day witness another. The Quivett birds—*my* birds I already hear myself ridicu-
lously calling them—return on March 23. Or at least that's the first
day I see them. Theirs is a dramatic homecoming. I'm out on the
marsh early on this hazy morning, sitting in my lawn chair, blue-

berry muffin and tea in hand, when they catch me by surprise. With the weather the way it's been, I didn't expect them back this early, but here they are. As the sun comes up and burns the fog off the marsh, a great bird—a male, I suspect—lifts up, his wings underlit with glimmers of silver, flying right toward me. His full outline shines when he gets closer, as if water is still drying on his primaries, the thirteen long feathered fingers that extend on the outer half of his wings. As he banks I see another gleam, like the flash of a knife blade, and notice the fish in his talons—a flounder, it looks like. He flies low, banks again, then flutters high so that I have a fine view of his vivid white belly and breast. Now the female joins him—*they're both back!*—and one behind the other they glide in from below the old nest, rise up, flap, and land.

He tears at the fish with his curved beak while she begs with the characteristic cry that the renowned early-twentieth-century ornithologist Edward Forbush called "a complaining whistle." Her cries fill the marsh the way no other sound has this cold month, and, despite the edge of irritation in her voice, it feels uplifting to be in the presence of ospreys again. Such proud-looking birds, with their white heads and dark masks. The field guides often describe their coloring as black and white, but today a dark chestnut brown seems a truer description. This color, contrasting vividly with the thick white of the chest, covers the tops of the wings before working its way up the back of the head and encircling the yellow eyes in a dark raccoon mask. I notice that, despite the speckling of dark spots on her throat, she seems to have more white in her than he does, but perhaps that's simply because she is larger and her white chest is more expansive. On the other hand, his mask is definitely fuller, covering a greater part of his face.

I marvel at their size. Ospreys are enormous birds, reaching twenty-four inches tall from head to toe, with wingspans between fifty-eight and seventy-two inches—five to six feet. By contrast, a red-tailed hawk (the hawk casual bird-watchers see most often) has a wingspan of about fifty inches, while a peregrine falcon's wings stretch between thirty-six and forty-four inches. On the other hand, a bald eagle's wingspan can reach between seventy and ninety inches, and it can weigh up to ten pounds more than an osprey. That said, beginning osprey watchers often can't get the word *eagle* out of their heads. The combination of coloring and majesty won't let them.

I watch through the morning. The pair lie low, likely exhausted from the journey, and later take short foraging trips for sticks to bolster the nest. As well as they fly, as brilliantly athletic as they are, they sometimes seem to have a difficult time landing on the nest, particularly when carrying large sticks. Before landing they drop down ten feet below the platform, almost to the ground, then fly straight up into the wind, hovering, and finally land with a great flapping of wings—beautiful, but the antithesis of smooth.

At first, as the morning passes, they both work, but before long I notice a division of labor along gender lines: he flies out and gathers, then hands—or *beaks*—the sticks over to her. She places the sticks with her bill, sometimes delicately, sometimes not, then hectors him if he hasn't already flown off for more material. Later he preens on a nearby post while she tamps down the inside of the nest. In no time their home is being built back up, and this early active domesticity gives me hope for the pair's success. Certainly these two at least look like they know what they're doing.

But the next day the rain pours; the next night lashes. I worry and fret, knowing a rainy spring means a greater chance of a failed nest. Then, on March 25, the third morning of the birds' return, the sun breaks through, and for the first time the bushes and briers surrounding the marsh appear more green than not. While most of the trees' buds still aren't open, they are poised, ready to burst. The resident great blue heron flies by in pelican profile, and the nesting Canada geese honk down for a hard landing. Having survived the last two days, the ospreys look proud, if rumpled, their heads up; she on the nest, he on the crossbar below. It's the warmest, least windy day yet, the real first day of spring, and the birds seem to be enjoying themselves. The morning is spent patiently resting, scratching feathers with bill and talon, soaking in the sun. They don't work as much as you might expect, though occasionally she pleads with him and he flies off to scavenge a stick or two. I've been told that words like *hector* and *plead* are examples of anthropomorphizing, but watch the nest for a morning and it's clear what is happening: she communicates a need to him, insistently—*I want this*—while he rests, ignoring her as long as he can. There is something of Dagwood Bumstead in the male, and he only reluctantly gives in to her commands, preferring to indulge in the osprey equivalent of hanging out on the couch. After a while he does lift up, taking a swing around the marsh, coming back with what looks like the shining tape of an unspooled cassette. She takes it for more tamping, but it is clearly not what she had in mind, and she lets him know. So he is off again, wings backlit, banking, gliding, as if still enjoying the sun. It isn't hard work. Sticks are easy prey, after all, much easier than fish, and this pair has the luxury of foraging close to home. He drops off another branch and returns to his crossbar.

This seems to me a morning well spent, a morning of Beston's "essentials," just what I came back to the Cape to find. "Feel that sun," the gas station attendant said to me on the way here, and for a while I do just that. As it soaks into my skin, I close my eyes. When I open them again I notice broken glass glimmering along the marsh's edge. At first I wonder if I'm seeing beer bottles from a teenagers' party, but, as I get up and walk over, I find that what I thought was glass turns out to be the purple-blue shine of broken mussel shells. It was a party all right, but the partiers were gulls; twenty-five shells or so spread over the rocks and spartina. On my way back to my seat, the sun paints the pines behind me olive and gives a landing crow its distinctly oily black shine.

The ospreys let off their cardinal-like warning cry at my stirring, but they aren't really alarmed. They rest next to each other, companionable. It has been my—and I suspect their—best morning yet. The three of us are all large animals, not frenetic like hummingbirds or mice, and, resting on top of the food chain, we can afford to lie back occasionally and let the sun stun us. But if I feel lazy, it's laziness tinged with excitement. My uneasiness and boredom of a week ago have vanished. Though I sometimes self-mockingly succumb to the stereotype of the nature lover as dull dodderer, and of bird-watching as boring, I know this is preposterously wrongheaded. What could be more exciting than the essential drama of these birds? What better than their return with the sun after all the cold winter months?

IN 1960, 10 TO 20 pairs of ospreys nested in Massachusetts. In 1996 there were over 300 pairs. At last count we were up to 350, and observation tells me the numbers are still increasing, at least locally. It makes sense. After fledging in New England in late summer, the young birds migrate to South or Central America, where they will spend the next two years. Then the two-year-old ospreys will return to their natal nesting grounds to attempt to breed. With between one and two birds fledging each year from our local nests, and around 40 percent of those surviving migration, we can expect more and more ospreys back in our neighborhood over the coming years, the numbers held in check only by the availability of nest sites and food supply. At the same time established pairs will keep breeding, and since ospreys live long lives, sometimes up to twenty to twenty-five years (though more often into their teens), most pairs will produce many young. This all adds up to a healthy return.

Meanwhile, with DDT long since banned on the Suffolk

County marshes, the place where the first legal war was waged, the ospreys are back. Dennis Puleston writes, "In 1992, a post-1948 record total of 226 nests on Long Island, including over 60 on Gardiners Island, fledged another record of 260 chicks." Though DDE remained in their systems, it turned out that a minuscule difference in the amount of the chemical made a world of difference for the birds. As the organochlorides disappeared, the percentage of the chemicals in the ospreys' systems lessened and the birds gradually returned, again breeding at the rate they had before the pesticides were introduced.

Nothing excites like a comeback. In sports, you may hope the home team wins in a blowout, but it isn't nearly as exciting or satisfying as an improbable escape from disaster. In love, what's better than the sparking of near-dead flames? In religion, we need look no further than Jesus emerging from the cave. Mythologically, the hero goes into the underworld and comes back alive, reborn. This has been the role the osprey has been fated to play: a modern-day, fish-eating phoenix staging a feathery revival. Drive down eastern Long Island, where DDT was once repeatedly sprayed, and you'll find a road dotted with nests, ospreys flying overhead with stripers in their talons. On Cape Cod even the most somnolent tourist occasionally wakes from his summerlong trance to notice the birds with the six-foot wingspans and ask: "What are those, some kind of eagle?" Ospreys have once again become the symbol of the New England coast, and many of us feel protective of our neighborhood pairs. They are, as they have long been, an emblem bird. And a status bird, too. Celebrities on Nantucket and Martha's Vineyard have platforms erected on their properties (so that we now have James Taylor's osprey or Carly's), and newspapers continually feature the good news of their return.

If there is a feel-good element to this story, it's at least partly deserved. For once we did something right, we can say to ourselves: for once we didn't screw up. But as miraculous as it is to have the birds back, it isn't hard to imagine the opposite, the route we've most often taken when interacting with other species or peoples. For all the joy of the ospreys' return, we need to understand just how tragic the alternative would have been.

Or maybe, in this case, we don't. Maybe, just this once, it isn't the dark side we need to keep reminding ourselves of. Maybe most of us remind ourselves of that enough. While the litany for pessimism is familiar—thinning ozone, depleted resources, acid rain, extinction, the intractable crush of population—here, in this case, we've given ourselves a reason to feel hopeful. Here is an example of a group of human beings who fought the will of an industry that stood to make millions and millions of dollars, and of human courts and government who handed down verdicts on the side of a bird. While I'm a cynic by nature, maybe once in a while we need to focus on our victories, not our losses. By looking toward the ospreys we can see a little light. We can see what can occur if we are able to exercise restraint. Can see something truly hopeful in the miracle of what we managed *not* to do.

MAYBE WE SHOULD all allow ourselves hope for at least one season each year; it seems to do some good, like the occasional shot of tequila. I try to hold myself in check, feigning sobriety, but it's no use. I'm drunk with the season. Now, as March becomes April, the world stages its full green resurrection. The rush is no longer slow, nature no longer opening in orderly fashion, single file, one thing at a time, but bursting in intoxicated glory: tadpoles, riotous birdsong, herring shooting up the silver of the tidal creeks. Our third spring here puts the lie to Heidi Schadt's rule: buds unclench and explode with meaty green and streaked red. One morning I head down to the beach as the sun rises over Brewster and stains the sky salmon, bathing the world below in a yellow light as I jump from one barnacled rock to the next. A gull flies by with a starfish in its mouth; then a crow comes close, its wings beating out a husky whisper. The harbor porpoise, chewed down to its black and red ribs, eyes and blowhole poked out, still smiles its perfect, small-toothed smile. Then, at the kettle pond up past the bluff, I hear a joyous though eerie symphony. For a brief second I think I'm listening to an insect's song, a cricket's maybe, but I quickly recognize the singers for who they are—the spring peepers. They are late, almost two weeks behind last year, but they make up for their tardiness with gusto. The tiny frogs sing to one another, to the world, as if trying to communicate what spring means at the top of their lungs. When I walk the path inland the song rings through the depression between the sloping sand hills.

Over the next week Sesuit Neck fills with ospreys. The birds claim the lopsided nest at Chapin, the midmarsh platform at Simpkins Neck, even the parking lot pole directly across the harbor. The neighborhood echoes with the upward whittling of their high-pitched cries—*kew, kew, kew*—cries I can now hear from my bedroom when I wake in the morning. The harbor pair seem dawdlers, not nearly as efficient or industrious as the Quivett birds, but it's still nice to have them back, flying near and sometimes directly over our house. Every morning I head to Quivett, nodding when I pass my father's gravestone, watching as the birds carry on with the essentials: nesting, feeding, and mating.

There's a thaw in the air, a certain smell of the land unlocking and the first cut grass, a smell that sends me back to childhood, that almost gets me reaching for my baseball glove under the mattress, where it's been breaking in. Out back, grackles posture with the puffed-up chests of bullies, and a tufted titmouse pecks at the food below the feeder. A kind of healthy mania is taking hold of the natural world, and I'm part of it, up at dawn and walking down to the bluff, hoping to see if the swallows have joined in the season's revival. They haven't, but no matter. As spring's excess overwhelms the simplicity of winter, life's usual doubts are over-turned. I know those doubts will return soon, but for the moment I enjoy the mindless surge of confidence, the sense of renewal. Right now, watching the ospreys, at this moment, both the world and I are back in place.

Building

There are some enterprises in which a
careful disorderliness is the true method.
—MELVILLE, *Moby-Dick*

An osprey nest is a giant pile of sticks, seaweed, grass, and whatever else the birds can get their talons on, a seemingly random mess of crosshatching and emphatic Jackson Pollack splatterings and slashes. People have found everything in the nests from the heads of rag dolls to beer cans to toy sailboats to doormats. Alan Poole has compiled a list that includes "corn stalks, hunks of dried cow manure, empty fertilizer bags, and discarded rubber teat holders from milking machines," as well as "sections of TV antennas, hula hoops, remnants of fish nets, old flannel shirts and rubber boots, styrofoam cups and buoys, a broken hoe, plastic hamburger cartons, and bicycle tires." Samuel Johnson was of the opinion that literature was worthless unless put to use, and the birds apparently agree. In 1932, writing in *National Geographic*, Captain C. W. R. Knight reported finding a book called *Lucile, Bringer of Joy* in one of the Gardiners Island nests (he immediately dubbed the female bird Lucile). The captain added, "Ospreys are much addicted to the habit of bringing to their nests various decorative oddments, such as dried carcasses of birds, crab shells, pieces of board, derelict shoes, bits of clothing, and so on." This was a kind way of saying that ospreys are indiscriminate pack rats. I've noticed that our local birds have a particular fondness for the shiny and artificial: plastic shopping bags, string, twine, the green fluorescent stuffing of an Easter basket, and large, dark green garbage bags that fly off the platforms like flags off pirate ships. All these have become parts of the nests I watch as building intensifies with the season. The early neighborhood prize for the most original choice in building material goes to the pair at Chapin Beach, who have added a nearly naked Barbie doll to their nest's northeast wall.

A slob myself, I feel a kinship with the ospreys. Not for them the artistic subtleties of the African weaverbird, who can tie at least a half dozen different stitches and knots and construct elaborate tunnels. Ospreys aren't minimalists, preferring sheer mass to dainty perfectionism. From up close their nests sometimes look more tall than wide, up to four feet high and weighing close to a quarter of a ton. Dennis Murley, the naturalist at the Wellfleet Bay Wildlife Sanctuary, reports word of a nest ten feet high and six across. Like eagle aeries, the nests usually weather the winter and are built up higher and higher with each passing year. Most are not as big as eagle aeries, however, or nearly as sturdy, as Alan Poole found out when he attempted to make like John Muir and climb up into one after it had been deserted for the winter. Poole's report is that they barely support the weight of a man.

One of the most striking things about the nests, other than the preponderance of tacky materials, is how such big birds disappear into them. Three or sometimes four almost full-grown fledglings, along with a parent bird or two, fit in the nest, apparently comfortably. Despite the fact that I've been told the nests don't really have much of a cupped depression, the birds can vanish almost completely out of sight. Considering the ospreys' size, this is extraordinary. More than once I've thought of Snoopy's mythical doghouse, and how he would disappear inside it to take a dip in the pool, look at his van Gogh, or shoot billiards. I've already made plans for spending a little time up in the nest during the fall, once the birds have flown south. Then I hope to get to the bottom of their mysterious depth.

As well as building *with* anything, ospreys will build *on* almost anything. Telephone poles, windmills, buoys, electric towers, billboards, duck blinds, and even shipwrecks can serve as homesites. In their book *Raptors,* Noel and Helen Snyder relate the story of an osprey pair that built their nest in a temporarily inactive construction crane: "The owner, to his everlasting credit, retired the crane from active duty, allowing the Ospreys to follow through with their nesting efforts." Despite this willingness to adapt, modern ospreys often opt for artificial platforms built by humans. For instance, in Massachusetts, 97 percent of osprey pairs sit on top of platforms, the poles and pallets frequently provided by Commonwealth Electric.

This year I plan on observing four nests: Quivett, Chapin, Simpkins Neck, and, finally, my home nest at the harbor. The ospreys are all returnees, coming back to nests they have built up in years past. While all four of the nests I watch are built on top of artificial poles and platforms, each has a different character. For instance, the nest across the harbor is the highest, sitting atop a thirty-foot pole above the noisy, exhaust-filled parking lot. Being brand-new, however, it's also the shallowest—and the sloppiest, the harbor pair apparently the least concerned with aesthetics: long sections of rope trail down and plastic shopping bags billow like parachutes in the wind. This confirms my belief that the harbor birds are the youngest pair I watch. While the urge to build is instinctive, tied to hormones triggered by the warming weather, skill in building increases with age and experience.

Early in the season, just after the Quivett pair returned, I was convinced that I saw the harbor birds, and I peered long and hard through my binoculars, taking earnest notes on coloring and habits. "Ospreys at the harbor still lying low," I reported in my journal on the third day. It was only on closer inspection on a particularly clear afternoon that I realized that the birds I was seeing were in fact Hefty garbage bags. I dug out Poole's book to find out what was going on and discovered that abandoned nests are common early in the season, as some birds shop around or create secondary sites and, recovering somewhat from my embarrassment, was reassured that if I hadn't seen actual ospreys then at least I'd seen evidence of them. When the harbor pair did return, Nina and I took to calling them the "lazy, good-for-nothing" ospreys, because they exhibited many of the classic characteristics of osprey immaturity. For instance, the male didn't share his food as readily as the more "responsible" Quivett bird, sometimes eating a whole fish right in front of his mate, and they both seemed generally lackluster about getting down to the business of nesting. Playing the early spring oddsmaker, I gave them little chance of successfully reproducing.

As for the nests themselves, the most interesting one to me is at Chapin, and not just because of the naked Barbie. Like the other three nests I watch, it sits atop a man-made platform. This platform, however, slants dramatically to the west, and the birds, as if to overcompensate, have built the west side of their nest even higher than the east, so that it now slopes in the opposite direction. The whole affair looks precarious, like a boy balancing on a skateboard. A more fastidious animal might abandon such an absurd homesite, but I never hear the Chapin birds complain, at least not about architecture. Like the lairs of the villains on the old TV *Batman,* their home is permanently, drunkenly tilted.

APRIL'S THEME is building. Unseen by most of us, nests of every variety are being constructed, from the hanging sack of the oriole to the rooty ball of the winter wren to the small eggcup of the redstart. Variety thrives not just in the final products but in the arts of construction: woodpeckers drilling, ovenbirds baking, chimney swifts practicing masonry by gluing their semicircle saucers with saliva onto brick. So many strategies and techniques, from marsh wrens creating dummy nests in the cattails to house wrens nesting almost anywhere—in the skull of a cow, for instance, or even in the pocket of a coat. One of the things we come to nature for is quiet, but if these birds had our human tools and machines the roar would be deafening. In the spring all of nature becomes a vast construction sight.

Even among birds of prey variety in nest building thrives. The most famous of raptor nests, of course, are eagle aeries, giant battlements on remote cliff sides. Christopher Leahy's *The Birdwatcher's Companion* informs me that "it would not be incorrect" to refer to an osprey's nest as an aerie, and I can see why as the sticks pile higher and higher. Watching the ospreys add to their huge nests, I experience something like the childhood pleasure I felt building forts with couch cushions and blankets in the living room and, later on, with branches and boards in the woods.

Raptor homesites fill almost every niche: ground, crag, cliff, church (a kestrel favorite), and tree. I prefer the habits of the osprey to those of most falcons, who take over the nests of other birds (both occupied and unoccupied), or the notoriously unhygienic vultures, who contradict the old maxim by constantly soiling their own nests. On the other hand, you can't help but admire the flourish of the red-shouldered hawk, who will place a sprig of greenery on its newly adopted home, a tasteful way of saying "Occupied." In Brown and Amadon's *Eagles, Hawks and Falcons of the World,* I read, "The possession of a green branch seems to be connected with heightened excitement." The last phrase, *heightened excitement,* captures the feel of this building season.

Though much of the works remains invisible, there's evidence of activity all around. Flickers rattle the phone poles, and a beautiful chestnut-brown house wren pokes a hole into the windowsill of our shed. On a kayak trip up the Herring River I find a red-winged blackbird's nest interwoven with strands of grass, and on the path down to Quivett I watch a chickadee carry twigs into a perfectly round hole high in a dead red pine. The bark is peeled off halfway down the tree, the wood barkless and smooth near the hole, and the little bird flits in and out, back and forth to gather material, dipping inside and arranging frenetically, showing only its bobbing tail to those outside its home. The bird virtually vibrates with movement, activity, effort. This, in a more hyperactive variety, is the same energy that sends the ospreys off on their relatively unhurried, loping flights.

While I understand the energy of the chickadee, nervous for its success and the success of its mate, I prefer the luxuriant sprawl of the osprey nest. Though they can make up to a hundred flights a day in pursuit of nesting material, they take their time about it. If there's an urgency to the season, for these large birds it's a fairly lazy urgency, particularly for the Quivett pair, whose nest remains mostly intact from the year before. The birds remind me a little of our cats in the way they lounge, preening, scratching, and soaking in sun.

By early April the marsh begins to show hints of green, though for the most part remaining the red-brown of the red-tailed hawk's tail. I sit on the other side of Quivett Creek, watching as the female lines the inner cup of the nest with softer materials, sod and grasses. At times she appears hulking compared to the male, a bulky pheasant, while he looks more delicate and hunched. She also seems on the tall side, maybe twenty-five inches. I can't make her size, particularly when she flies close by, jive with a fact I have just learned from my books: that ospreys weigh only about four pounds. This strikes me as nearly preposterous, since she looks like she could easily scoop up our house cat, Tabernash, who weighs three times as much. My book explains this away by saying that birds have hollow bones and bodies streamlined for flight, but it's still hard to swallow.

While the birds do sit a lot, she on the nest, he on the crossbar, they don't exactly sit *still*. The binoculars reveal the birds as less Zen-like than first glance would indicate: they fidget, look around, listen, let go with their peevish warning cries. At one point the male chases a crow away from the nest, tailing it, brilliantly mimicking the flight of the smaller bird. When he tires of the chase, he retreats to the nest and the female takes over, tag-team style, flying just as beautifully, the sun backlighting the dark-light pattern of her primaries. When the excitement dies down the male turns to foraging, flying out and then coming back to the nest with a clump of grass, which the female immediately sets to tamping down as lining. The next trip he brings back a veritable cudgel, knotted at one end and long like a tail. He has trouble dipping then rising up to the nest, delivering it only with a powerful exertion of wings. His heroism goes unrewarded, however, except by a glance that seems to say, "What am I supposed to do with *that?*"

Though there are exceptions, nest building among birds of prey follows a simple rule: males bring and females build. Females most often dominate the process, from site selection on, nest building being inextricably entwined with mating. As with humans, osprey males seem at their most energetic when hoping to procure sexual rewards. Osprey courtship isn't subtle. While a male red-tailed hawk begins each year shyly, involving himself in an elaborate, almost bashful, courtship ritual, ospreys are more direct. The open plains that the sage grouse use for their courtship dance are called the "strutting grounds," and male ospreys strut too, though not on the ground. They prefer a wild up-and-down flight, the "sky dance," a glorious display often performed with fish in talons.

While the dance *is* glorious, the act itself is more simple and direct. More and more frequently, I find myself voyeuristic witness to osprey intimacy. As with the first time I saw it, the whole action of mating takes a matter of ten or fifteen seconds, both the birds on the nest, the male flapping in from behind and the female tilting up. The male, perching on her back, continues to flap his wings throughout the act, for balance probably, and balls up his feet to make sure not to claw the female with his talons. They aren't shy about sex, the whole act fast and without noticeable foreplay, other than the bringing of food. The male, once sated, will often fly off immediately afterward. Alan Poole points out that much osprey mating occurs at the nest not because they are exhibitionists but for a very commonsense reason: that is where the female spends most of her day.

OSPREYS ARE cosmopolitan birds. The building and breeding that I watch on Cape Cod is also taking place all over the world, from Corsica to Scotland, from Florida to Siberia. As the pairs I watched flew up from South America over the Caribbean, European ospreys migrated from Africa over the Mediterranean. Every spring the great feathered exodus occurs, and every spring nests like the ones I watch are built all across the planet.

But for all their worldliness, when it comes to locating their nests ospreys have just a few unshakable criteria. For one thing, they insist on living near water, a choice that I respect entirely. Living by water has such attraction that I'm always baffled when animals, particularly humans, make other arrangements. Admittedly, for a bird that survives by catching fish, this is a practical as well as an aesthetic choice. Like humans, ospreys are fond of islands; and on islands without natural predators, they will happily build their nests right on the ground. Since there are fewer and fewer places on earth untouched by man and the species he brings along in his train, there are, naturally, fewer and fewer ground-nesting ospreys.

Before man-made sites cluttered the landscape, their preference was for the tops of tall dead trees, especially over water. Like billboards and platforms, these older sites were created by another species—in this case, the beaver. Flowing water would be stopped up by beaver dams, and when it rose it killed trees and simultaneously created dream homes for ospreys—island poles surrounded by predator-protecting water. One reason for this preference for dead trees is because, as powerfully as they fly, ospreys can't maneuver well in tight quarters and so need to have open space above their nests.

Platforms provide this. This is the upside of poles and platforms, along with the fact of their greater stability, making them much less likely to blow over than tree sites. The downside is that platforms increase the birds' dependence on humans, and create a less wild home. Despite this unfortunate fact, platforms seem to be the only real alternative at this time on places like Cape Cod, where the bird's old nesting habitat is still being destroyed daily. I have friends in the West who spit out the oxymoronic words *wildlife management* and who might think a platform bird a compromised bird. But in the crowded East the ospreys could never have come back to anywhere close to their old numbers without the efforts of a fairly heroic band of platform builders. The banning of DDT let these birds live, but the platform builders gave them homes to live on.

Massachusetts has been lucky to have two particularly tireless groups of platform builders. By 1963, Gilbert and Josephine Fernandez of Dartmouth had already become concerned with the small colony of ospreys along the Westport River. Over the years they erected dozens of platforms, making sure that, when breeding rates increased after the banning of DDT, the new birds would have places to nest. Unlike the power poles, these platforms are low structures that blend in well with the marsh, like old duck blinds. The Fernandezes' work has led to Massachusetts's largest colony, with over seventy pairs, and our most dense concentration of birds. The second group, led by Gus Ben David, is made up of amateurs and professionals from the Audubon Society's Felix Neck Wildlife Sanctuary on Martha's Vineyard.

When I visited Ben David at the sanctuary, he interrupted our conversation to point out a red-tailed hawk to a group of children touring the grounds. A compact, energetic man, he shouted like a carnival barker as he gestured up at the hawk. This same energy has served him well over the years. In 1970, with only two pairs of ospreys left on the entire island, he helped erect an artificial pole after a pine tree with a nest on it blew over in a storm. The next year that pair returned in March to build their nest on the platform, and the revolution began. Ben David, aided by Tim "Rangus" Baird and a band of hearty volunteers, began the long hard work of "shepherding" (in his words) the ospreys back to the Vineyard. "It's been a story of people," he said. "Of cooperation. And, of course, of birds." Ben David and his gang have erected over a hundred platforms all over the island. Now, almost thirty years later, seventy-five pairs nest on Martha's Vineyard. Last year ninety young fledged.

The nests that the Felix Neck volunteers erect are thirty-foot-tall poles with four six-foot pressure-treated crossarms that form the nesting platforms. Mounted on the pole with center bolts, the crossarms are further strengthened by metal braces, capable of withstanding even hurricane winds. As on the Cape, these poles are provided by Commonwealth Electric. At the risk of sounding like a booster for the electric company, without Com Electric supplying the platforms, the comeback would have been much more difficult, if not impossible. Recently, searching for a birthday present for a neighbor of ours who had everything (including beachfront property), my mother and I called the power company and asked them to erect a platform on his property, which they promptly did.

It seems to me that all those who built the platforms did good work, work that intertwined them with the world and put to healthy use our constant human need to meddle and build. While I'd prefer to be watching the birds in more purely natural settings, there is something appealing about the result of the platforms: a teaming of human and avian construction, a marriage of domestic and wild. In the end, the platform builders have created a wonderful sort of organic architecture, a bridging as well as a building. In their efforts to aid those whose original homes other humans destroyed, they have rebuilt the stages on which osprey dramas play out.

A FEW WEEKS AGO, back in March, I made a pilgrimage to Westport, Massachusetts. I did this in part to see the site of Massachusetts's largest colony—dozens of platforms, many erected by Gil and Joe Fernandez. Unlike other raptors, ospreys are social birds, happy to nest near one another, just as they did on Gardiners Island when Dennis Puleston first saw them after World War II. Though the birds hadn't yet returned to the Westport marsh, it didn't take much imagination to see the place as it would be later in the summer: the air filled with a hundred large raptors, high-pitched cries, and beating wings. A wild community filled with osprey concerns and osprey interactions.

As good as it felt seeing what humans had helped hammer together, my real reason for going to Westport was to meet Alan Poole, whose book had become my guide and practical bible. I was happy to discover that Alan's own nest was a delightfully proportioned one-bedroom cabin right on the shore, nestled in the surrounding trees and briers, with a bedroom door that looked out at the water, and a telescope aimed directly at the osprey platform that jutted up out of a tidal inlet not three hundred feet away. Alan turned out to be a thin, handsome man whose blue eyes and high forehead reminded me of James Taylor. He had the kind of natural quiet composure that I, a born blowhard, always find somewhat disconcerting. I'd wondered if he might be somewhat territorial about his osprey knowledge, but he couldn't have been more helpful, answering all my questions as we sat in his glassed-in living room, sipping tea, listening to the wind howl, and enjoying what there was of the March sun.

Now at work on editing a massive modern version of the life histories of the birds of North America, he happily recalled his early osprey days.

"I started at grad school and I came on the scene in the late seventies," he explained. "The birds were just starting to get the DDT out of their systems, just starting to recover, and it was a fantastic time to be working on them. They're resilient birds, no question about it. It was a hopeful time for environmentalists, and ospreys were kind of the star players. They were coming back, nesting on platforms, getting an article in the *New York Times* at least once every summer. They were the golden boy."

Despite a calm scientific demeanor, his words were spiced with an unavoidable romanticism as he recalled the seasons out at the nests, seasons of observing behavior, inspecting the nests themselves, even once almost losing an eye when he was dive-bombed by a bird that didn't want him so close. Becoming increasingly aware of the patience required for fieldwork, I listened to the stories with admiration. Then, when he was done, I asked him about the migration that was already under way. I'd been wondering how the birds knew when to start.

"The sun's the clock that determines when they begin migrating," he said. "Weather determines how quickly they move, though the older ones pretty much do it on schedule no matter what the weather is. Of course they may not get around to nesting as quickly, if they come back and find it like this. They may stop in Long Island or New Jersey, but essentially they're being driven by the sun.

"By and large the birds that were born here all come back to the same area. Fifty percent come back to the exact areas where they were born. What we don't know is if *all* the Westport birds always come back to Westport, and then some sort of look around and say, 'Not enough room' and move on."

Alan explained an aspect of osprey migration unique among raptors. Fledgling ospreys, just a few months old, will fly down to South America for the winter, as do their parents. But unlike other birds of prey, the young ospreys do not return north the next spring, waiting another year, until they are two going on three, to return north. On the tape recording I made of the conversation I, at this point, hear myself interrupt and blurt out a rhapsodic spiel about how "miraculous" it is that two-year-old ospreys, who have last been in the Northeast when they were only three months old, somehow manage to make their way back to their natal nesting grounds. It wasn't my first such interruption, and it is followed by a pause on the tape, during which Alan was likely staring at me and wondering whether I'd come to talk or to listen. However he felt, he responded politely. While admitting it was remarkable, he stopped short of declaring it a miracle, quietly making the point that those three-month-old birds were, in fact, adolescents: "If you could fly and you were a teenager and spent the summer flying around Cape Cod, you would certainly know that landscape. And when you came back there, there would be certain things you'd recognize—obvious landmarks. What we don't know about ospreys is what they recognize: is it the configuration of the marsh and beach . . . or what exactly?"

Despite my interruptions, I quickly began to feel comfortable with Alan. Soon we finished our tea and took a walk down the path to the beach, into the sting of the wind, and watched the dark blue swell of winter waves. On the way back he pointed out birds for me. When we returned to the house he demonstrated with his hands how a joint in the osprey's foot allowed the bird's reversible outer talon to swivel and grab a fish from behind, and he described

the feeling of raw power of holding an adult osprey during band-
ing. He also talked about a thesis by a student who lived among
the Senegalese tribesmen, and how the tribesmen would paddle
out to fish and watch the ospreys dive. At my prodding, he spec-
ulated a little about the roles that ospreys might have played in the
mythic life of primitive man. The idea, mentioned briefly in his
book, had caught my imagination: this fierce hunting bird becoming a totem for people whose survival was dependent on their
hunting or fishing skills.

Before returning to my car I mentioned all the platforms I'd
seen while driving to Alan's house, and my newfound respect for
those who dedicated their lives to giving new homes to the birds.
Alan spoke admiringly of the platform builders—"They're the ones
who have fueled this whole renaissance"—before adding: "But
they aren't *biologists.*"

That was a telling sentence, one that I got the feeling he could
have applied just as easily to certain nature writers. If I left his
house exhilarated, full of new knowledge and excited about
getting down to watching my birds, I also left it with a minor
sense of healthy chastisement. It's possible that as a biologist, he
found the species of nature writer on the whole a tad romantic and
unscientific.

He had a point, particularly in my case. Though I love to take
any opportunity to rail against specialization, I am pure hypocrite.
I stopped taking science courses in high school, turning all my attention to literature. This now seems to me an unhealthy split, particularly as I hope to learn more about the natural world. At one
point Alan mentioned something about those who write about
nature without having a rudimentary concept of evolutionary biology. I took it personally, as perhaps I should have.

"They don't understand what's driving all this. And what's
driving all this is *reproduction.* Read Darwin, for God's sake, read
natural history magazines. There are basics in biology that you

need to have to understand it. Sometimes I don't see any inherent curiosity. For me, it's about fascination."

And so I drove away from Alan Poole's not just with a new sense of excitement and deeper possibilities but with a reading list. If I was going to really learn about ospreys, I'd need to fill in some gaps in my learning. As well as observing the birds, I'd have to get out some basic texts and sit down and study. For the first time in my life, I'd need to learn some science.

WHICH I'VE TRIED to do over the past few weeks. Despite a sometimes comic ineptitude, I've set myself a fairly ambitious task of learning—biology, ornithology, geology.

At first I found myself rebelling. There were times when some of the texts, particularly the ornithology books, seemed to confirm what I saw as a rawly materialistic view of the world. I read about test after sadistic test: "Young chickadees were offered water that made them sick and learned not to drink the water. . . . A bird's eggs were taken from the nest and we observed great distress on the bird's part. [Duh!] . . . When we killed a bird's mate, we learned . . ." And on and on and on. That's when I closed the pages and headed out to the marsh, full of outrage. Who needs to know these things? Especially when the tests only prove the obvious. Isn't too much justified by our constant hunger to unearth every last fact? Don't we overly respect merely scientific truths? Aren't we too in love with so-called hard facts? Science quickly becomes technology, losing its purpose and direction. And science, at its worst, ignores the validity of the intuitive, of the artistic approach to nature, forgetting that we don't just get data in the woods, we get stories.

But having gotten that off my chest, I gradually began to learn from the books, and despite my objections and fears, my whining and kicking, it hasn't been so bad. Happily, I find that again and again the facts confirm my best instincts. For instance, consider the deep intertwining of osprey breeding and osprey nest sites. Most ospreys are monogamous, but as Alan Poole explained to me in Westport, this is a monogamy based on the pair's joint commitment to a nest site, as much as to each other. In other words, it's the building of their homes that makes mere concept corporal. To the ospreys, love of place is more than a fancy idea; this is commitment as biological imperative, a deep instinct for home. While the birds may be compelled by the drive to reproduce, it's significant that familiar ground, a home turf, dramatically increases, indeed is vital to, their chances for reproductive success.

Of course, even here I'm using science as story. The truth is that while I've tried to open my mind to more solid facts, I know I'll never look at nature as a scientist. At best I can hope to wander that unstable but rich territory between science and art, though even to get to that murky place I have a lot of learning to do. But if I can put aside my defensiveness, my tendency to polarize, I might begin to understand that the richest territory is just this land in between.

LET'S BE HONEST. Sometimes sitting out on the marsh for hours on end is simply boring. Even Alan Poole must have occasionally thought so. One of the things I'm learning, one of my profound scientific conclusions, is that April is colder than I remember. The *Cliffs Notes* to my current mode of life would read like this: "The ospreys sit; I sit. The ospreys build; I scribble in my journal. The ospreys fly off to fish; I watch."

For all the surface dullness—and it's true my life wouldn't make a good miniseries—there is still something exciting, even *thrilling* about it. To put myself out here, to *watch*, on the chance that I'll be lifted out of my own life and into a world where the chief concerns are the birdly ones of procuring fish and fortifying the nest. And then, occasionally, to actually become immersed! This, when it happens, is anything but dull.

Take this morning, April 11, for example, when the Quivett male returns with what looks to be a trout. He flies right over the nest twice, the fish gleaming, while the female cries with greater and greater agitation. But instead of bringing the fish to the nest he suddenly ascends forty feet, hovers, drops, floats up, and hovers again, wings flapping wildly in extravagant display. Like a giant hummingbird, he stays in one place, rearing back and flapping like mad. I've seen this courtship ritual—the "sky dance"—before, with the jetty pair, but never from so close. It's a kind of avian chest beating, a testosterone-driven celebration, with the clutched fish signifying competence, the male announcing to all the world both his capacity to provide food and, of course, his intention to mate. Later, the fish devoured, he will do just that, and the wild beating of the wings will repeat the flapping of the dance.

But that is later. Now, having teased her with the fish, he alights on his roost twenty feet from the nest to dine alone. Despite the dance, the fish still has some life in it and flops back and forth more than once. The male, barely glancing down, ignores this death flurry, content to grip it in his enormous talons and let it slowly die. After a minute he begins ripping into the flesh, starting with the mouth area, tearing the fish apart with savage screwdriver twists. He makes short work of it. In ten minutes he is down to the eye, the pink inner meat revealed. This is when the female, who has been silent, begins to beg again, but he still ignores her. I'm impressed by the savagery of his appetite. He is halfway through the fish and still going strong when her begging intensifies. Finally, he delivers the slimy, glittering prize, what is left of a decapitated and mostly detorsoed fish.

THE TIMES OF change—spring's bursting and fall's death— are the most arresting times, and April, even more than March, is a time in between. It's a month of uncertainty, of unpredictability, of opening. The mania for building continues to pulse through the animal world, the season waking the urge to construct in humans, too. Mid-April is also marked by excitement in another way. The big news here is that I've bought some boots, black rubber and knee-high. While I might look even more ridiculous now, decked out like a nineteenth-century English explorer with only my pith helmet missing, the fact is that they make life on the marsh easier. And with each day I'm getting more comfortable being out here.

There are few places that undergo as many daily changes as the salt marsh. It's a true land-in-between, particularly at this point along Quivett Creek, close to where fresh water alchemizes to salt. Change is the constant here: flooding, drying out, flooding again, an environment for both creatures of land and sea, a place overly rich with life and a hundred stories. Furthermore, the Quivett nest is in-between in one other way, the ospreys having chosen to nest almost exactly on the town line, so that until they register to vote no one can be sure if they are in fact Brewster or Dennis residents.

Spring on the marsh constitutes a great resurrection. The marsh itself is a "detritus-based" ecosystem, powered by the rot of marsh grasses from the previous year. As winter ends, the marsh prepares itself for ospreys. It begins with the sun warming the mud. Bacteria comes alive; plankton and algae grow and feed the small fish, which feed the large fish, which feed the ospreys. In this way the birds are perfectly a part of their place, demonstrating what Alan Poole has called "the conversion of sunlight into ospreys." On the salt marsh there is more of everything; the marsh is an ecological phoenix, rising to life off its own death.

BIRDS AREN'T the only ones building on Quivett. Each day the sound of hammering thumps through the quiet of the marsh, a sound that would usually send me straight out of my revery and into a grumbling antidevelopment diatribe. But because I know where the hammering comes from, it doesn't bother me. I admire both the builder and home in this case. Since spring green has not yet filled in the trees, the foundation of the slowly rising house across the way has served as my backdrop while I've watched the Quivett birds these last few weeks. And because Don MacKenzie respects this place, I take the construction as natural, no different from the male osprey lugging another huge stick up to its nest. If the instinct of spring is to construct, then MacKenzie's home seems not so different from the ones I draw in my journal: the red-tailed hawks' tree nest, the herons' roost, and the Canada geese's ground nest near the creek.

Almost two years ago, the first July after Nina and I moved back to Cape Cod, I tramped through what is now MacKenzie's land but what was then the ruins of a place called Sealand. Sealand had once been an aquarium where I'd come as a child to watch ocean animals on display: dolphins named Salty and Spray jumping through hoops, fish behind glass, seals barking and clapping. The park had closed in the '80s and had been abandoned, so that by the time I hiked through it in 1997, it felt like walking into a lost civilization. Tree branches reached like pickpockets through broken windows, glass glittered along the old paths, weeds and vines crawled the walls, and everywhere the wild broke up into rooms that had once tried to contain it. Walking toward the old turtle pool, which had become an algal swamp more aptly called an insect pool, I scared a little bobwhite with a yellow head and the brown-black speckling of a hen, setting it running down the path on its short comic legs before it attempted a kind of brief fluttery flight. Once the bird had scrambled into the bushes, I followed some ivy vines into what was once the "fish library." The place was well vandalized: pink insulation showing like wounds on the walls, and glass and plaster spread across the rotting carpet.

The remains of a twelve-pack of Miller Lite lay scattered over the occasionally gouged floor, and these appropriate words were spraypainted on the wall: DESTROY SOCIETY.

After inspecting the library's moldering remains, I walked over to the building that had previously housed Sealand's main attraction. In faded letters—or, actually, in the space below where the letters had once been—I read the words DOLPHIN POOL. Admission was cheaper than it had been when I was a kid: there was a gaping hole in the wall I could easily climb through. The pool itself, empty except for trash and puddles of black rainwater, was about thirty feet at the deep end but still struck me as absurdly small, hardly enough room for what I remembered as being nearly jet-propelled dolphins. The reeking debris at the pool's bottom consisted of old fertilizer bags, several cinder blocks, a long pole likely once used for training the dolphins, and a dead skunk.

As I climbed through the ruins I couldn't help but feel that that was a more satisfying trip to Sealand than my childhood visits. The dolphins were amazing, and they did delight me when I was young, but I'm sure that now I'd see them through the usual haze of captured sadness. Though I've never gone on a whale watch, I'd always wanted to, at least until last summer, when one of the boats accidentally killed the whale they were "watching." Voyeurism can be costly, I remind myself; watchers are complicitous, too.

But that July, as day turned to night, I did my share of greedy watching. That was the day that I had my memorable twilight encounter with the mother osprey protecting her young. After I turned away from the depressing space of the dolphin pool, I headed down, past the library, to the marsh. It was dusk by then, and I noticed that marshland had encroached on Sealand, phragmites whispering behind the backs of the buildings. Red-winged blackbirds flitted across the tops of the grasses as I climbed atop an abandoned refrigerator and stared toward the tidal inlet, catching a glimpse of the osprey nest. Not satisfied with a mere view, I crashed down through the reeds, trampling a path through breakable grasses that grew five feet above my head. Between the phragmites I could see a nearly full orange moon rising over Quivett Creek. It was appropriate, I thought, that the marsh bordered Sealand, as it, too, was an in-between place, caught between land and water, and it might easily have been called by the same oxymoronic name as the park. The richest zones of food and life are those between the tides, places not quite water or land, living places that give off the constant smell of death and decay. By the time I emerged from the soughing grasses my shoes were encased in black, stinking muck, and I found myself surprisingly close, too close, to the osprey nest. It was then that I saw the mother osprey swooping back and forth, warning me away.

As moving as being close to the osprey was, it was Sealand itself that I thought about as I walked back up to my car. On the ride home I tried to make sense of the satisfaction I felt with the park's dilapidated state. Crossing the marsh on Bridge Street, catching a glimpse of our neighborhood mute swans like bright question marks in the dark, I decided that the thrill came from the reversal of the place's nature. That is, it came from seeing a place that once contained wildness now being contained by it, a place that had been for merely watching nature now overrun with it. And a place where human debris was on display, where wilderness, or half wilderness, had won for a while, as if it had thrown over the cages and exhibits and broken free.

Liberation stirred in my chest for all of five seconds, until I turned right, off Bridge and onto Sesuit Neck Road. At that corner a huge square barn of a house stood on a manicured lawn, and it, like so many places on the Cape, served only to remind me of what had once been there. In this place I remembered a copse of locusts that I had tramped through as a boy, reminding me of the

Cape's diminishment. Maybe that was another part of Sealand's appeal: it was one of the few places on Cape Cod where what was was more wild than what had been.

BUT, AS ALWAYS, the future intrudes. Now it is 1999, two years later, and the ruins are no longer ruins. Not long after that July day I drove by Sealand and noticed the real estate agent's sign. A year later the bulldozers were at work, plowing down the old structures to make room for what I supposed would be condos. A quaint stone wall sprouted, a wall that I feared would mock the values it mimicked. I responded to this loss with the usual anger, and felt great relief upon finally learning that it was the MacKenzies who would be building there. It's true, dozers did plow down a couple of the old ruins, but, as it turned out, this was a labor of love, not cash. The best arts make healthy use of what is already there, and, like the Quivett ospreys, MacKenzie built on an already established foundation, relying on found materials to construct his home. A man who crafts violins, Don MacKenzie and his son have spent the last year involved in the most organic sort of architecture, raising a home built not just on the land but on the human past. The foundation of their two-bedroom house is the aquarium's old foundation, and they have made ample use of all that was there before. What once was the corridor between the tanks, where children stared through green glass at sand sharks and blowfish, is now a walkway of stones between a garden, where pink zinnias, strawflowers, marigolds, and bachelor's buttons will soon bloom. The old fish library has lent its foundation to a vast barn, with white pine floors that smell of sawdust; part of that barn will become a studio for Don and his violins. Not long ago seventeen friends and neighbors helped him move the deck that was by the turtle pool, so that it now juts off the barn's back, providing a perfect view of the osprey nest. Old benches from Sealand dot the yard that slopes down to the marsh, placed in shady spots under trees. And near another flower garden, by some rocks, is the spot where the first two Sealand dolphins, Salty and Spray's predecessors, were buried. Throughout the place the old serves the new, compost for growth.

Just a week ago, on April 23, I pulled into the MacKenzies' driveway to ask them some questions about the ospreys, since they were, with the exception of the Canada geese, the birds' closest neighbors. Don and his son stood by a bonfire, into which they fed brush. Smoke turned our view of the marsh rubbery while Don told me about the drama of the previous year, when one of the young ospreys had refused to leave, staying at the nest until November. He then described watching ospreys chase a coyote away from the nest, battle with great blue herons, and fish close to home, plunging right down into Quivett Creek. And he spoke proudly about the short-eared owl in the neighborhood, and pointed across the street at the pine where the red-tails nested. As he talked, it was obvious that he and his family weren't just physically close to the birds. As surely as the ospreys built their wild nest on a tame foundation, the MacKenzies had built their new home on a foundation of the wild.

Don gave me a tour of the stockpile of the old Sealand materials that they planned on reusing: two-by-fours, two-by-eights, walls, shingles, window frames, windows. Even the bricks could be reused, because the original mason had stuck with the old formula, which, unlike the modern one, made it easy to chip mortar off individual bricks. The old masons understood the fact that materials could be used again, as do the MacKenzies. Even the thick blue-green aquarium glass was going to be put back into use; Don didn't see why he couldn't use it for showers, or as kitchen counters.

One of the things Don and I discussed during my visit was a bit of bad news. Coming out daily to the marsh behind his house has been a bit like reading a good book, right down to the surprising plot twists. Two weeks ago in early April, it had looked like the Quivett ospreys were down to some serious nesting: they had mated, and the female was spending her days down low, only occasionally relieved by the male, presumably incubating the eggs. But then, after business took me away for a few days, I came back to find the nest temporarily abandoned. Don filled me in on the date, around April 18, that they'd suddenly left the nest and we agreed that something—a raccoon, probably—must have gotten to the eggs.

The birds came back a day later and are back at it now, re-building the nest and mating again, but when I called Alan Poole to report on what had happened, he told me that it's likely their second efforts will fail, too, since failure is the norm for osprey second clutches. Though it may seem odd, given the many warm months ahead, ospreys that start late are often unsuccessful, as if their genes, anticipating fall's cold, understand that they are too far behind schedule. Those born late have less time, before fall migration, to learn the skills that help them survive, and this somehow translates to the parents of second clutches, who often look, in Poole's words, "as if they just aren't trying as hard," as if they know that their offspring are doomed. In other words, though they were back first, at Quivett the early birds may get nothing. This came as a shock, and I'm not quite ready to accept it. It's still only April, after all, and they are carrying on with such patience, with such earnestness, that I can't help but believe there is reason to hope. Of course, ospreys whose clutches fail, like young ospreys, still funnel their reproductive energy directly into the nest, spending hours gathering and fixing up the walls—"housekeeping," as it's called. It's almost as if, having failed at their main goal, they throw themselves into the second, and, to the human eye, there is something almost desperate about all this building. But, as I say, I'm not ready to concede defeat at Quivett yet.

Meanwhile, there are early signs of success at all the other nests. At the lopsided nest on Chapin, the female is nesting deep, rarely switching places with the male and depending on him almost exclusively for food. The scene is repeated at the Simpkins Neck nest and, to my surprise, across the harbor. Two weeks ago I'd written off the harbor birds, but one morning, while stretching my back, I heard the familiar *kew-kew* coming through our walls. I walked outside to find that they were both on the nest and that the nest itself had somehow bulked up while I wasn't looking. Perhaps they will not prove so good-for-nothing after all.

Still, while the other nests flourish, I return to Quivett, sticking to my routine, coming to the marsh daily, like a supplicant. I sit in my spot where the grass is matted down and watch and wait, occasionally flicking ticks off my sweatpants. As the season deepens, the flush time is almost here: everything is blooming except the hoary post oak (which takes its stubborn time), and soon the smell of honeysuckle will permeate the air. Downy woodpeckers fly like swallows up at Scargo Tower, and barn swallows, of course, fly even more like swallows: they zip and dart over the marsh, flashing bellies the color of cooked mussels, carving up the air. They seem intent on expending as much energy as possible at every moment, the opposite of the ospreys, who pick their spots.

I sit here, watching the birds bolster what may be a doomed nest, and listen to Don MacKenzie hammering on his house in the background. MacKenzie's house helps me organize my thoughts on human building and helps me answer a question I consider vital: how do I use my own instinct for building to the best purpose? I like nothing better than to rail against those who construct enormous dream houses in our neighborhood, destroying Sesuit Neck's character, but I know I'm driven by similar impulses. MacKenzie's house reminds me of the need to root my ambition in the natural world, to keep in touch with the earth. Certainly his house is ambitious, the result of an obsessive project my he will likely work on for the rest of his life. Though his energy to make a home is not rawly instinctive, it does spring from an animal base, like the osprey's instinct for home. But he has also given consideration to what is to be done with this instinct; he has married it to thought, to reason. This is an ambition that remembers its roots in the wild but also embraces the particularly human gifts of imagination and foresight.

At the moment I am more falcon than osprey, settling in another's home, though the other is my parent. I live here for free, squatting in a family house that would otherwise go abandoned. But I'm bothered by my inabilty to make my own home. Besides a few minor repairs, I've constructed nothing. I suppose it's building my life here with Nina that really concerns me. This project involves patching together various, random means of support as we attempt to live close to the ocean and close to our passions. At times it isn't easy, like the other day, when I discovered that we had a balance of $3.25 in our joint checking account. But at other times I'd like to nail a sprig of greenery to our door to convey our heightened excitement. The key seems to be that, like the MacKenzies, our lives are built on a foundation of the natural world. Before starting to write each morning, I take my tea out on the back deck to see the sun rise, and for a break I walk down to the beach to greet the seals. This may sound romantic, but it's also practical. More and more I find that not just my work but my life depends on this direct connection with the world. It may be as simple as this: human constructs, whether architectural, philosophic, scientific, or literary, are strongest when nature serves as their base. The best of our creations are a marriage of the human and the wild, thought and instinct, the product of a place in between.

And if it's the places in between that are most interesting and the most nourishing, then they are also the places that hold the most hope for the future. Though the footing is uncertain, I know this: it is in these lands—the lands between sea and water, science and art, low tide and high—that I'll gather my own material. There is a life that is between our present and our past selves, our self-consciousness and our wildness. It's a better life, I'm convinced.

Though I know I'm supposed to be out here looking for science, not stories, I can't help but find one more lesson to be learned from house and nest. Both build on a foundation of what has come before, relying on found materials. The ospreys get what they need where they can: lately they've added a mesh potato sack, yellow marine line made of nylon, a white plastic grocery bag. Like the ospreys, I am somewhat sloppy of method, taking what I can, picking randomly, haphazardly. I, too, gather found materials to put to use in my life, driven by an instinct to build something, however unkempt or goofy, and I, too, frown on the persnickety, the neat, the overly proper, preferring to build a large and unkempt nest.

Fishing

We hunger for a kind of experience
deep enough to change our selves, our form of life.

—JACK TURNER, *The Abstract Wild*

I love all men who dive.

—MELVILLE

Ospreys are the only raptors that dive fully into the water to catch their prey. Try to imagine the physical sensation. To skim across the sky, above the ocean, peering down with eyes that can see into the shallows from forty, sixty, even a hundred feet up. To catch a glint or the shadow of a movement and know it to be a fish, the one thing that keeps you alive. To hover, adjust, beating your wings so that you stay in place, like a giant kingfisher or hummingbird. Then to dive, to commit, to tuck with folded wings and plunge downward at over forty miles an hour while still keeping your eyes on the prey, calculating its size and movement. To adjust in midair, redirecting, considering even the refraction of the fish's image in the water, before pulling in your wings and diving again. And then, at the last second before hitting the water, to throw your wings back and your talons forward, striking feet first. To plunge in, splash, immerse, and make contact at the same time, trapping, piercing, clutching a slippery, scaled, cold-blooded creature.

Now imagine what comes next. Securing the fish, aided by the sharp, horny scales on the pads beneath your toes. For a moment being out of your element and in your prey's, feeling wet, awkward, ungainly. Then lifting off from the water with a great thrust of exertion, soaked and heavy, hefting an animal that may weigh half of what you do. Beating your wings furiously and rising, shaking the water off like a wet dog, already using your reversible outer talon to adjust the squirming fish, turning the fish so that it faces forward to reduce drag as you lift into the air, triumphant (or at the very least *successful*), shaking off silver flecks of spray.

To even imagine a dive is to get excited. *What a bold way to live!* To find one thing you do well and then to stake your life on it. It's as simple and direct as passion. It *is* passion. Peter Matthiessen wrote: "Simplicity is the whole secret of well-being." If so, the ospreys have got it figured out. It isn't hard to picture a band of primitive osprey tribesmen watching the birds and learning from them. One thing they might have learned, and one thing that appeals to me, is how the osprey's dive weds calculated patience to wild aggression. He who hesitates is smart, at least if when he finally commits he commits fully. For the ospreys, the hesitation is as important as the dive. The birds have a remarkable success rate, some catching well over 50 percent of what they dive for (like humans, athleticism varies; a few particularly adept birds catch close to 90), and this is due in good part to the predive patience, the search for the right target. This careful adjustment will often carry over into the dive itself. After the bird has tucked its wings and dropped down thirty feet, it may pause and readjust, and it may repeat this a time or two again, as if descending imaginary stairs. But while the predive ritual demands control and calculation, the plunge itself is about the opposite of control. It is a moment of full commitment, of abandon, and, finally, of immersion.

BUT NOW a confession. So far I have witnessed dives only in my imagination. Despite having spent the past two months roaming the marsh and the last two years walking the beach, I've never seen an osprey dive. This is a fairly major failing for a budding ospreyologist. By all accounts the dive—the search, hover, tuck, and foot-first plunge—is the pinnacle of osprey artistry. It's also how the birds survive. An osprey is built for fishing, and over the last fifteen million years or so has been perfectly honed by evolution to get its food solely by diving from the sky. While most raptors hunt a variety of prey, and in a variety of ways, ospreys eat fish almost exclusively. Despite the nearly constant vocalizations of the Quivett female to her mate, one question she never asks is, "What's for dinner?"

An osprey nest is ideal for the beginning bird-watcher. It's big and conspicuous, and the birds, who are also big, go about their behavior in a fairly obvious, even-paced manner, as if winking and making sure you get it. With a pair of binoculars and a little patience you can be a perfectly successful voyeur, watching them mate, nest, feed, preen, sleep. But seeing a dive is another matter. The foraging range of an osprey can extend as far as fifteen miles from the nest, depending on the weather and what's running, and ospreys fish in the ocean, ponds, lakes, and tidal inlets. I've spent a good part of May kayaking up the creeks, along with the herring, hoping to put myself in the right place to watch a dive, and jumping on my bike and desperately chasing the male as he flaps inland toward the Brewster ponds.

Despite my failures, and a creeping sense of inadequacy, something about the activity itself excites me. For the first time in my life I'm taking what I know about nature—about wind, water, weather, and animals—and trying to put this knowledge to use to achieve something. Though what I'm mainly finding out is that I don't know much, there are times when I feel perfectly content, consumed with the process of hunting for the hunt, fishing for fishing. There's a primitive satisfaction in reducing life to one goal, and I sometimes remember Alan Poole's speculations about a Neandertal or Cro-Magnon osprey people. Think of the raw simplicity of a hunter's life. *Get food,* as a commandment, is thrillingly reductive. If there is anxiety about the task, at least it's specific anxiety. To track, to hunt, means to focus on one thing, the prey; but to focus well, the whole world must be taken into account. My own commandment over the last weeks has been only a little more complex than primitive man's. Mine is: *See bird dive.*

Alan Poole relates a missonary's story of how a Bolivian Indian "slipped a warm bone" from an osprey under the skin of his arm, "apparently in hopes of absorbing hawklike skills at hunting." That seems a little drastic, but it might be worth slipping a bone under my forearm, at least if it instills an enlivened sense of purpose. As it is, I'm not above sniffing the air or playing my hunches. One thing I hope for is that I'll soon have osprey dreams. I fully expect to, not out of any mystical alliance, but because osprey is what I do all day. It's been my experience that dreams steal from life, particularly life's more exciting parts. When I played Ultimate Frisbee in college, I'd sometimes spend the better part of the night skying or diving after discs. In *The Snow Leopard,* Peter Matthiessen writes about his young son's artwork: "Ecstasy is identity with all existence, and ecstasy showed in his bright paintings; like the Aurignacion hunter who became the deer he drew on the cave wall, there was no 'self' to separate him from the bird or flower." This sentence may also be less mystical than it sounds, more practical and obvious. To be good hunters we must look at what we're aiming at, seeing and becoming what we stalk.

WHILE I HUNT the world opens. It's impossible to jam all of May into my journal, the month refusing to be organized. Too much is happening too fast. A yellow-shafted flicker rattles its jungle call off the top of a telephone pole, a red-winged blackbird slides down a cattail, and two red-tailed hawks breach the clouds, spiraling and whistling upward in a graceful love dance. Hundreds of feet above the Quivett marsh, they circle and circle, letting off their unearthly cries as they disappear upward beyond the limits of human vision. The other day a pudgy bobwhite flew behind the house, and both types of orioles, northern and orchard, are back, splashing the air with bold colors: tangerine and black, black and blood-red. A chickadee is building its nest under our bedroom windowsill, emitting a loud clicking, as if someone were perpetually knocking on our door. In the mornings the world explodes with birdsong and you wake to a noise so clamorous you wonder how you ever slept.

One day in early May, on the way to the beach, I startle a whole woodwind section of mourning doves, and they break from the phone line with a hushed sound like the rapid opening and closing of an umbrella. In the woods I see more grackles posture, puffing up their chests in a mating ritual, iridescent colors in their black feathers like flying oil slicks. The spring seesaw notes of chickadees, the upward twittering of cardinals, the peals of thrushes. The songs sound pretty, but, armed with my new knowledge, I know them to be laced with testosterone, with claims of property and braggadocio about gonad size. This is the less-than-proper truth behind the dainty doily melodies. Songs of power and sex. With all this boasting about sexuality and territory, it's almost too loud to think, which may be the whole point.

And not just songs but dances, often elaborate. Among raptors these spring displays include chasing, plummeting, hovering, butterflying, volplaning, and soaring. The osprey's fish dance is impressive, but perhaps the most spectacular of rituals, bordering on pure ostentation, is that of the bald eagle. Pairs of eagles can be seen flying together, one *upside down,* linking talons in midair, looking like mirror images of each other, one above and one below. And this is just the beginning of their hotdogging. Next they begin to roll over and over, like a sideways Ferris wheel, whipping each other around in a technique called whirling. Ornithologists Leslie Brown and Dean Amadon elaborate: "With wings at full stretch, tautly connected by the outstretched legs, the great birds come tumbling down in a series of cartwheels, over and over one another, often for several hundred feet, finally separating close to the ground and water and flying upwards again."

MEANWHILE, AT THE marsh, green shoots sprout next to last year's brown phragmites, like seven-foot-tall tulip petals (for the moment I forgive the plant its invasive nature). It's a different marsh than the one I walked around just two weeks ago, almost lime green in places, nearing the peak of fruition, of what John Hay calls "prodigality." Even the tardy oaks now join the budding, and in the mornings I listen to a massive soughing through new leaves. But while the wind blows, and blows hard at times, it doesn't phase the birds or me. Warm and pleasant, it has lost its bite. At dawn on May 6 at Quivett, as this new wind laves the land, I look through the haze toward to the north, toward the ocean, and see two deer, almost chestnut red in the morning light, grazing their way across the spartina, slowly picking through a line of dew.

This is the time of year when life fills every void; if I put my tea mug on the ground for half a minute it crawls with insects. Sometimes it seems that watching the ospreys is just an excuse to be out in this rushing world, an excuse to watch the different shapes that buds take—some delicate, some hooflike, some bloody purple things like animals just being born. At home the honey-suckle sweetens and tenderizes the air, and while our post oak is the one tree that stubbornly refuses to fully bloom, its tentative buds finally dribble down. Nina and I spend more and more time outside, watching the green procession. At night we take our drinks and dinner out on the deck and listen to the waves lap, the puttering of lobster boats.

While I haven't seen an osprey dive yet, it seems I've watched every other avian fisherman go about its work over the past month. From Bridge Street I witnessed the black silhouette of a heron spearing its own reflection at sunset, ripples wavering in the molten red water as it emerged with something silvery and small. And I've seen a kingfisher holding perfectly still in the air, though *still* only in the sense a hummingbird is, hovering, wings beating faster than sight, before plunging. At the beach near our house, terns dive like thrown darts, living check marks jabbing into the water.

But the birds I most want to watch dive keep teasing me. I've seen many close calls but no successful dives, and there are moments when my search seems a bit frantic. I spend a lot of time wandering Wing Island and Paine's Creek, where the herring have begun to return, wriggling back to the source. I know that to the ospreys the herring present an irresistible feast. And ospreys do come, though at first I have trouble telling them apart from gulls, at least from any height or distance.

On Alan Poole's urging I pick up *Hawks in Flight,* by Pete Dunne, David Sibley, and Clay Sutton. This book, as I understand it, is the state-of-the-art guide to raptor identification. "An Osprey seems unlikely ever to be confused with another bird, but it is," the authors write, adding that ospreys "can plausibly be confused only with a Bald Eagle or a large gull." I will testify as to the plausibility of this confusion. While we don't have many bald eagles, gulls crowd our neighborhood. If you think of the ends of the wings as hands, and the end feathers as fingers, an osprey's wing's distinctive identifying trait is that, unlike other raptors, it bends at the carpus, or wrist, giving the hawk-watcher—even the beginning hawk-watcher—something to look for, an easy "search image." This crook, along with the distinctive black and white markings, small head, and somewhat labored "arthritic" wing beat, do paint a fairly unmistakable picture, and as the month of May goes on, I get better and better at spotting ospreys, even from a good distance. But during those first weeks I make the mistakes of the beginner, running across marshes and scribbling down field notes while staring up at a herring gull. The problem, at first, is that gulls also have a crook in their wings, though, it seems to me, their crook forms more of a V, closer to the "elbow" than the wrist. Gulls, particularly great black-backed gulls, are also a lot bigger than I remember, and often are marked in near-osprey patterns of black and white. There are clear differences, however. As the hawk boys put it: "The wing beat of the larger species of gulls is methodical, languid, and shallow, with overtones of effortlessness or unmindfulness. The wing beat of an Osprey is stiff and labored and seems the product of concentrated effort. On the average, gulls flap a good deal more than do Ospreys."

At night I continue to bone up on osprey facts. I learn that ospreys have been clocked flying between twenty and eighty miles per hour, at times breaking forty when they dive. Though they can't match the speed of the fastest raptors—peregrine falcons, for instance, are believed to exceed two hundred miles per hour in a stoop—their angled wing design, along with their long and numerous wing feathers, have been particularly adapted for the jolt of diving into the water and the exertion of lifting out. While accipiters (a group that includes goshawks, sharp-shinned hawks, and Cooper's hawks) prey on and carry birds significantly smaller than they are, ospreys have been known to lift fish matching their own weight. "The wings of an osprey are remarkable," writes Floyd Scholz in *Birds of Prey*. "The long, high-arching design allows the osprey to carry much heavier weight loads in relation to body size than any other bird of prey." The feathers are also especially adapted for fishing, the plumage dense and oily, keeping them dry during their multiple daily immersions.

The capture of a living fish would be impossible without powerful, specialized wings, but the bird's toes and talons do the real dirty work. This is fairly standard procedure in the raptor world. In *Eagles, Hawks and Falcons of the World*, a beautiful compilation of all things raptor (which I've taken to simply calling "the hawk book") Brown and Amadon write of raptors, "The actual killing of prey is achieved by the feet." An osprey's feet, like a pergrine's, look grossly oversized, but they are perfectly task-efficient. The toes are scaly, the bottoms of the toes studded with projections called spicules. The spicules barb down into the fish, and the grip is sure and spiky. Moreover, an osprey's legs are exceedingly long, so that they can stretch down into the water with what Pete Dunne calls a "boardinghouse reach." The long legs also act as shock absorbers, muting the impact upon hitting the water.

WHILE I'VE YET to see what I most want to see this spring, these early weeks of May offer other unexpected pleasures. I try to stay alert to the world beyond my goal. Though I focus my energies on one species of bird, I unintentionally learn about many others. For instance, I'd always looked at gulls the way I look at robins, their commonness rendering them invisible. But now I discover that gulls are better fliers, and more generally interesting, than I ever gave them credit for. A few times I've watched a pause and a dive, impressed by the aerial acrobatics, before realizing that it was "just a gull." This "just a" keeps cropping up, like the day I excitedly tried to identify a mysterious seesaw note before discovering that it was "just" the spring song of the chickadee. Squirrels, grackles, sparrows, and Canada geese also suffer from this justness, or injustness, all carrying on with their own lives, oblivious that they have been assigned a lesser position on the human scale of interest. Somehow they manage to continue nesting and mating without letting what we think bother them too much.

Other times my search for the osprey's dive leads me to sights entirely new. One afternoon during the first week of May, Fred Dunford, the archaeologist at the natural history museum, mentions that while driving on the bridge over the Herring River in Harwich, he saw an osprey fishing. The next morning I'm on my bike, map crumpled between my right hand and the handlebar, scouting around the dirt paths that circle Swan Lake and follow the sinuous river. The air hangs thick, gray and cloud-scumbled, and reflections of branches undulate in the dark water. The swans are out, but last year's osprey nests remain unoccupied. This is the day I see the kingfisher skim over the water with its rattling call, then plunge under and come up with a fish. The sight just presents itself to me, unbidden. I decide that it will take a similar act of grace for me to see that singular graceful act, the osprey's dive, and that perhaps I'm trying too hard. But pedaling home along the path, I startle a bunch of grayish birds that I first assume are gulls. They don't behave like gulls, however, flying off in a loose flock before landing in another tree. I get off my bike and try to creep closer, and when they fly off again they look like slivers of blue against the gray sky. This time I walk more quietly toward them, keeping my distance. I've seen a lot this spring, which should have made me calmer, but I still tend to run impatiently toward what I see. I don't sit still or hang back, lacking a predator's patience. Now I manage to get close without scaring them, eight birds scattered through a tall red pine, all sitting fairly close to each other. My field guide tells me they are black-crowned night herons, roosting and resting up for a big night of fishing. As I pedal home I remind myself to be patient. I haven't seen a dive yet, it's true, but each time I come out I'm more filled with the expectation of it.

A couple of days later, on May 10, I kayak all the way up Quivett Creek to the osprey nest. One thing I've learned this spring is that kayaking is the right way to enter the marsh. Low and quiet. Not the usual crunching over stalks and crabs that sound like eggshells breaking, warning every animal within two miles, or, the alternative, sloshing through knee-deep muck. Though I'm hesitant to use the word *flow,* attended as it is by New Age chiming, here I can't resist. To kayak is to be invited, pulled, tugged into another world, a world where I'm a stranger, though a stranger who feels curiously at home. At Quivett the tide is with me and the current tugs me in deeper, into narrower winding paths that curve and convolute, my paddle barely lapping the water while the spartina rustles. It seems important that I come at this place from below, deferentially, though it's taken me many years to begin to enter the marsh in this way. As I turn a corner I see a yellowlegs walk along a shallow shelf of mud, pecking down at minnows that come in with the tide.

Despite being outside for much of this spring, I know I'm just beginning to enter the marsh. So much goes on that I don't see. This food-rich inlet teems with mussels, moon jellyfish, barnacles, scallops, mud snails, skeleton shrimp, turtles, and, of course, fish and fry of all varieties. Above me minuscule spiral shells dot the eelgrass and gulls colic the sea hay with their nests and owl-faced harriers hunt and coyotes roam and howl at night. Even the walls of mud are alive: black seaweed hangs from the ledges like the wet wings of a bat, fluttering in the wind. As I paddle I have the sense that if I'm trying to get away from it all, I've come to exactly the wrong place.

I make the journey along with the herring, hundreds of them, though still not at full surge, bluish squiggling masses pushing toward their end. Stripers pulse by, too. Just as the tide pulls all of us in, Quivett pulls me out of self. That's saying something, for I'm not easily pulled, clinging as I do to the first person. But here it seems almost effortless, almost graceful, and there are moments— and on the best days more than moments—when nature apprehends me. At times I don't want to give in to this place, I really don't, but it doesn't leave me any choice. This spring has been my coming-out party. Sometimes I feel as if I can string together not just moments and hours but whole days, immersing myself and letting this feeling spread throughout my life. When the sea grass hisses and I turn a corner deeper into the marsh, I can't help but suspect I'm rounding a corner in myself as well.

Fortunately, my nose keeps my brain from reaching too high. The marsh provides this consistent irony: from the town's most lively, food-filled place, the smell of fresh death emanates. Here there's always plenty of murder and intrigue: fish killing fish, birds killing fish, birds killing other birds. But there's life alongside death. I watch a muskrat scramble up into its hole, knowing that ospreys have occasionally taken them as prey during their rare— and possibly accidental—breaks from fish. Horseshoe crabs mate everywhere, and light plays and pulsates off the muck banks. Nature repeats herself shamelessly, and the walls of revealed muck look almost exactly like the desert canyon walls of Utah, even down to miniature cliff dwellings, though here wetness, not aridity, is the theme. While the tide comes in, water still trickles out down tiny waterfalls, playing a clear, hollow-sounding song.

As I near the osprey nest I pick up the bird equivalent of a police escort, territorial Canada gesse paddling in front of the kayak and honking. This alerts the ospreys, who swoop off the nest, flying down low, their six-foot wingspans looking even wider from up close. They are such beautiful birds, black and white tinted by the sun's silver, that for a moment I wonder how I could ever mistake them for gulls. The creek winds right by the nest, giving me the best view yet of the Quivett pair. The nest itself rises mountainous from down here; with no young to incubate, piling up massive amounts of *stuff* has been the Quivett pair's principal activity. I paddle beyond the nest, to Sea Street, once a working road that spanned the marsh but now a decaying ruin, phragmites breaking through the concrete. The creek runs right up to the old rusted sign that divides the towns of Dennis and Brewster.

These marshes wind through our towns like a mucky subconscious, and I love the fact that it's hard for people to build on them. Here there's no foundation; you can never rest on certainties for long. On the marsh it's easier to accept the fact that there are no set answers, that everything is variable, each case particular. The month of May also helps make uncertainties easier to accept, making it easier to form a new philosophy almost hourly, as fits each particular case—each day, each moment. I pull the boat up onto the muck below Sea Street, waiting to turn back with the tide. In this way I retain the sense of flow while cheating myself out of a workout. Feeling as lazy as the afternoon, I glide back out. On the way I drift up to the shore, sending black-bellied plovers and ruddy turnstones running off over the grass. I paddle easily back to Crowe's pasture, where the creek flows into open water. The wind picks up slightly on the bay, but the water remains calm and flat. I am lying back in the kayak, looking up at pale blue-white cloud formations and thinking of nothing except the burritos we're having for dinner, when an osprey suddenly materializes right above me. It's no gull, I can tell right away—no "just a." It's a single large osprey, and it is hunting. I don't sit up but watch from my recumbent position, a fish's-eye view of the hunt. From this angle the bird looks menacing, as it must be for a herring or a flounder, a death-bringing shadow. But this angel of death ignores me, obviously focused on movement right near my boat. He adjusts his primaries, the thirteen long flight feathers looking like ragged fingers. He hovers, dips, appears ready to make the final plunge, while I hold my breath. At one point he draws his wings into a tuck, but then he pulls up at the last second, flies, treads air again, kicking his feet out. I feel tension in him, and in me: *will he plunge or not?* He starts to dive again and pulls out, the tension breaking in both of us. For ten minutes I hunt with him—treading, hovering, half-diving—then nothing. Each time he stays still and starts to flap I tense. Each time we are both disappointed. Then, with a few strong flaps, he banks on the wind and starts heading back toward Dennis, toward my house, perhaps toward the harbor nest. Less than a minute later he's out of sight.

The moment of first seeing the bird was one of raw joy, but already, as I paddle back to Paine's landing, I know that I'll label this day as a failure. I almost saw an osprey dive. *Almost.* How idiotic to judge the experience only by this. While I didn't see a dive itself, I came closer than I ever have, feeling as if I were part of the hunt. To judge the day a failure is to judge the hunt itself as failure, to understand only the ends of things, not the process. It is, I think, a universal idiocy, but particularly a modern and American one. Despite seeing so many new things, learning so much more, I've been falling into a trap, reducing the complexity of nature to a single goal. But these tidy bits of philosophy notwithstanding, I *do* feel dissatisfied by not having seen what I've come to see, unable to check that item off my list. At the same time I try to remind myself of the amazing patience the osprey showed as he prepared for the dive, and to know that the same patience is required of me.

THERE ARE OTHER moments when the monomania of my quest loosens its grip. A few days later I have another close call, again at Quivett. This May evening I decide to circumnavigate the marsh, this time by land, not water. As the sun lowers itself delicately toward the bay, the spartina and phragmites shine. Last year's reeds might as well be van Gogh sunflowers, while spring green—a bright, almost silly, suburban green—lights up the marsh edge. I hike down the west side of the marsh, jumping over muck canals and covering myself in mud, at one point stumbling into what I'm pretty sure is a muskrat hole. As I walk I keep one eye on the Quivett nest, not quite able to get my mind around the fact that this nest will likely fail. On top of returning early from the Southern Hemisphere, these birds made the very sensible choice of nesting out here, protected in the middle of a marsh, rather than living over at the harbor. And yet the harbor female is down low, nesting hard, contradicting what I saw as her "lazy" nature, while these two continue their frantic housekeeping.

At the beach shadows of eelgrass wave over beige sand. I walk straight into the water in my silly rubber boots, the tide low enough to wade across Quivett's mouth. The evening shimmers, tides fidgeting against each other. The water is copper-colored, though spotted with deep mahogany patches. On the other side of the creek, near Wing Island, I see a deer, beautiful, tawny, white-tailed, walking quietly, almost pensively.

I veer east, onto Wing Island itself. The hump of land called Wing is an island only in the sense that water fills the salt marshes surrounding it at high tide. Fred Dunford told me the local Native American tribes would come to Wing Island in summer, after wintering inland in the woods. Though they lived deeply in their place, they had two distinct seasonal homes, following food and weather to their advantage. It's above the raised woodland of the island and the winding tidal creeks of the marsh that I see today's ospreys. Three of them, interweaving like skiers cutting tracks in fresh snow, their underwings lit up reddish in the low light. They form a hunting party, though at first I think it's too late to fish. But then I see one of the birds dive and pull up, right near me, and later one flaps wildly, screeching, while the other two fly over to see what the commotion is about. I watch several dives, but the shoulders of the marsh obscure the final results. The sky fills with chipping warning cries, and I think again how easily the birds cover great distances, as I spastically run this way and that over the marsh, trying to keep them all in sight through my binoculars. I fail, of course, and pay for it. Soon one of the three is flying by, straightening out a herring, while the other two follow, screeching and complaining. Now I've seen everything—the preparation, the dive, the caught fish—everything except the plunge itself.

Tonight, however, as the sun reddens the creek and the ospreys fly off, I don't feel depressed. The sunset helps me focus on the successes of the spring. For instance, I can now tell an osprey from a gull, even from a half mile away, and with more and more frequency I'm seeing them fish. It's only a matter of time, I tell myself, until I see a dive.

AT NIGHT AFTER my hunting ends, I jump back into my books, trying to learn more about the birds, particularly something that might aid in the next day's hunt. All of the air treading, hovering, and half-diving I've been watching is, according to Stephen Carpenteri's *Osprey: The Fish Hawk,* "part of the seek-find-commit sequence that makes a successful hunt." It doesn't escape me that this is the same sequence I'm trying to emulate. "Careful observation and imitation of animal habits enhance the hunter's chance of success," I read of Neandertals in Carelton Coon's *The Story of Man.*

The more I read, the more I love the romance of the old bird books, the mythic style and anecdotal spirit of the old-time naturalists. Not as purely scientific as our present observers, they say things that sometimes sound a little silly to the modern ear. But even when they were wrong, they were wrong on their own terms. They saw what they saw with their own eyes. They were freer to speculate, to generalize and air it out, and what they lacked in accuracy they made up for in fun. They were also less stingy with poetry—the way, for instance, Arthur Cleveland Bent calls fish "the finny prey" and describes the "exuberant spirits of mating season."

Of course, for sheer outlandishness the old stories can't match the modern science books. For the first time I can understand why creationists are skeptical of evolution. In my ornithology text I read how birds developed from reptiles: "the scales on the forelimb became elongated, and their posterior margins frayed out, in time evolving into feathers." *In time evolving into feathers!* As if this were the natural course of events—for feathers to appear! But if this sort of change is hard to imagine, it could also provide Bible-thumpers with conclusive evidence of the miraculous. If they were to actually embrace theories of evolution, they would find miracles that made loaves and fishes pale by comparison.

My reading always leads me back to the ospreys and their dives. Bent describes the osprey's plunge as "dashing," and he isn't alone. Mervin Roberts's *The Tidemarsh Guide* reports: "This is a tremendous bird to be hovering and precision diving like a circus stunt man from a height of 100 feet into a rainbarrel, but that is just what an osprey does, and he does it well." Roberts repeats the oft-repeated story of the large carp caught with an osprey skeleton still attached to it. This is an example of that most embarrassing of osprey deaths, being taken under by a fish too large to lift, reminding Roberts of "one of the closing scenes in Melville's 'Moby-Dick' where the harpooner Tashtego captures a sky hawk and pulls it down with him as the stricken *Pequod* sinks." There are those who consider the carp story apocryphal (Alan Poole, for one, remains skeptical.) But even if an osprey has never actually drowned this way, it remains a useful myth. It reminds us that diving has its risks, despite the best calculations and commitment. There is always the chance that once you dive under you'll never come back up again. That immersion will be permanent.

MY OLD FRIEND Hones comes down for a week of fishing in the middle of the month. He's here for his birthday week, as he has been the past two springs. The first spring was difficult, the weather bad. Despite our old, comfortable friendship, our styles clashed. I was protective of my morning writing time and didn't like his intrusions, as good-natured as they were. I felt cramped, unable to sprawl through the day as I was accustomed. At night I tried to keep up with his eating and drinking, but constitutionally I was no match. I'm a sprinter, wolfing down meals, but he's a marathoner, able to gnaw through dozens of ribs at a slow pace, and, at six-four, he has more storage space for booze and food. By the visit's end I had bags under my eyes from trying to eat and drink with Hones and still write every morning.

Fortunately, the next year we developed a routine. While I wrote in the morning, he fished. Then we would get together in the afternoon to exercise, *then* eat and drink. This year, for the first time, we decide to cut back further on the latter two activities. I used to describe Hones as part Gargantuan reveler, part meat-grilling Sasquatch, but that's changed since his health scare in January. He now checks fat content, keeps notes on what he eats and, subsequently, is nearly back to the beanpole days of his youth, weighing about what I do despite the fact he's four inches taller. "A type A personality trapped in a type B lifestyle" is how Nina de-scribes me, and the same could be said of Hones, though in a different way. He's always had an obsessiveness that rivals my own and, until recently, that obsessiveness tended to involve putting things in his mouth: booze, food, cigarettes. But now, like the os-preys, Hones has whittled down his obsessions from the plural to the singular. Rather than a variety of interests he now has one rul-ing passion, and that passion is fishing.

All spring, while I've been tramping through marshes to watch the birds, he's engaged in a similar activity, taking off after work and on weekends to fish at the Wachusett Reservoir near Worcester or along the Cape Cod Canal. He's called me frequently to report the sizes of the fish he's caught or his near misses. Again, like the ospreys, Hones is an opportunist and doesn't focus on a single species of fish and, just like the birds, herring are one of the first things he catches. He wades into the Charles River near his house and nets them for bait fish. One day he called to tell me what it felt like to hold one in his hand below the water, the unbelievable power, squirming vitality, and force. Though he doesn't have reversible talons, Hones was built to fish: he has the necessary hardiness and patience. When he catches nothing, he's philosophical. "That's fishing," he says. We all have friends

who we say were born too late: Hones excels at concrete things—
tying knots and packing and building fires—and would have made
a fine pioneer.

As a child I never liked fishing much. Fishing meant long boat
trips out on Cape Cod Bay with my father and a couple of other
men, all of them smoking Lucky Strikes and wearing hats and
drinking. Those were less politically correct and health-conscious
times, and the men never thought to bring along water or even
soda. They drank cans of beers into which they'd dropped the pop
tops, making me wonder how they didn't ever cut their throats.
When they were done they filled the cans with seawater and sank
them to the ocean floor (which, in its day, was considered the environmental alternative to just tossing them overboard.) When I
was thirsty they offered me a sip of warm Schlitz or Miller. My first
reaction to beer was revulsion, something I've since gotten over.
But for fishing I've never developed a taste.

THIS YEAR ON his birthday, smack in the middle of May,
Hones gets up at dawn to fish for trout at Scargo, while I check
in at the Chapin, Simpkins, and Quivett nests. We both quit early
though, so we can get over to Paine's Creek at the right tide. We've
decided that health-consciousness can take a vacation for a day
and, before loading the kayaks in the car, Hones prepares several
racks of ribs, setting them inside his wood smoker, a three-foot-
high grill that looks like R2-D2. Nina has agreed to occasionally
baste, and the ribs will cook all day long while we paddle, giving
us incentive to return. Keeping with the festive spirit, I smuggle
along four Red Hook beers in my backpack.

Last year we got the tides wrong when we tried to paddle all
the way up Paine's Creek to Stony Brook and its source. This year
we hit it right, flowing with the incoming tide. There's no better
way to quickly immerse yourself in a place than to paddle up its
creeks. As we enter, a green heron flies off from the spot on the

bank where it had been hunting, its blood-purple neck extended and orange feet hanging down, landing farther up the creek, far but not too far ahead. We see a rose-breasted grosbeak and a towhee, and as we paddle past Wing Island, the split-tailed barn swallows shoot low in front of our boats, hunting insects.

The first part of our trip is lazy, uneventful, until we portage over Route 6A and put in on the other side. There, trying to lower himself into his tipsy boat, Hones manages to act out a classic pratfall, flipping the kayak and spilling himself and all his belongings into the creek. This would be the occasion for curses and teasing, and it is, until we realize that, along with his shoes and baseball cap, his glasses have fallen into the water. I climb down the bank, get hip deep in the dark water, and, somehow, with the first swipe of my hand along the bottom, feel the metal frames. This is a stroke of preposterous good luck, serendipity not skill, finding the frames in a rapidly moving stream. We laugh at our good fortune, sure that the day must be blessed. We also rescue his boat shoes, and find his favorite striper hat floating a hundred yards downstream.

Once we've pulled ourselves together, we paddle under the bridge near the natural history museum, past a platform where osprey pairs have tried to nest in the past. When we cross under the bridge I can taste fresh water mingling with the salt. The banks close in with briers and overhanging poison ivy, giving the journey a feeling at once more cramped and more secluded. A muskrat streams along, heading right toward us until he notices the kayaks, and dives under.

We take a break from paddling so that Hones and I can indulge our individual obsessions: I lie back in the kayak and stare up at the sky, looking for my birds, while he peers down into the creek, or what is now a lightly salted brook. At first he has more luck. He finds a bullhead catfish in the shadows below the bank, and several perch. Most of all he finds herring, in greater and

greater numbers, their bluish forms squiggling and darting upstream. As the creek gets shallower and melts to copper, the fish
become more and more obvious, and Hones follows them into
the shady hollows below branch and bush, where they rest for the
great climb ahead. Alan Poole tried to drill it into my head that reproduction is behind everything, and here that lesson comes
through clear. As creek becomes brook the tide gives way to the
seaward flow of the water. The fish expend a fierce, almost
unimaginable effort against the flow, particularly during the last
stretch, where they will climb stone and water walls, all in hopes
of getting back to where they were born so that they can spawn. If
it's hard to understand how young ospreys return to their birth-
places, this is all but unfathomable. The herring squiggle en masse
to the source. As inelegant as the metaphor is, it's a bit like watching the animal equivalent of sperm.

Unlike Hones, I can take only so much fish drama. I tell him
that I'm going to laze awhile and that he should paddle ahead. But
before he goes I pull out the beers and hand him his first birthday
present, a warm Red Hook. He looks pleased despite the beer's
temperature, and we slurp them down as if they'd just been pulled
from an ice chest. When he leaves I imagine someday bringing my
own son or my nephew Noah on a kayak trip like this one.

Walls of vegetation, catbrier and poison ivy, hem in the spot
where I've chosen to stop. Here the creek narrows to six feet, and
I let my boat drift in a side pool, pull off my shirt, and stare at the
sky. It's one of those mid-May days when you know winter's heavy
cloak has been lifted off your shoulders, and when you can feel
pretty sure it won't be back for a good while. As with any time
when a great weight is taken off, the reaction is one of lift, energy,
spring. I kill the beer, and a feeling burbles up in me similar to that
of the shadows I see pulsing off the underside of an overhanging
oak. I chalk the sensation up to equal parts alcohol and weather.

Two orioles flash overhead, and for a while I watch some

gulls, once or twice thinking I see an osprey, and then—right in the midst of a pack of gulls—suddenly sure, I see one. My search image has been refined over the last couple of weeks, and I manage to pick him or her out of a crowd over a hundred feet up. The gulls scatter, and the first osprey is joined by another, both of them seeming to focus more and more on my particular spot, and coming down to within thirty feet of me, hovering, looking ready. *Go ahead, dive,* I think, *there are fish in here.* They look ready but then, perhaps because of my presence, they bank off and head away to less crowded fishing grounds.

By looking for one thing you can miss many others. There have been days this spring when my goal of seeing the birds dive has gotten in the way of seeing itself. I've let the worry that I'll never see a dive nag and obsess. This isn't very Zen of me, I understand. But if there are days when my own brain limits me, there are other days when spring will not allow self-consciousness, and this is one of them. With Hones out of sight, I decide to indulge my taste for the ridiculous. If the ospreys won't dive for herring, then I'll do it myself. I dock my boat in some reeds, strip off my shorts, and wade upstream to where the bottom is sandy and the water hip deep. A skinny-dipping human male rightly fears snapping turtles, knowing exactly what they'd chomp on as dangling bait, but I quell my anxieties and climb up on a small bank above the sandy section of stream. It takes only a minute or so of waiting, crouching, until the first pack of herring arrive, twenty or so strong. So many fish that I figure I might have an actual shot of at least touching—if not actually catching—one. Trying to put myself in an osprey frame of mind, I tense, wait till they're right below me, then pounce. Part dive, part belly flop, I splash into the water with a pure and sheer inelegance that only *Homo sapiens* could manage. Of course I land no fish; they likely darted away before I even hit the water. Evolution has not been as kind to me as to the ospreys, at least when it comes to catching the finny prey bare-handed. I have no spicules or scales on my fingers. Theoretically, I've been dealt a big brain, but I let that brain stay shut off for a while as I do a dead man's float in the stream, opening my eyes and watching weeds weave along the brown bottom. I swim for ten minutes before pulling on my pants and paddling hard upstream to catch Hones.

By the time I reach him the water runs so shallow that the kayaks can barely move. We pull the boats up on a bank and then walk straight up the brook, still escorted by herring. Soon we hear the barking of gulls and then the gull-like barking of the tourists who've come to the Stony Brook Mill to watch the last stage of the herring's journey: the miraculous leap up the rock rapids to achieve their final goal of the spawning lake. But before reentering the human world, Hones receives another birthday present. We begin to notice a sparkling in the water, a sparkling that shines stronger and stronger the farther we walk up the brook, like a pile of dimes below the water.

"What the hell are they?" I ask.

Hones drops to a knee and reaches under the water, scooping up a handful of sand and silver. He studies them.

"Scales," he says finally.

And that's what they are. Thousands and thousands of fish scales, peeled off by the current and bottom. Left behind by the herring during their struggle, thousands of them forming a shining underwater mosaic.

Reluctantly we leave the scales behind and trudge up the last section of water. What was a wild place becomes a tourist attraction as we emerge at the bottom of the human-aided section of the run. Here parents point at the fish and their children stare and scream. This is evolution as entertainment, and I'm hoping we add to the spectacle. We must present a fairly startling picture as we emerge from downriver: two bearded, muck-covered, near-naked men walking out of the wilds. But though we don't mind being part of the show, we don't linger long at the mill. We quickly re-treat and cross back down through the water to regain our boats.

I let Hones paddle ahead while I scoop up a handful of the herring scales, the water sifting through my fingers until only some sand and the thin, glimmering jewels remain. These scales are the day's prize, its treasure, its reward. They say that money can't buy happiness; maybe fish scales can. Whatever the case, hap-piness is briefly mine.

And I am happy, even after tossing the silver back in the wa-ter. As dense as I can sometimes be, I'm not quite stupid enough to think that not seeing a bird dive has ruined this refulgent spring. I also know that I've been hunting not just for the hunt but for moments, moments exactly like this one. If I haven't witnessed an osprey catch a fish, then these times, when I feel empty but full, are coming with more and more frequency, and that, as my father would say, can't be a bad thing.

But it isn't just moments I'm after, and not just moments I've found. It's gradually begun to dawn on me that what I'm really hunting for is knowledge about my place, and that is coming, too. For instance, a year ago when we kayaked up this same creek, the site of a green heron startled me, and I had no words for what it was. But now green herons sproaking across the marsh are an everyday sight; I recognize the bird by ear before even seeing it. So while I haven't watched an osprey dive, at least I feel like I've gone deeper into this place, and that—slowly but clumsily—I'm learn-ing more about it. By spending more and more time outside I have, despite myself, begun to change in ways I can't yet put into words.

If this process—being outside, walking around, biking, watch-ing the world, kayaking—is an end in itself, it's also a sort of fishing. At the very least I'm fishing around the edges of my consciousness for my own best thoughts. On most days these thoughts don't come at all, and when they do they never seem to

come in an orderly way, even-paced, predictable, but rather indi-
rectly, in bunches, and in a rush, like this hurried, overfull month.
I don't know how to logically produce these thoughts, but I do
know the habits that tend to conjure them up. They're the habits
of a fisherman: getting up early and going out alone, throwing my
line in, waiting patiently by the water's edge.

As it has for Hones, this spring for me has been a quest, a
search. With all due respect to those privileged few who have
found "it," we all know that humans are happiest when in the act
of searching. What does a searcher search for? Something larger,
more vital, more meaningful; something outside of self. Some find
God. This spring I've begun, however tentatively, to find ospreys,
though I could just as easily, like Hones, have been on a pilgrimage for stripers. It's been said a hundred times before but bears re-
peating: the object doesn't matter as much as the process—being
part of a process. Putting myself out here is the important thing.

Now, however, comes the time to turn around. If the way
back out is always anticlimax, it is anticlimax spiced by sights of its
own. By the bridge we witness something I've never seen before.
An osprey is flying by with a fish when, suddenly, a red-tailed
hawk drops from above, diving viciously toward fish and fish
hawk. For a minute we watch a true aerial battle; when the hawk
dives again, the osprey veers off beautifully. But as the osprey
banks, something shining drops from its talons, and the red-tail
loses its motive for battle. The fish gone, the hawk relents, and the
osprey flies off, making no effort to retrieve its hard-earned dinner.

This reminds Hones of an osprey he saw dive on a lake by his
parents' house near Mount Lassen State Park in California. As
graceful as an osprey's dive can be, a fish hawk in the water often
looks awkward and ungainly. Water weighs down their wings and
they seem to need to *heft* themselves back into the air. The bird
Hones saw had speared a fish but found it too heavy to lift back
out of the lake, and so used its wings to row through the water,

dragging its prey to shore. There it lay exhausted next to the dying fish, while a half dozen human fisherman, including Hones, looked on. One of the fisherman, a particularly indolent and repulsive member of his breed, took the opportunity to walk over and try to plunder the osprey's dinner. "We all yelled and swore at him," Hones says, "Told him to get the fuck away." When the interloper relented, the osprey, strength regained, picked up the fish in its talons and flew off.

Hones finishes his story just before we portage back across route 6A. No mishaps this time. Again, we've gotten lucky with the tide; it's just turned, and we flow out with deep water that rises up over the banks of muck into the spartina. Now the creek spills over with herring. We pass thousands of fish, all working against the tide, heading to the place we've just come from. The water bulges blue with herring, and though it would be impossible for me not to see them, Hones, terrifically excited, keeps pointing them out to me as if I were blind.

When we get home we re-create the day for Nina, worried that our adventures don't seem quite so adventurous in the retelling. But beer and rum drinks quash the worries and on we blab, for one night allowing ourselves to regress to our older, less healthy habits. Hones takes the beautiful red ribs off the grill and we sit down to a ritual feast. We gather around the dinner table, toasting the birthday boy with red wine and gumming meat off the bone. A full moon the color of a skinned plum rises over the harbor. We drink until just after midnight before heading to bed, happily stupefied. Despite the fact that I still haven't attained my purported goal of seeing a dive, it's hard to look at today as anything but a success, and, trying to keep hold of our journey as long as possible, I refuse to shower, sleeping with the day's salt still on me. Before dozing off I think one last time of the scales we found near the creek's source. The glittering silvery prize that was momentarily able to satisfy even my deepest, greediest needs.

The Dive

A fish hawk dimples the glassy surface
of the pond and brings up a fish.
—THOREAU, *Walden*

W hen I finally see it this is what I see:

It's near the end of May and I'm out at Bells Neck, chasing af-ter birds. The weatherman says rain, but it holds off, though the day grows steadily colder and windier. Earlier I biked up the short section of road near Scargo Tower, climbing up, coasting back down, over and over, like a hamster on a treadmill, trying to sim-ulate one of the steep rides Nina and I used to take in Colorado. Then, my brain flushed clean, I listened to my instincts. They told me to come here, so I pedaled up Old Bass River Road to the bike path. Now I ride along the Herring River again, over familiar paths that cut through poison ivy, back to Swan Lake, the place where I saw the night herons roost and the kingfisher dive. I smile at the sight of three ospreys hunting in the sky above river and lake, interthreading like the hunting party I watched not long ago above Wing Island. While most raptors hunt alone, ospreys will occasionally hunt near one another, bunched up just like their prey.

Used to being alone out here, I start at the intrusive rumbling of a car over the dirt road. I'm on a footbridge, staring at the sky, when three teenage boys pull up in an old Cadillac and watch me watch. The boys get out of the car and speak Spanish to one another. After a minute I walk over to them and point out a nearby nest. I spread my arms wide and describe an osprey, and they again speak to one another in Spanish. As they talk I only hear one English word. It's "eagle."

His two friends look bored, but one of the boys, who wears a thick metal necklace of chains, seems impressed by what I tell him. He's seen one before, he's sure of it. Before they climb back in his car he points at me.

"That's what I gotta get, man. Binoculars."

Alone again, I catch sight of one of the birds, wishing the kid were still here so he could see it, too. But the osprey doesn't wait around long. With a slight movement of his wings, just a mild alteration of a few feathers, he banks and rides the wind almost out of sight to the west. I'm guessing that, hunting this late in the nesting season, he's a male, since most females are settled on their nests. I'm also guessing he's off to hunt the shallows that lead into Swan Lake. Following this hunch, I hop on my bike and pedal up the dirt road, then ride down the hill to another, larger bridge that crosses the river. I stop there and find what I'm pretty sure is the same bird.

He's in full hunting mode, hovering, unconsciously adjusting his flight feathers, searching. The bird, starkly brown-black and white, with his bandit mask over a white eagle head, looks magnificent, pulling his wings in, letting them out, then beating hard, staying in one place despite the blustery wind. At times the preparation for a dive surges like music—building up, building up, then a near plunge, then building again, themes that increase in power with repetition, as in a Beethoven Symphony. My own mood rises and falls with the hunt. Today my mind is clear of everything except the bird's pursuit, and I'm sure we are truly building toward something. *I'm going to see it,* I think, *I'm going to see it, I'm going to see it . . .*

Unfortunately, a red-winged blackbird, emboldened by territorial instinct, interrupts the osprey's symphonic buildup. The blackbird calls these reeds home and won't stand for interlopers, no matter their size. He dives right at the osprey, spearing him squarely on the back. Much smaller and more fluttery, the blackbird actually herds the osprey closer to me and the bridge, until, having protected his turf, he leaves the larger bird alone.

Then I see it. The bridge stands maybe twenty feet high and the osprey floats right in front of me, another thirty feet up. Suddenly he notices something. Hovering, adjusting, he stays stock-still in the air. Then he rears back, flapping wildly, kicking his white pantalooned legs forward. I hold my breath as the tension builds, the air filled with fluttering and circling and anticipation. I root the bird on: *Yes, yes, yes, go, go, go.* Next comes the part when the birds I've watched always pull up, but not now—not this time. This time he sees what he's looking for somewhere down there in the copper-colored water. He draws his wings into his sides, taking away that which kept him floating in the air. He tucks and dives and I see the whole thing right in front of me as clearly as if he were putting on a show: the tucking of the wings, the sudden acceleration, the violent splash and immersion.

As he hits the water I yell something foolish—*"Hoooo!"* I think—a kind of instinctive letting go. A second later comes the ascension, the heavy flap of wet wings and silvery rising up. He flaps into the sky not a hundred feet from me, shaking off water, the silver tint of a fish, a herring, snared in his talons. He adjusts the fish, turning it forward, and flaps steadily over to an oak tree about a quarter mile away. I can still see him clearly through the binoculars: he ignores the fish awhile, keeping it pinned in his talons.

While he rests and readies himself to eat, I indulge in a few postdive celebrations. I let go with another little victory hoot and raise my hands up over my head, as if I'd caught the fish myself. Of course, this is an everyday occurrence for the bird—it has to be for him to survive—but for me there's nothing everyday about it. The moment has unwrapped itself like the most generous of gifts, and I respond to it with a heady mixture of emotions: the excitement of witnessing the dive itself, the satisfaction of achieving a goal, and, finally, a dramatic relief. Alan Poole describes the dive as a "release of tension." He's talking about the bird, of course, but it's a release I'm experiencing, too, after so many false starts. My springlong sense of inadequacy lifts. Now I don't have to spend every day running around like a crazed great white hunter, pedaling, paddling, searching. It doesn't mean I'll stop watching for dives—but it instantly takes the edge of desperation off.

The osprey perches in a slow-budding oak. He seems content to wait, holding off on his well-earned meal, and I find myself thinking that the Spanish-speaking kids were right: from this distance, perched in the tree, the osprey looks almost exactly like a bald eagle. Finally he tears into the fish, starting with the head. To the victor goes the herring.

The osprey's way of getting food is just one of many evolutionary possibilities, and others soon present themselves. A crow lands a couple of branches down, demonstrating another feeding strategy, trying to horn in on the fish. Then two more crows land close, like a group of hyenas, or like nothing so much as crows. The first crow nudges closer, hopping to within two branches; then a gull lands, and before long the osprey has attracted a small convention of gulls and crows. The fish hawk looks noble among the other scavenging birds, a king among fawners, beggars, and jesters. Not to entirely put down the crows: they're smart and they thrive on opportunism and adaptability. You can see this demonstrated, for instance, in the way they've learned the rules of the road, barely hopping to the other side of the yellow line when a car drives up. Crows know all the angles and will be around for a long, long time.

But ospreys may be around for a while yet, too, and with all due respect to corvids, I'll take the way the fish hawk gets his dinner. Evolution has shaped something far different for him than for the other birds, something far better, in my judgment. What a supremely athletic way to find food. Of course for this particular osprey, the dive I witnessed will need to be just one of at least two or three daily victories, meaning he needs to do something astounding with regularity. On top of my osprey books, I've been reading a biography of Ralph Waldo Emerson by Robert Richardson. Richardson writes of Emerson's "workaday exaltation." This is a quality that ospreys have in spades. Everyday daring and dash.

I watch until the hunter finishes feeding and flies off, the scavengers moving in, scraping for leftovers. Below me herring gather under the bridge, and pale beige phragmites hiss. Just before I'm ready to leave I hear a sound that I first mistake for the hissing reeds. Then it grows louder behind me, as if the phragmites were moving closer. I turn to see two mute swans flying toward the bridge, their wings beating out a strange noise, an unearthly humming and vibrating—*hunnhhh, hunnhh, hunnhhh.* Silky gray undersides, slightly soiled whites pass close to my head.

I push off on my bike, riding along the edge of the lake. Swallows dart among sunken tree stumps, and painted turtles, sunning on logs, plop off when I get close. All of a sudden I hear another odd noise—the sound of myself laughing out loud. I saw a dive! Despite having spent all these hours out here, it still seems a fluke. How did I get so lucky? I ask myself. Yes, people see ospreys dive every day, but so what? I do feel as if I *got lucky.* It may be pushing the metaphor, but if Thoreau could rhapsodize about making love to an oak tree, maybe I can be forgiven for feeling like lighting up a cigarette after seeing a dive. Who knows? Perhaps I'll now experience a new degree of intimacy with the birds. I'll likely see more spectacular dives during the spring and summer—sharper-angled dives from greater heights, and larger fish caught, wings flapping violently with water—but as I pedal home I know that, no matter what I see, I won't forget my first time.

I SHOULDN'T MAKE light of the sexual metaphor. While an osprey's dive doesn't arouse me, at least not carnally, the experience of watching it does share something with sex. In both cases what we are after is union, attempting to be part of something beyond, marrying ourselves to the world. And union begins with contact. We touch an arm, throw ourselves into the ocean, feel cold rain on our skin. Touch wakes us. Contact is the cornerstone, at once physical foundation and assurance that a world exists beyond—or at least apart from—us.

Contact need not be subtle. It can be as jarring and violent as the sinking of an osprey's talons into the back of a herring. The other day my friend Brad Watson was jogging and heard a fluttering of wings. He looked up to see a mourning dove taking off from a phone wire. Despite the commonness of the sight, something in it held his eye. The dove hadn't made it ten feet off the wire when it was taken out with a powerful *thwunk* in midair by a Cooper's hawk. This is the same accipiter that we sometimes see from his back patio at cocktail hour, watching as it pirouettes across the lawn, hunting low over the bluff.

My own taste for contact, sometimes violent, comes out in a love of sports. As I get older, I find myself growing more critical of our country's too passionate love affair with professional sports, but the thing itself—the joy of running, jumping, throwing, jostling, hitting—still brings me joy. Like a sudden rainstorm, like wild nature, like sex, sports insist on direct contact with the physical world, and with others. My own interest in sports was so intense that for thirteen or fourteen years, approximately the span of an average osprey life, I dedicated myself to being an athlete. My sport of choice was Ultimate Frisbee, considered on par with hula hoops or tiddledywinks by many, but serious and consequential to those of us who played. If the word *Frisbee* conjures up games of catch on the beach, this sport was anything but casual, combining the running of soccer with the positioning and contact of basketball. Best of all—the thing that hooked me and led me for years into a the sport's subculture—is the fact that a Frisbee floats. Because a plastic disc will seem to wait in the air, hovering at a plateau, the sport lends itself to diving horizontally and leaping high, "skying." It's these moments—the moments of leaving the ground and committing, moments of wildness and abandon—that led me, and thousands of others like me, to give up normal goals and dedicate myself obsessively to the game.

The first fall I played seriously, working as a carpenter while living on Cape Cod, I often trained on the beach, tossing a Frisbee ahead of me on the sand and diving after it. During those days I began to have flying dreams, and once, jumping off a dune during a hurricane, I really thought I'd managed to get some lift. The intensity of these feelings was enough to cause me to stick with the sport for over a decade, to the detriment of my career and relationships. At the time I often worried and fretted about what I was doing, but looking back, I like the choice I made: it seems to me now that it mirrored the osprey's dive. A plunging, a full immersion, diving in and worrying about the difficulty of flapping out later on.

OF COURSE, during the time I was playing Ultimate I knew there were thousands and thousands of better athletes in the world. Throw a Frisbee high in the air and put me up against an NBA player, and the results would be comic. And, as huge as the gap is between me and the best human athletes, it's a hundred times greater between humans and animals. At our best we can jump forty-some inches off the ground, run twenty-five miles an hour for a short burst, climb fairly well. For a real athlete, I'll take the osprey. They can migrate for thousands of miles at a speed as fast as our sprints, dive like an arrow, lift fish nearly their own weight high into the air.

"Ospreys are graceful fliers that seem capable of finding lift when other birds cannot," I read in *Hawks in Flight*. "In a kettle of Broad-wingeds, they will rise almost twice as fast as the milling buteos and will begin their glides much earlier." If migration is the great osprey feat of endurance, their marathon, then the dive is their sprint. In rare instances, ospreys have been known to begin their dives from as high as two hundred feet up. Think of the eyesight required to pick out a fish from that height and then the sheer daring of the plunge itself, hurtling down toward the water at forty miles per hour. Then imagine what we would call the hand-eye coordination; the eye must calculate the refraction of the water and anticipated route of the fish, like a quarterback leading a receiver, and once the plunge is made the talons can shut in 2/100ths of a second, "so fast they might be a tactile reflex not a voluntary one," according to Poole.

For sheer speed, of course, ospreys can't match their falcon cousins. But they make up for it in strength and, it seems to me, independence. Unlike falcons, ospreys have rarely had their athleticism tapped by humans. While peregrines have been trained to hunt by man, ospreys will not be *used*. If they are willing to live near us they'll only take the human thing so far.

Ospreys, like humans, vary, some being more athletic than others. For instance, I've read of an osprey actually coming up with a fish in each talon. I already have the sense that the male at the lopsided Chapin nest is the best local fisherman, based on how frequently and quickly he brings back food, sometimes a mere twenty minutes after he leaves. While we need to factor in the weather and the supply of fish, it doesn't seem too far-fetched to imagine that there are individual birds who are simply great athletes, who catch fish easily where others might have problems. Of course, the less coordinated are weeded out more viciously in the avian world than in the human, birds suffering a worse fate than being picked last in gym class. But again, like human athletes, those that survive naturally get better. Experience counts, and experienced hunters are better hunters.

It makes sense to me that the males are the leaner of the birds. The female lives on the nest from spring through midsummer, while the male becomes the primary hunter. In some raptors the difference in size allows the male and female birds to hunt different prey, as well as protecting the female from the male's aggression, though this isn't the case with ospreys. Some have argued that a female osprey's larger size helps her defend the nest from intruders, since she is the primary nest guard during the breeding season. Whatever the case, there is a cleanness to the male's body, a Spartan simplicity. Sports teaches sparseness, and the best athletes make themselves into arrows, serving one purpose, carving off excess from their lives as they carve fat from their bodies. This is a lesson the ospreys live.

The great wonder is that this supremely athletic feat is at the very center of daily osprey existence. There can be no days off or off days. This spectacle I saw once happens over and over again. To eat is not to walk to the fridge but to become involved in the most savage and direct of hunts. Modern humans miss the link between our actions and our food. We miss *directness*. For the ospreys, eating doesn't mean ordering out. It means performing an act of great improbability and brilliance several times a day.

ALAN POOLE WRITES, "Wolof tribesmen living along the beaches of Senegel chant of the Osprey's hunting skills as they paddle canoes through Atlantic surf to tend their nets. Skilled fishermen themselves, they share fishing grounds with Ospreys born thousands of kilometers away along Swedish lakes and Scottish lochs. These people clearly admire the prowess of a plunging fish hawk. It is an everyday sight for them, woven into the fabric of their culture."

If ospreys aren't exactly woven into my culture, then at least they have become, more and more, woven into the fabric of my life. When I wake I make a point of lying in bed until I hear the begging of the harbor female. Each morning I check in on my four nests, and each afternoon I kayak up the creeks. I'm not naturally patient—I doubt anyone is who grows up in our culture—but I suspect the birds themselves are helping me learn to wait and watch, to not to rush things.

This morning, Memorial Day, Hones and I decide to kayak up the Herring River to the spot where I saw the first dive from the bridge. Hones wants to look for turtles, while I hope to see more dives. The river shines even more coppery today, like a stream of melted pennies, the surface thick with yellow pollen that our paddles break through. We watch swans rip out stalks of marsh grass, showing their young, called cygnets, where to eat, probing deep into the water with their muscular necks.

Ferns grow thick below the oak where I watched the osprey eat after its dive. Marsh wrens sing as we paddle past, bobbing their tails, and a kingbird skims for insects. We come up along one loud man in a canoe whose voice carries across the water, going on about CNN and stocks. We're amazed when we get closer and see that he is talking not to his canoeing partner, who sits quietly in the other end of the boat, but into a cell phone. It takes restraint not to ram him and sink his vessel. I suppose, in evolutionary terms, it's likely that this man is a good hunter, a successful provider. I had a roommate in college who's now a millionaire, his millions made by playing around on a computer with other people's money. On the simplest animal level you can say this about him: he catches a lot of fish. He would be a good osprey perhaps, but a distinction must be made in the case of human animals: we can, to a degree, decide what it is we fish for. Instinct doesn't compel us to get our food only one way; we have a choice. Ultimately we must decide, whether by hunch or by long consideration, thoughtfully or thoughtlessly, as to the *value* of a thing.

I am learning what I value. I value the osprey's dive. And, after we portage up by the herring ladder to the lake, I'm treated once again. It happens almost the instant we put the kayaks back in, as if conjured by thought. A hundred feet above us an osprey fakes a dive and I prepare for the usual tentative ritual of search. But after the first fake, there's no wait, no hesitation. He tucks and dives, adjusts for a split second twenty feet from the water, then darts down and lands with a splash. For a minute he's a waterbird, until, with a great flap, he rises up with a fish, shaking off dramatically, water cascading back down to the lake.

The day is made, and Hones and I point and laugh, both making sure the other saw it. Then Hones heads off on his own, looking for snappers among the tree stumps by the shore. While he hunts for turtles I watch the sky. It isn't long before I see another osprey dive and pull up, dive and pull up again, before flying off. A third bird rests on a stump near the middle of the lake, ignoring me even when I paddle close. He, or she, is beautiful, with a vivid white chest and head and the thinnest mask I've seen yet, looking even more like a bald eagle than most. A fourth bird, plumper and darker, perches on the lake's edge in a dead tree. After a while both birds rise up and hunt together. I watch from below as they ride the wind, swooping down on the currents, their shadows banking off the pines of the lake shore.

Though my second dive may lack the novelty of the first time, it still moves me. The bird remains indifferent, unconcerned with my gratification, but that doesn't matter. What matters, to me, is having made contact, having briefly, through the very human act of empathy, entered the bird's world. No longer desperate, I lie back in the kayak and stare up at the blue sky. When Hones returns he tells me he saw a snapper in the shallows the size of manhole cover. I congratulate him. We have both found what we came to see, and we paddle home.

On Osprey Time

Exaltation takes practice.

—JOHN HAY

I'm feeling good after seeing the dives, satisfied, maybe too satisfied. If I'm due for a comeuppance, Alan Poole provides. I brag to him over the phone about the spectacular sights of my last two weeks. He takes a moment to respond.

"It's fine to be running around on your bicycle or kayak and seeing a dive here and there," he says finally. "But you've got to slow down, and spend hours at the nest. You've got to live on osprey time."

When I hang up my reaction is, at first, defensive. I'm not a scientist, and this isn't a science experiment: I don't need to record the nest's minutiae, how many bites of herring the female takes or what type of fish flavored this morning's guano. While I respect Alan Poole immensely, our goals, I tell myself, are different.

But after a few minutes of rationalizing, I realize he's right. Something's missing. My encounters with nature tend to have a vehemence, or even a violence, to them; I like to jostle, move around, dive into. "Nature apprehends you," a friend said to me, and that phrase makes nature itself sound aggressive, like a perpetrator. I need to stop rushing and being rushed. To put away the bike, take a deep breath, and slow down. Despite my choosing to live in a quiet place, worry often wars with peace, and worry often wins.

Nature hardly guarantees peace of mind. It's easy enough to make our "wild" experiences as anxiety-filled as anything else. Look at the campers who might as well be at home or the office, neatening up every corner of the tent, loving their gear and their lists. Or the competitive birders who could be playing Monopoly, so intensely do they go about identifying ("Aha, a ruby-throated warbler!"). This year I've tied my fate to the fate of the birds, and so I get anxious about "how they will do," as if I were hoping they'd get into a good prep school. While this hasn't turned me into a basket case, it has given an edge to the experience. I look at the way I made seeing a dive into a overweening goal, heaping all the necessary anxiety, panic, and intensity on the outcome. Now that I've seen a dive, and checked that item off my list, it's on to the next worry. For the last week I've been fretting that none of the nests I watch will be "successful." Success, in osprey terms, means having young that fledge, that is, fly from the nest.

We can see only so much when in movement, and I've been running between my four nests like a nervous nanny. To keep an eye on the immature "good-for-nothing" birds at the harbor I need only walk out my back door, but to see the other nests I now drive our fake-wood-paneled Chrysler station wagon to the sites. Since I don't have much confidence in the harbor male as provider, I spend most of my time away from home. It's been hard for me to give up on the Quivett nest, since the ospreys returned there first, but I must face the fact that that nest will fail. Though she might be sitting atop a second batch of eggs, my books caution me that success is unlikely. That means my hopes lie with the lopsided nest at Chapin Beach and the Simpkins Neck nest, both of these built atop platforms anchored along the winding tidal inlet known as Chase Garden Creek. Because Simpkins requires a twenty-five-minute hike through thorns and ticks, Chapin has become my regular viewing spot, and the repository of most of my hopes. Even though the other day I saw both birds off the nest at Chapin, further fueling my worries, I believe in the Chapin male's hunting prowess. Because of this and, honestly, convenience I find myself focusing more and more on the lopsided nest to the exclusion of the others.

As I sit and stare at the Chapin nest, it slowly sinks in that Alan Poole is right. I need to take his words as a prod to go deeper, to slow down. I've always liked my nature on the move, but it's time to stow my kayak and get off my bike, and see what I can learn from stillness.

Alan has described how he and his colleagues would watch ospreys for whole days, trading on and off in four-hour shifts.

"It's a good life the birds lead," he said. "You've got to watch them do nothing. And they do a whole lot of nothing. You've really got to spend a lot of time at the nests to get to know them."

And that's what I'll do. I've forced myself to do many things before, though those things have usually been of the active variety. Now I will stay still. Despite myself, I will live on osprey time.

AT FIRST IT isn't so easy. One thing that sometimes gets in the way of seeing, of settling, is writing itself. There are times when I look down to see my hand moving, scribbling in my journal all on its own, like Cousin It of the Addams Family. Isn't this need to capture every detail a type of greed? Isn't it, as much as moneymaking, a symptom of unquenchable acquisitiveness?

Back in early April I tried a small experiment at the Quivett nest. I wondered if I could put my journal aside and sit still, sinking below words for a while. Stowing my watch, pens, tape recorder, and journal in my backpack, I hiked out near the nest, sitting on the bank above the creek. I tried to empty my mind of thought, tried to stop narrating my own life for just a short while.

My goal was to see the place, and nothing but the place, and not let the mosquito-like hum of worry interfere.

I hunkered low, out of the wind, and watched the nest. Two Canada geese landed in the creek in their silly way, like awkward puppets held up by wires, and as I watched and thought—wanting desperately to grab a pen and write down the bit about "awkward puppets"—I realized just how ingrained my need to scribble had become, how deep my fear of *losing* my thoughts by not writing them down. But I didn't let myself run for my journal, and I resisted the urge to carve sentences in the mud with my boot. Instead I tried to quiet myself again and stare at the opposite bank, focusing on the pockmarks of muck. They looked like something out of a dream, miniature Anasazi dwellings.

For a short while my experiment seemed to work. I stared at the incoming creek with dumb wonder, not letting any thoughts adhere or cling, ideas soughing like the wind through the phragmites. In no time I felt reawakened, felt I was beginning to achieve the stillness I desired. Then, soon enough, the old sensation of uneasiness replaced that of peace. I got antsy and cold. But I forced myself to sit still. Finally, after a seemingly interminable period went by, I gave in. I walked over to my backpack, took out my watch, and stared at it. Seven minutes had passed.

IF I WANT a role model for patience I need look no further than the incubating female ospreys. For all four females, even the Quivett mother and her second batch of eggs, this is a period of concentration and the slowing down of time. In some species of raptors, females lose even the instinct to hunt and kill while incubating. All food is provided by the male. While the osprey males do all the hunting, they are relatively modern fathers, taking occasional turns at incubating. But most of the sedentary work is done by the female and, according to Poole's book, the distaff bird always takes the night shift. In the "hawk book," Brown and Amadon write that more observation needs to be done on the incubation period, but they note that watching incubation is "an exceedingly boring pastime." After a whole lot of "boring" time at the nest, Alan Poole calculates that incubation lasts from thirty-five to forty-three days, with an average of thirty-nine. That's a long time to sit. While other birds of prey spend time off their eggs without harming them, at the nests I watch the eggs are rarely left uncovered, perhaps, I speculate, because an osprey nest is so open to both the elements and enemies.

At Chapin and Simpkins Neck deep nesting has been going on since just past mid-April, which means they should be hatching and makes me worry that something has gone wrong. The eggs, if there *are* eggs, would have been laid at intervals of a day or more, the first being the largest. *First laid, first hatched* is the osprey rule, giving the eldest a great competitive advantage of age and size. Among birds of prey, the smaller species generally have the largest clutch size—kestrels, for instance, sometimes lay half a dozen eggs or more—and ospreys follow this precept, usually laying three eggs, though sometimes two or four.

Every expert weighs in with a different description of the eggs, probably because there is some variety, but basically they are large, white or whitish, and splattered with brownish or red markings. The three eggs that I see, in a box in a drawer in a back room at the natural history museum, are beautiful: creamy yellow-white freckled with chestnut blotches that clump together at the ends of the eggs. The spotting and clumping of the freckles reminds me of my father's back after too many summers shirtless out on his boat. The eggs have been drained through a tiny hole in one end, leaving them nearly weightless, and I delicately turn them over and over. The small sheet of paper within the box tells me that they were found seventy feet up in a live cedar fir on May 11, 1900, almost exactly ninety-nine years ago. Back then naturalists and bird lovers were just as likely as poachers to want to add these beautiful eggs to their collections.

Eggs just like these are now, hopefully, being incubated in at least three of our neighborhood nests. Osprey eggs spend a month or more in the soft grass padding at the bottom of the nest, resting below the female's belly or, more specifically, her brood patch, a patch of skin that develops specifically for incubation. This featherless spot thickens and pumps full with blood vessels, producing heat, and is common among all birds.

The ospreys seem to be hunkering down even further as May nudges toward June. At the Simpkins nest I can barely see the mother's head and hooked bill, and even the harbor pair is getting the hang of it. Though their home is still a slipshod mess, like the remains at the end of a bad yard sale, there are encouraging signs. While I can't shake my prejudice against this trashy couple, living in the midst of a construction project, by June 1 the female seems to be nesting deeply, lowering herself and tightening the seal, and the formerly irresponsible male has been more conscientious about bringing home the fish.

IF THEY CAN do it, why can't I?

In my attempts to be more still I enlist habit as my ally. Without habit, after all, I wouldn't be able to do anything. Perhaps the most important lesson that daily writing has taught me is the iron strength of routine. Nonwriters have funny ideas about "inspiration," about how it must catch a person up in a romantic frenzy and send them running for their pen. Of course, this does happen once in a great while, but more often it's just a case of sitting down at the same time every day. Strangely enough, the simple activity of placing your butt in a chair with some regularity can start to fool the mind into mimicking the "inspired" state. "Workaday exaltation" doesn't just apply to Emerson and the ospreys.

If inspiration can become habitual, why not patience? I've

tried to bring more of a sense of ritual to my osprey mornings. My routine consists of getting up at dawn, stretching my back, and putting on water for tea. While the water boils I walk out on the back deck to check in with the harbor nest. When my water is ready, I take binoculars, boots, journal, and field guides and throw them in the back of our station wagon. Though I feel a vague, occasional prick of disloyalty, I rarely check in with the failed Quivett nest, instead heading directly to Chapin. I drive down roads lined with just-blooming rugosa roses and lilacs that drip like grapes from the trees, sometimes growing as high as the phone wires. As I head north toward the beach I pass a stone wall from another life, a wall I built with my younger brother for ten bucks an hour. Then Wild Hunter Road comes up on my right, a sign that I usually note with pleasure (hoping secretly, as I do, to become a wild hunter myself). Next I pass Joe Mac's, its sign, in the maroon and blue color scheme of an old Schlitz can, featuring a cartoon clam with big eyes. Sometimes I remember my miserable days working as a dishwasher within those walls; most times, thankfully, I don't.

I pass Gina's by the Sea, our local bar-restaurant, and take a left on Dr. Botero's Road, which constitutes the home stretch to Chapin Beach. If ospreys are sometimes called "trash birds," then the last streets leading to Chapin are trash streets. Old sandy roads where my father occasionally got stuck on his way to fish, roads lined with dune shacks giving the area a scraggly, forever-summer feel, places constructed in a sloppy osprey style of architecture. I park in the Chapin lot. While ospreys could live in the houses along the road, this parking lot, with its Porta Potti and over-spilling trash-littered dunes, is the kind of place where gulls would congregate if gulls were people. It's a hot spot for four-wheelers, and from here the oversized cars bomb down to the beach, windows rolled up, air conditioners and radios blasting. This lot acts as their launching pad, where they make final preparations, letting air out of their tires before setting about destroying plover and tern habitat. It doesn't do any good to try to convince them that the time the birds expend avoiding their monster cars means less for eating and resting, that is, less energy for survival. Most of them remain happily combative, conceding nothing, and sport bumper stickers that read PIPING PLOVER TASTES LIKE CHICKEN.

While the four-wheelers drive to the beach, I, after pulling on my rubber boots, set out in the opposite direction, to the marsh. On foot now, I follow the road for a bit, past beach plum and bay-berry. I climb down onto the marsh's edge, over mussel shells and spongy glasswort. Poverty grass, sea lavender, and marsh elder usher me into this place between water and land, and crab shells litter the spartina, some baked orange by the sun, some bleached white, so well cooked that they crumble, not crunch, under foot. Then comes the standard osprey greeting: as I get closer to the lopsided nest they let off their shrill warning cries but, used to me by now, remain on the nest. This pair is smart and understood quickly I would come only so close. Which is another reason I've begun to watch Chapin almost exclusively.

I set up camp at a respectful distance, a hundred feet or so away. Mine is a fairly amateurish operation, and, still waiting for my mail-order telescope, I use only my old binoculars. I unfold a nylon beach chair with a blue-and-white checkered pattern, take out the binoculars and journal, and set to watching.

Despite the consistency of my new routine, the first few days are failures, at least as far as living on osprey time goes. I've man-aged to spend more time than I ever have before "in the field," though not nearly what Alan Poole recommended. My mind con-stantly races back home to obligations, to my things-to-do list, to the computer that's been gathering dust. I agree with the hawk book authors on the frustrations of watching incubation. What is the point of just sitting here? The birds, for their part, do very little.

Finally, on June 3, during the second week of my attempt to

live on osprey time, something unusual occurs at the lopsided Chapin nest. The ospreys greet my morning arrival with more than the usual vocalizations, both of them lifting off from the nest and buzzing me, warning me away. Showing respect, I stay farther back, but I worry that this is a dire sign, especially when the female stays off the nest for a full five minutes. It occurs to me that she would never leave her eggs for that long if she were still incubating. The implications are obvious: *she can no longer be nesting,* and I unhappily conclude I'm watching another failed nest.

"They are definitely not nesting and they don't seem to have any young," I write despairingly in my journal.

EVERYTHING CHANGES the next day, June 4.

Tired of my halfhearted efforts, I promise myself that today, finally, I will live on osprey time. In keeping to this promise, I'm out on the marsh early. Beach grass shines silvery green against the ocean's blue, and, as I slosh up to my watching point, the Chapin birds greet me as they did yesterday, both flying off the nest, leaving me with a sinking feeling. Today's warning is even more aggressive, the female expressing a higher degree of agitation, whistling a singular whistle, not the *kew-kew-kew* of standard warning. When she dives near me, tucking and darting, I decide to take her seriously, and back off a full fifty feet from my usual spot. She settles down just after I do; by sitting I signal I'm coming no closer, and she, understanding this, retreats to the nest. The thing that puzzles me most about this new greeting is that they'd grown so used to me just a week ago. Even if the nest has failed, her adamancy strikes me as odd.

Two minutes later she's forgotten about me and proceeds as if I'm not here. It seems I've interrupted a meal, which may, I decide, be the reason for her agitation. It's sushi for breakfast again, and I watch her tear into what might be a trout, pinning the fish with her talons and ripping at it with her sharp bill. "They must like fish a whole lot," Nina said the other day, and I couldn't argue. The female bends down to tear and then lifts her head to swallow, bobbing slightly. Occasionally she bends low in the nest in an unusual way, a behavior I haven't observed before. I note this in my journal.

After the meal the morning lags. For the next two hours the male mans the ground roost thirty feet from the nest while the female putters around on the nest itself, occasionally dipping her head low. Practicing my own new art, that of patience, I watch the long shadows and shifting sun, the spartina lit up an Easter-basket green. Over the course of the morning the sky's blue gradually erases last night's sliver moon, while I sit, listening to the whine of the nearby aquaculture plant and watching a small band of green herons hunt. The morning's big event occurs when a kamikaze wood duck flies by, looking for a minute like it will crash into the nest.

I watch swallows indulge in their usual sky dances, racing their own shadows over the grass. The swallows actually provide more entertainment than the ospreys, which makes sense, given their hyperactive lives. The small birds peep as they fly near, little rocket bodies feinting and jabbing, then darting away. The other night I wasn't surprised to read that some swallows, like swifts, mate in the air. It makes perfect sense since air is their element, and to do anything while attached to the ground would seem against their natures.

But, I remind myself, I'm not here to watch swallows, and I'm not here for "entertainment." I'm here to slow down and settle, to watch the ospreys, and so I train my binoculars on them, blocking out the rest of the marsh while the birds laze through their morning. As with looking for the dive, and as with an osprey searching for a fish, a goal by definition limits and simplifies the world. I now limit my vision to the nest. Though little happens, I watch it closely for two hours, then three, then three and a half. If scientists can do it, I tell myself, then so can I. For good stretches I even manage to lose myself in their world, noting that from some angles the male looks almost like an enormous pileated woodpecker; from others, briefly, part vulture. By contrast, the female appears partridgelike and dowdy, browner, duller, maybe because she hasn't had the chance to wash much while nesting (the male, of course, takes several daily plunges). At one point an intruding osprey flies over, a neighbor or migrant perhaps, and the Chapin pair rise up into the air in defense, letting off agitated guard calls that slur together with a sound close to clicking. The intruder, larger than the Chapin female, slowly circles up and away, toward the sun, revealing the angular band on his underwing and long feather fingers.

Though for moments—for glimpses—I'm drawn into osprey time, for the most part sitting here is an act of will. I glance at my watch, again drawn back to the business of the ordinary human world. Then, right before the four-hour limit is up, right before I've fulfilled my Alan Poole requirement and am ready to pack up and head home, the male flaps off toward the bay, leaving the female alone on the nest. I decide I should wait until he returns so that I can witness a second feeding, giving my long morning some closure. A half hour passes before he returns over the dunes and settles on an old wood post, his secondary perch, by the aquaculture plant, almost a quarter mile from the nest. This time I'm sure it's a trout, though I wonder at this, since he'd flown off in the direction of the ocean, not the lake. Whatever it is, it flops under his great snowshoe talons while he glances around casually, letting his prey die its excruciating death. As well as ignoring the fish, he ignores his mate, who shoots her piercing begging cries across the marsh. Finally, he starts tearing into the trout's mouth, revealing its shining inner white, ripping the skin free with characteristic savage screwdriver twists. He makes short work of the fish and in ten minutes is down to the eye. The female's begging cries increase in intensity until they sound almost frantic, like a high-pitched whelp. Five minutes later, the fish half eaten, the male flies back to the nest and hands off what's left. She snags it in her talons and takes a short hop-flight away from him to the nest's other side, while he alights on the crossbar, a foot above her.

This is where I came in this morning, at this point in the feeding, and I can leave feeling I've watched a full cycle. But something about the way she feeds keeps me in my seat. The nature of what I'm actually seeing is finally beginning to dawn on me when she doesn't dip quite as low with the next morsel of fish, and I see—or only half-believe I see—a quick flash of something pop up toward her bill. Though every ounce of me wants to believe that what I just saw was a nestling, I can't quite bring myself to—not yet. But as I watch the female tear off another piece of fish and then bend low, tilting her head and delicately placing the food, it occurs to me that this *must* be what I'm seeing. Now her behavior makes perfect sense. It explains not only this new style of feeding but the recent intensity of the pair's protectiveness. And of course, if she's no longer incubating, it also explains her new willingness to leave the nest entirely.

I watch closer, excited now, though still doubting. When she gobbles the next few pieces without dipping down I start to lose faith in what I saw. But then I see it again. More clearly. First one, then another little ball-like head reaching up on a thin uncertain neck, popping up over the nest's rim and into sight. There *are* nestlings here! Unbelievably, stupidly, I've somehow managed to completely misread the signs of what I was seeing, taking what was success for failure. Now the mother—*mother!*—tears off another strand and dips down to one of the little heads and I have my best view yet. This act of feeding beautifully marries savagery and delicacy. If the tearing of the fish is savage, the feeding itself is the most gentle, loving act: she reaches down with a bill more delicate than a debutante's pinky finger and places the torn morsel into her child's mouth. Sometimes after she's placed the food and the nestlings are swallowing, she'll study them with a cocked head, as if to say, *Have you had enough?*

While she hunches maternally, attentively, feeding first one, then another, the male stands aloof on the crossbar, feathers ruffling in the wind, as if these matters barely concerned him. Most of the time I can only see hints of the brood, the female ducking down out of sight with the fish, and when I do get glimpses of the nestlings they look not so much like birds as inverted exclamation points. They wobble uncertainly, rising up for only a second or so on their brand-new necks. But as tentative, as purely goofy, as these cartoon silhouettes look, they fill me with excitement. There is something so basic, so archetypal, about this act of feeding. While understanding that new life is an ordinary thing, I can't help but feel that what I'm witnessing is extraordinary.

I watch for another hour, thrilled every time I catch a glimpse of the newborn birds. But when the feeding ends, so do the sightings. From reading Alan Poole's book I can roughly imagine the situation in the nest: the nestlings have now collapsed, exhausted from the effort of lifting themselves, falling back down into a downy bundle to sleep away most of the day, brooded by the female. Of course, they have already been through a great struggle to get just this far in life. It often takes a day or more of chipping for the newborns to break their way out of the eggs. In the raptor world, unlike the human one, parents don't help much, maybe occasionally, almost inadvertently, giving a little aid in breaking open the shell with their own feet or bills. Most of the work is done with the egg tooth, the small hard knob on the upper mandible of the bill, which the emerging chick wields like a small spiked mallet. Following evolution's perfect timing, the egg tooth will disappear over the next week, as will the mother's brood patch.

If the chicks emerge tired, they also emerge hungry. The next month will be a constantly changing adventure of growth, a challenge not just for the young but for the parents. For instance, no sooner do the female's incubatory efforts end then the male's increased hunting requirements begin. I find myself experiencing a funny sense of companionability with the male osprey as he rests on his primary post. To put it simply, I am confident that this particular dad—sinewy, wily, a jock—will be up to the task ahead. To put it even more simply, I like and trust him.

My reading has taught me some things about the nestlings, but what I don't know is just how old they are, and I excitedly flip back in my journal, trying to see if there were earlier days when I recorded the female coming off the nest. I figure they're a week old, tops, maybe only a day or two, but I can't be sure. I know that newborn chicks are covered in their first down—"a short, thick, buff colored plumage" according to Poole—but my binoculars don't allow me to truly determine the coloring; from this distance they just look dark. Whatever their exact age, what concerns me most is that they are *here*. That I've seen my first young of the season.

On the way home I feel like pulling over to buy cigars. I can't get over my good fortune. The moment of seeing the nestling's head was so surprising that it rivals watching my first dive. If I'd left the nest after three hours, even after four hours, I'd have thought it was just another day, usual except for some minorly aberrant behavior. But because I stayed longer I was allowed to witness a great drama, a spectacle. Though it runs a far second to wonder, I also feel a little pride regarding the morning's immersion. It wouldn't have happened if I hadn't kept in one place, and though it was an enforced patience, it was patience still. And it lifted into something higher, the last hour and a half at the nest passing in no time at all, a blink. If this morning I felt annoyed, peevish, as if having to stay at the nest were an obligation, an item to be checked off a list, then watching the young feed was anything but. For a short while I felt absorbed in the world of ospreys, knee deep in meaning, exalted even, part of a larger cycle of birth and return.

THE NEXT DAY it's a little harder to feel quite as exalted, in large part thanks to the gnats. They think I'm the greatest thing to hit the marsh since fish guts. While yesterday's fall-like wind kept bugs away, today is summer still, and as I write in my journal my hair and arms, and the journal page itself, crawl with insects. I've settled back farther away from the nest now, though the birds greeted me with the usual lap or two of warning flight this morning. Today, of course, I didn't take this as a sign of despair.

Excited by what I've seen here, I've decided to ignore the other nests for the day. I've been here four hours, since dawn, and despite the film of sweat and insect corpses covering me, it's been another absorbing morning. One of the best sights was a tiny chick perched high on the nest, peering over the platform's side as if off the edge of the world. At that moment I caught a glimpse of the bird's tail, discovering it was a little bigger than I'd imagined yesterday. (Of course, given the furious rate of growth, it isn't impossible to see day-to-day change.) When the chick got too close to the nest's edge, the female bustled over to keep it from falling out, herding it back with maternal pips. I don't think this demonstrated overly paranoid concern on the mother's part, given the generally spasmodic nature of the chicks' movements. They awkwardly propel themselves around the nest, flopping and flailing. Their necks wobble, and their wings, not really wings at all yet, flap out of control in a caricature of flight. So unwinglike are these appendages, in fact, that the first few times I see them flop I fear that one of the young birds has broken its long neck.

I still can't be certain how many nestlings there are. I've seen at least two above the nest rim, and once thought I saw three. Whatever the number, they're insatiable little creatures. When father brings a fish to the crossbar, they stumble, stretch, and strain toward it, the embodiment of yearning. I still can't get over what a delicate operation the feeding process is—the ripping tear and gentle placement by the mother—and I try to get the head tilt just right when I draw it. I also find myself calling this movement "human," as if members of our species were the greatest practicers of all things delicate and gentle. Given the fact that even human locomotion, the way we walk, is little more than catching ourselves after stumbling forward, this might be a false assumption. And given the tools the female is working with, a hooked, cutting beak and sharp jagged talons, I doubt many humans could manage such delicacy. How many of us would want to try feeding a baby with hedge clippers?

When the migrant intruder makes his daily visit, the young disappear below the rim of the nest, as if on Mother's order. Today she stays with them while the male drives off the strange bird. Later, the threat passed, she settles down low with the nestlings, and I take a break, walking over to the beach for a swim, hoping to clean off the heat and slime of the marsh. The water's warm over the flats, but cold enough to rid me of the layer of muck and bugs. Since no one's around I dry naked for a while. With the wind blowing over me, and two days of witnessing miraculous sights behind me, I'm feeling particularly strong and hopeful, but I've barely got my pants back on when I'm brought down to earth. A four-wheeler bounds and charges down the beach in my direction, its windows rolled down, blaring Neil Diamond's "Turn On Your Heart Light."

I hurry back to my seat on the marsh, worried about having left my journal on the lawn chair. On the way back to my chair I imagine the male osprey swooping down and snaring my journal in his talons, bringing it back to the nest, handing it off to the female. Then I imagine the female tearing my pages into small pieces with her beak, delicately feeding my words to her young.

• • •

FOUR DAYS LATER the nestlings are entirely different animals. They grow at an absurd rate. They will become almost full-grown ospreys in thirty days, the most dramatic change coming over the next three weeks. I note that June 9 is the first time they look like real birds, like miniature versions of the adults. And that is the day that, for the first time, I can distinguish size differences between them, one definitely larger and stronger, as well as more alert, than the other two. When the male flies a short lap to defecate and then alights on the crossbar, the strongest nestling pops its head up quickly to see if it's fish yet.

I find it easier and easier to get up early, to spend time out on the marsh. In *The Snow Leopard,* Peter Matthiessen writes of watching mountain sheep in the Himalayas: "I chew bread, in this wonderful immersion in pure sheep-ness." This has been a week of pure osprey-ness. I don't pretend that a handful of days watching the nest through binoculars has transformed me; I make no claims to enlightenment. But I can say this: the more time I spend like this, the more days I spend outside, the closer I become to the creature I'd most like to be. Getting outside—both out of doors and outside my own brain—is how it starts. And the more I discipline myself to slow down, to notice things, to stay still, the more confident I become that I can really live a life in closer touch with older ways and older rhythms.

The discipline, of course, is the hard part. It's easy to look back at the first day I saw the nestlings and only remember the joyous sight of the first head popping up. But for hours that day the most interesting thing about the nest was the naked Barbie doll plastered to the northeast wall. As with with almost anything worthwhile, it's the dull hours spent staying in your seat that are the foundation, the fundament. The seat of learning, in this case, is the butt. We talk about patience as if it were an innate trait, like being tall or blue-eyed, a thing we either have or don't, not something learned. But while I'm naturally about the least patient person I know—always wanting it all *right now*—I've gradually come to see that I can *train* myself to slow down, to look, listen, and occasionally actually *be* in the present, holding back from shooting off to future plans or retreating to past comforts. Real patience means putting in the dull hours and trusting that the occasional lift will come. And while you can't force grace, you can put yourself out where grace is.

That's the central paradox of slowing down: it leads to excitement that is often dazzling. What, after all, surprises and delights us? Speed. Growth. Quantity. Vibrancy. Variety. These are the qualities the natural world presents if we simply sit still and open our eyes. This world may seem dull at first, but when it opens to you, it opens like spring, in a great rush: rapid, enormous change flowering in a thousand ways. Like the growth of the birds over the last few days, it presents everyday miracles. In this respect, living on older rhythms proves to be a bit of a cheat. It turns out you *can* have it all: when you live more slowly, the world's excitement intensifies, and you end up walking around smiling like a man with a secret. I only have to think of all the things I've never seen until the past two months to elicit that same smile: An osprey dive. An oystercatcher. A marsh wren. A green heron's hunt. Grosbeaks and towhees. A red-winged blackbird's eggs and nest. And if I really want to grin, I can think of that moment when I saw the nestling's head pop up. I'll put that up against a good day on the stock market anytime.

"TIME IS MONEY," I joked to Hones once when he was lagging during a hiking trip in the White Mountains. Time can be money, or power, or control, or lots of things. For me there have been plenty of occasions when time was writing, working frantically to erect monuments of words, sentences, books. Sometimes, taken by these ambitious moods, I like to secretly plot out the next two, three, or even five years: imagining the books I'll write, the dates I'll finish them. Like many of us, I have a hunter in me who enjoys throwing spears at targets, and targets fill life with a certain juice. But, having said that, I find that being too goal-conscious, looking too hard for the dive, leads to a rigid way of seeing, a constant comparison of some fictional life to the actual moments you're living today.

On the one hand, goals greatly reduce our chances of living on osprey time. Out of fear we put blinders on, forever narrowing the scope of our concerns. We forget that the concerns that seem so passionately important to us are just concerns, not too different from those that other creatures have. When the Chapin male flies over toward his hunting grounds, he couldn't care less about me. Money and success, seen through another set of eyes, are just so much fish. On the other hand, fish are how ospreys live. Fail, and they die. In fact, you can't get much more goal-focused than the ospreys, particularly at this time of year. They live by killing, by achieving enough kills per day, every day. I admire the Chapin male because his life seems as focused as an arrow; I laugh at the younger harbor birds, who fritter away their precious energy.

If watching the birds makes me question specific goals, it doesn't make me question the importance of goals themselves. I am still ambitious; it's just that my ambitions are changing. Why not go directly to the root of the thing? Our complex relationship with time, our many names for it, revolves around the fact that someday our time will end. I need to directly face the fact that this body that holds me will rot—has already begun to rot—and to not run from this fact. Of course, this leads to the inevitable pun on "settling." We get jittery when we commit to a place because it reminds us of our final commitment. My father has settled in East Dennis in a way that I can't yet hope to rival.

Though I want to slow down, I'm not quite ready to sink into the dirt. If I don't believe that I've managed to completely live

on osprey time—and I don't, nowhere close—I do believe that being with the birds and watching their lives has made a difference.
Over the last week or two I've become a little more patient, and
I'm beginning to understand a little better what patience is. For
now I'll just keep driving myself out here, putting my butt in
the chair, and keeping my eyes and ears open. That, at least, is a
start.

Neighbors, Good and Bad

In its relations with other species the osprey is
a peaceful, gentle and harmless neighbor.
. . . If unmolested it attends to its own business,
in which it is very industrious.

—ARTHUR CLEVELAND BENT

Ospreys make good neighbors. Not just for humans, but for almost every other animal. There are some notable exceptions: raccoons, owls, crows, the occasional Canada goose, and, of course, nearly all fish. But it's precisely because their diet is almost exclusively piscine that ospreys are more tolerant than other raptors of small mammals, rodents, and most birds, which is to say they don't attack and kill them. Studying ospreys seventy years ago, A. C. Bent reported that meadow mice sometimes made their homes in osprey ground nests, an arrangement that certainly wouldn't work if the bird were a kestrel or merlin. "The fish hawk bears a good character in the avian world," testified Captain C. W. R. Knight in his 1932 *National Geographic* article. "He is harmless to most other birds, and so well do they know it that smaller species often build in the interstices of his bulky home. Although courageous in defense of his nest and young, the osprey is seldom an aggressor." At Quivett, Chapin, and the harbor, house sparrows occupy the downstairs apartments of the osprey nests, building their own homes, not exactly as Knight describes, but in the gaps between the slats of the platforms. You can watch them work, zipping in and out—building, copulating, fighting—while the ospreys sit, relatively impassive. To a certain extent the birds mirror each other: the sparrows bringing back twigs instead of sticks, string and thread instead of rope and boat line, but the smaller birds, besides being substantially neater, are industrious to the point of hyperactivity, needing to make use of their shorter time on earth and not able to survive on just a few fish feasts a day. The sparrows look like a kind of pilot fish for the larger birds, darting around the nest with a wingspan measurable in inches rather than feet, busily housekeeping, the males flashing their formal black bibs. But they lack a pilot fish's function. While ospreys provide a kind of built-in big brother, protecting the sparrows from other raptors and raccoons, for instance, it's not quite as clear what the sparrows do for the ospreys. Maybe what they do is amuse them, I decide during my idle time at the nests. Maybe their fast-forward lifestyles seem funny to the larger birds. Nest life is a fairly dull life, after all, and the house sparrows are the closest thing the ospreys have to TV.

The most social of raptors, ospreys also get along exceptionally well with their own kind. "Where possible, Ospreys like to nest near other Ospreys," writes Alan Poole. "Good nest sites are often clustered—in swamps, on islands, or on power pylons, for example. In such situations, pairs breed colonially with nests 50–100 meters apart, although loosely spaced colonies are more common." According to Poole, one of the reasons they cluster may not be particularly neighborly, as ospreys sometimes hope to usurp existing nest sites. But the fact is that the birds usually manage to coexist quite well, to the extent that neighbors often fish together, as I witnessed in the hunting party over Wing Island this spring. Once again they owe this sociability in large part to what they hunt. The fact that they eat fish is what allows for colonial living, because, unlike most hawks and eagles, they can't readily establish and defend a feeding territory, since fish are always on the move. For this reason ospreys, while still territorial about their immediate nest areas, can be more tolerant of their fellows who nest nearby.

A less harmonious relationship exists between the ospreys and red-tailed hawks, at least at the Quivett nest where the hawks' hunting grounds overlap with the ospreys' immediate nesting territory. Red-tails are powerful, short-tailed birds with broad wings, usually identified by their chestnut-red tails, though the coloration of this area often varies. In fact, almost everything about red-tails varies—from the coloring of their breasts and bellies to the nests they build to what they prey on—so much so that the bird we now call the red-tailed hawk was once thought to be several different species. If the osprey is the hawk world's great specialist, the red-tailed hawk plays the generalist—the utility infielder, adapting to whatever situation presents itself. This adaptability, combined with the red-tails' less chemical-heavy diet, allowed them to continue thriving throughout the DDT era, becoming our most well-known hawk. The Quivett red-tails nest less than a mile from the osprey platform and hunt the small mammals in the marsh, enchroaching on the ospreys' nesting area. The hawks have shorter wings than the ospreys by ten to twenty inches, but they are strong fliers who seem to give the ospreys all they can handle. I've witnessed a couple of aerial battles, but more often what is involved is a whole lot of threatening and warning, upward spiraling punctuated by the distinct high-pitched cries of each species.

Great horned owls are far worse neighbors. These nocturnal birds of prey are a mortal threat to both ospreys and their young. At first I was doubtful that a bird with a plentiful food source of rabbits, mice, and voles would attack another raptor. But, in response to my skeptical e-mail, Alan Poole wrote back, "I don't think owls will kill adult ospreys just for food, or at least not often, but I suspect they may do so when adults are protecting their young. . . . I have found dead adults near nests, obvious victims of owl predation (puncture wounds, head missing)—but not often. Maybe 3–4 times in 5 years of checking 80 nests per week at least one time. This, of course, doesn't include the amount of times that owls preyed on nestlings without evidence."

Stealth and night vision, as well the power of a surprise attack, apparently make up for the owl's slightly smaller size. Also talons that, if not as long, are just as sharp and deadly as an osprey's own (as well as sharing the same sort of reversible toe). Not long ago I found a great horned owl corpse on the beach, the talons so black and piercingly sharp that to touch them gave credence to a story I'd always thought apocryphal: that an owl hunting in tall grassland had mistaken a boy's scalp for prey, and had killed the boy by taking off half his head. Dennis Murley, the longtime naturalist for the Wellfleet Bay Wildlife Sanctuary, tells of a naive woman who excitedly related how she had watched a mother osprey teaching its young to fly at dusk by carrying it through the air. Murley explained to her that it was likely an owl swooping off with an osprey nestling. When Murley and others erect osprey poles, they are careful to put them out in the middle of marshes, where the birds can have a good 360-degree view and some distance from the woods. To erect a pole and platform too close to the trees is to invite a night raid by owls.

One final enemy should be mentioned, this one more annoying than deadly. Not all raptors get their meals as cleanly and athletically as ospreys do. While an osprey will turn his or her nose up at a secondhand fish, bald eagles aren't above a little piracy. Where the two species coexist, the eagle will often watch an osprey do the work of fishing before swooping in to plunder. For those of us inclined toward ospreys, this gives us yet another reason to root for them. "The osprey is a clean sportsman and prefers to catch living fish," writes A. C. Bent. "It is not a carrion feeder like the bald eagle and will not touch a tainted fish."

While ospreys do have enemies, in the main they get along well with their neighbors. Perhaps more important for their survival, ospreys get along well with people. Despite the warning cries and agitated flights, ospreys are remarkably tolerant of humans and will nest in places other raptors wouldn't dream of. The harbor pair is a stunning example, going about their wild business while the harbor parking lot is being rebuilt, jackhammers and drills shaking the ground, dredges dredging and pile drivers driving pilings. While the other pairs are more shy, these two seem great extroverts, habituated as they are to all sorts of human movement. With the male's tousled crown, they seem a punk-rock pair, the least Thoreauvian of the birds I watch, comfortable with trash, crowds, smoke, and noise. Fortunately, the humans around them are also relatively tolerant. The harbor dredging crew, who begin work each day with a loud round of swearing, respect the birds they work next to, or at least that's what they say. When I ask them about the birds, they respond excitedly, telling me what they've seen while they worked. Though fish hawks were once shot around fisheries, we now know that their take of fish is relatively minimal, and the local fishermen that I've talked to see their return as a good omen.

EARLY IN THE SECOND week of June, Nina and I become involved in our own experiment in neighborliness. During the winter we live here as if it were our home, but in the summer it again becomes a family place. My mother migrates up from North Carolina, and we make the shorter migration to the upstairs room that I use as a study during the off-season. I'm not oblivious to the implications of moving back into what was my childhood room, but the view of the ocean and the sounds of the harbor ospreys counterbalance my anxieties. It is good to see my mother after a long winter.

As for my osprey neighbors, they're doing just fine. With increasingly greater frequency and reliability, my trips to watch the nests have brought me delight. I now enjoy spending time with the birds every day, and relish the feeling of easy intimacy that grows as spring turns to summer. One of the odd things is just how much I find myself *liking* the birds. Not just the Chapin male, my admitted favorite, but all of them, even the punk-rock pair.

If visiting the birds suits me, it's largely because I've always preferred fairly domestic adventures. One of Thoreau's less extreme lessons was that you can experience something profound in the natural world without going to the Himalayas, that you can find everything you need in your own backyard. In other words, you don't need to live with grizzlies or gorillas to live deeply. We need to love the near with the same excitement that we love the exotic. Besides the ospreys, I've found myself enjoying the intimacy of catbirds this spring, particularly the one who flew close to me on the deck the other night. I was drinking the night's first beer and watching a full moon dis-impale itself from a sailboat mast in the harbor when the little bird hopped to within two feet of me. I admired the simple and elegant lines of the wings, its little black cap and lighter gray-black feathers, but even more than that I liked the simple fact that it came close. If not particularly melodious, spitting out the mumbled mewings that give them their names, catbirds have the virtue of being the most neighborly of birds.

Despite the famous saying, familiarity is not always such a bad thing. Neighbors sometimes ask me how I can walk the same route down the beach each day, but what they don't understand is that the beach changes with every tide. "To find new things, take the path you took yesterday," wrote John Burroughs. While it might seem that the novelty would wear off during my trips to the osprey nests, the opposite has proven true. I'm constantly being surprised by what I see. This month, in particular, plays a leitmotif of variety. The weather continues warm and rainless, perfect unless you're a plant, and Hones, back home in Boston, reports that the fish are still biting. He's after stripers now, driving down to the South Shore after work and on weekends. Using his rod, a Shakespeare "Ugly Stik," he recently caught another keeper, this one thirty inches. With few storms and fish plentiful, it's no real surprise that the ospreys are thriving, and, a week after watching the nestlings at Chapin, I see two heads pop up over the nest at Simpkins Neck.

But it's my next-door neighbors, the harbor pair, that give me the biggest shock. Just the other afternoon the harbor male flew low over our back deck, pausing above me, as if showing off his vast wingspan, before banking and lapping around the house. Today, June 12, the shadow of an oak branch plays across my journal page as I scribble down notes at dusk. The cooing of the mourning doves sounds different this evening, too aggressive, almost savage, and the flapping of our flag provides a back beat to my viewing. I watch the female osprey, a lighter chocolate brown, exactly the color of our house's post and beams, as she rests alone on the nest. When she flies off, my long-held suspicions are confirmed; the harbor nest, the junk nest, is a failure. But having made this same mistake before, I hold off on judgment, and soon I'm glad I did. She circles back to the nest and takes up a begging call, and not long after, the male flies by with a nearly headless flounder in his talons, passing low over the nest once as if taunting her before circling back and landing. The light is fading, the water streaked with dark blue paint slashes, but something about the way she begins eating makes me shiver. She tears off a piece and dips low in the nest, her tail up, and I now recognize this as the sign of what it is: a mother feeding her young.

Despite the fact that I've never given this nest much respect,

I'm overjoyed by its success. It's a success I really don't deserve to have right out my back door, seeing as I've bad-mouthed this pair all spring, but I'll take it. Like many young parents, they invite second-guessing—he seems just beginning to get the concept of sharing, and just in time. As for her, though she started getting down to nesting later than the other pairs, the results are undeniable. Once again reality has contradicted my expectations.

As in the human world, appearances can be deceiving. The conscientious Quivett pair fail, the easygoing harbor pair succeed. I decide not to think about it too much, and jump on the bandwagon. This is my next-door nest, after all, my home nest, the only nest I can see from inside the house, the only birds I can hear begging from my bedroom. Also, now that they have young, it adds a new social element to my osprey viewing. During cocktail hour, I can hand the binoculars to my wife or friends and let them look in on what I've been seeing at Chapin. This gives me the tour guide's thrill of watching others watch, pointing things out. And it is a thrill: particularly when Nina first sees the nestlings' heads pop up and witnesses the mother's delicate feedings. She imitates the action with her head and mouth, as if it were beyond humans to observe this act and not mimic it.

Since the Chapin nest is two weeks ahead of this one, I have seen the future, and so can play the expert, if not quite a full-blown psychic. When the birds enter their reptilian phase, I predict they'll soon crouch, and sure enough they do. But it isn't just ego gratification I get from having a nest so close to home; there is also sociability. Now the people close to me can understand what it is I've been ranting about.

I ASPIRE TO BE a good neighbor, to be part of my neighborhood, and that means human as well as animal and vegetable. Despite a growing prejudice toward ospreys, I've also enjoyed the company of my human neighbors since returning to the Cape, and

I might even have learned some lessons from them as well as from the birds. In a tourist town, there's a distinct difference between your summer and winter neighbors. During my first year back, I feared the melancholy of February, but when the dreaded month hit I found that, surprisingly, I was settling in and really starting to enjoy it here. Winter insists on its own pace, dispensing with ambition. I felt curiously free. Sometimes I would eschew my writing altogether and split wood on a solid, perfectly flat chopping block of locust. The block was a gift from Danny Schadt, who ran, and still runs, the Northside Marina, across the street from us. When he dropped it off I asked him if he liked his job.

"Ya, I do," he said. "I like the fact that if I get bored pulling boats I can work on the computer in the office and if I get bored with that I can cut wood for the stove."

This confirmed my own impulse toward variety. Cape Cod in summer becomes run over by specialists, by orthodontists and stockbrokers, but my winter neighbors are generalists, jacks-of-all-trades. As the sun pulls away we move back in time, concerned again with the basics: wood and warmth. My neighbor Glen ex-emplifies this warm-blooded philosophy. After the big ice storm last winter he came by, hooded by a sweatshirt, with ice tinging his droopy mustache. We talked a minute before he started to chain-saw the branches and trees we'd lost during the blizzard. I pulled the wood down to the curb, stacking what I could use.

After we finished piling the wood, he talked to me about why he'd moved down to the Cape.

"When I came here one of the things I wanted to do was be neighborly. I fixed up our house and made some changes, but I think I did it with respect to the neighborhood. I didn't want to come in here and change the way it was. I just wanted to have a garden in the back and live by the ocean. Now these people come in who don't even live here and they tear down the little houses and put up big ones, ruining views and driving up property taxes. It's changed so much."

I nodded. He'd said everything I felt. Inevitably, talk of loving our neighborhood leads to anger, talk of paradise leads to the serpent. This is an unfortunate consequence of living in a beautiful place, but in one way at least it's a good thing: it simplifies the world. While we still have patches of wildness and while ospreys still fly over our waters, it's no exaggeration to say that all is threatened, and that the threat runs like a steady burbling undertone through our neighborhood gossip. Grumbling is our genre of preference on Cape Cod, and we have plenty to grumble about. New houses sprout up hourly, four permits per town per day, in fact. Sesuit Neck presents the extremes of both dramatic beauty and rapacious destruction. That is one thing becoming part of this neighborhood has done for me; it has telescoped the world down to this single place. My cosmology is simplified. Sesuit Neck is the world.

THE HEART OF that world is the bluff. A hump of land that rises from the beach like a great whale-backed beast, a jutting heath transported from a nineteenth-century romantic novel. This is the place where I first watched the jetty ospreys forage for sticks for their nest, making slow trips back and forth from the jetty's end to the land below the bluff and back. It's also a place that, due to a coincidence of wealth and geography, has long remained undeveloped, and so has become a refuge for many of my neighbors. Not all of us get down to the bluff, of course, but many do, some to walk their dogs, some to think, some to get away. Even those who don't actually spend time down below the bluff must be reassured by its presence, by the fact that our neighborhood contains, within it, a place apart. If the English had their commons, the best American neighborhoods contain within them a still-wild place. For many of us the bluff has been the epitome of a good neighbor: minding its own business, keeping quiet, giving much, taking little.

Just as the ospreys imprint images of their natal nesting grounds, the land below the bluff has been imprinted on me. I've walked the path to the bluff since I was a small child, first holding my mother's hand, then exploring on my own. All my life the bluff has stood in counterpoint to the development that has been a constant of Sesuit Neck. The sound of hammering is never far off on Cape Cod, but neither is the sound of the ocean, and the ocean insists on wildness. Approaching the bluff by beach from the harbor, you have the sensation of moving from tame to wild, first walking past the overdeveloped private beachfronts, then past the public beach and Bagley's beach, and finally leaving all houses behind. As an adolescent I had a distinct sense of relief when, moving past the last of the homes, no longer feeling windows or eyes staring down at me, I began to walk faster, excited, out to greet the bluff alone.

Part of what ensured this solitude was the rocky terrain. Except at dead low tide, the land below the bluff could only be walked by jumping from rock to rock, and most beachgoers, fearing bloody shins, didn't take the risk. But the brave were rewarded. Once past the sandy stretch and headed toward the point, anything could happen. Seals basked on Tautog rock, floats of eiders bobbed offshore, and, if you got there before dawn, you might see deer licking salt off the rocks. It was as if by walking less than a mile from the Dennis Yacht Club, you'd passed through a door into another world.

Not a quiet world. Weather reached the bluff first, and, often, summer turned to fall when you arrived at the jutting spit. The sky above would pile up with clouds, enormous cloud continents with dark violet interiors and flashes of gold escaping from the coasts. Long shadows shafted down the sand, my own goofy dark doppelgänger stretching out in front of me as I walked. Sometimes the open beach barely let me approach—warning me off with sand stinging my face. Gulls drifted by sideways. Trees and grasses bent and ran from water and wind. Light dry sand flew spectral over the darker sandbar sand like a curtain revealing the blue-gray ocean and purpled clouds. Even on the rare days when the waves rested, the rocks seethed with life. Barnacles hissed and crabs scuttled and swallows darted and swooped down from their cave homes in the brown cliff wall.

As with any good relationship, mine with the bluff deepened over time. Not long after college, I came to Cape Cod to work and write, and that fall, standing on the point like the bow of a ship, I watched as the wind swept out summer's clinging heat and ushered in the clarifying Cape light. When the real weather blew in, the leafy world reddened, poison ivy and sumac bloodying the edges of the cranberry bog. Not wanting to squander any opportunity for joy, I often reached the beach before dawn, and returned at sunset to catch the dying rays of light, sipping a beer and watching a pumpkin-orange moon rise.

This overindulgence, this binge of color, led to a long hangover, and I had to leave the Cape for a while. But over the years I've kept coming back. In 1994 I returned again to spread my father's ashes out on the bay beyond Stone's point (burying half of the ashes at the Quivett plot), after which I walked out alone toward the bluff at sunset. Now I am back with my wife, living close to the bluff again.

BUT THINGS HAVE CHANGED, the way they always do. Not long ago, just before Nina and I moved to the neighborhood in 1997, the bluff and beach were bought and we found ourselves with a new neighbor. Over the last two years I've stood by and witnessed that neighbor's methodical destruction of the bluff, first the tearing down of the old mansion that was the neighborhood landmark, and then the saddling of the bluff's wild whale back with a trophy house the size of a castle. Walking out on the jetty's end, I can no longer look in the bluff's direction without a twinge of despair. We all know the feeling: our dream places ripped up for someone else's dream house.

It's true I'm not above the urge for a dream house myself, and I'd have been happy for my new neighbor if he'd built a grand house, even an enormous house. The bluff is of such magnificent scale that formerly a mansion—a *mansion!*—was able to fit snugly into place. But the sad and frustrating thing, the thing that still causes me daily depressions and stabbing pains, is that a dream house or mansion wasn't good enough. My new neighbor could not tolerate merely becoming part of the beautiful bluff but felt compelled to dominate it.

"It's a goddamn desecration of place," another of my neighbors said recently. That's the word—*desecration*—that keeps coming up when I think of what has been done to the land. I don't use the word lightly, but accurately: a sacred place made profane.

When I walk below the bluff now I find myself repeatedly thinking about how "out of place" the building seems. Since humans first settled in Sesuit Neck they've built their homes low and strong, a logical and organic reaction to the daily assault of wind and water. This is how things grow on Cape Cod and how they've long been built, a response that evolved directly from place, and an intimate knowledge of that place. For inspiration, the new owner needed to look no farther than the pitch pines and scrub oaks that crawl mangily across the humpback of his new backyard, a yard he will find to be one of the windiest places on earth. If he'd been in a listening mood, the trees would have spoken directly to him, whispering, "Stay low," and, heeding that advice, he could have still built a large and beautiful structure. But, he may have reasoned, with modern building materials and techniques making the old restraints irrelevant, why not spread as far and high as I can go? Why merely become part of the bluff when I can rise above it?

Stifling the moralist's urge to tell him to go back and read the story of Icarus, I'll suggest that there may have been simpler reasons for restraint. He might have paused and considered his neighbors. Not just the deer whose paths have forever weaved through the brambles he tore down or the swallows who for countless generations have made their homes in the undercusp of the bluff where tractors now rumble, but the three hundred or so *Homo sapiens* who dwell here in different seasons. He might have—dare I mention it in this day and age?—minded his manners and said, Well, since I'm tearing down this mansion, this neighborhood landmark, I'll consider the others who live here and, while of course building a large place, will try to fit gracefully into my new home.

This was not the option my neighbor chose.

HAVING SPENT THE SPRING watching the ospreys, I believe that human beings could stand to become more territorial, that is, could stand to take a lesson from the birds. Destroy an osprey's home nest, and she will keep coming back to it. She will fight off geese, raccoons, coyotes, even humans. She doesn't care about trespassing laws. She will remain loyal to place, until you either have to kill her or let her settle.

"In most human populations, transgressions relating to spatial distribution and proprietary boundaries are enforced through courts of law," writes Pete Dunne in *The Wind Masters*. "In birds of prey, territorial defense is the responsibility of the birds themselves." Over the last two years I've begun to take things into my own hands, perhaps taking a cue from the ospreys. Recently I began to write articles, draft petitions, and attend conservation meetings; the other day, I wrote a long letter to my new neighbor. But if I've become more willing to fight for my place, I'd like to become more willing still. Loving these birds, this land, has led me to dramatically simplify my life, to pare it down. To remember what is most important and make my hours revolve around that. Ospreys teach passion, immediacy, directness.

In the cardboard box that I use as my "Neighborhood Fight" file, I also keep quotes and examples of osprey tenacity for place. "The Fish Hawk has a great attachment to the tree to which it carries its prey," wrote John James Audubon in *The Birds of America*. "It shows the same attachment to the tree on which it has built its first nest, and returns to it year after year." But it is an even stronger commitment than Audubon knew. Ospreys stake their lives on their places. In *Birds of Massachusetts and Other New England States,* Forbush writes of a friend of his who bought a farm in Touisset:

The house had been unoccupied for some time, and when the family moved in they found a great nest on the top of kitchen chimney with a pair of Ospreys in full and complete possession of the premises. Before starting a fire in the range it became necessary to remove the nest, which was accomplished by strenuous labor, as a great mass of material had been accumulated on the chimney top. Immediately the birds began to rebuild the nest. They brought large sticks and placed them across the chimney, and to hold them down they brought clods and stones. Destruction of their domicile did not discourage them in the least. At last in self-defense my friend was obliged to shoot the female. The male did not mourn long and in a few hours was back again with another mate ("just like a man," the good wife said), and the pair, having first reconnoitered the place, decided to recommence building. When they had finished, they had filled the chimney from bottom to top with sticks, stones and rubbish, so that it became necessary either to destroy those birds or give up the house to them.

Forbusch's friend ended up killing the new pair, though, based on the law of desire, he might have considered handing over the house keys to the birds, since they wanted to settle there to the point of dying while he only to the point of killing. If this shows a lack of flexibility on the ospreys' part (not to mention the humans'), it also demonstrates an admirable example of making a choice and staking everything on it. Forbusch gives another example of osprey tenacity, this one with a happier ending. A pair of birds insisted on nesting on a certain electric pole, despite a lineman's continued attempts to rid the pole of the nest. In this case it was the humans, not the birds, who gave ground: "The lineman tore down the nest but the birds persisted until one day the superintendent happened along and told the men to take the wires off the pole, and set up another pole back in the field and string the wires to that. This was done and the birds triumphantly occupied the nest on the first pole."

CURRENTLY THE GREATEST threat for wild animals is habitat loss, their places being methodically chewed up. What we don't seem to recognize is that every time we blindly tear up woods to build homes, we are destroying the homes of others on a massive scale. With each passing year our building, our *development,* as we unironically call it, has become more and more destructive to our wild neighbors—and to wildness itself. Of course humans feel the instinct to build as surely as birds do, but in some of us this instinct, unencumbered by a sense of proportion (and unlimited by modern technology), has run amuck.

Despite the platforms we've built for them, habitat loss poses a growing threat for ospreys. For the New England birds summer means living on the coastline, where all the trees are being gobbled up by and for homes, where platforms are the only option. Winter means flying to rain forests that, at the current rate, will be gone halfway through the next century. When a landscape is imprinted in you, how does it feel to be internally compelled to return to a place, only to find that that place is gone?

I know that this is a familiar drumbeat, and I know that when hearing it over and over again, we recoil into apathy, a kind of mental fetal position. Saving the rain forest is remote to us, impossible, a cause for rock stars and ice-cream tycoons. I, too, would rather not think about it—but that becomes impossible when they start to destroy places imprinted in me. Maybe it's healthy to take these losses personally, and then to act without thinking. The writer Jack Turner offers intimacy as at least the first part of an antidote for apathy. Fall in love with what you are losing and it will be harder to be blasé about the loss. "To reverse this situation we must become so intimate with wild animals, with plants and places, that we answer to their destruction from the gut," he writes. "Like when we discover the landlady strangling our cat." Exactly. Only when a thing is close does it become immediate, urgent.

IT MAY BE entirely presumptuous, but I believe that my new neighbor on the bluff has helped teach me a little about what habitat loss must be like to the birds. I may be oversensitive, but with each new building that goes up on Sesuit Neck I wince, as if they were developing on some part of me. Now the dozers rumble up by Paddock's Path, and there is one particular apple tree that I worry for. To love this neighborhood is to be constantly open to loss, like committing to a woman who keeps fooling around.

But I hold to hope. The changes in how we've treated the ospreys over the last thirty years give me faith in the ability of human beings to grow, though I'm not sure I have faith we can grow fast enough. Too often we have evolved too late. The trick, and it's quite a trick, is regretting *before* the fact, imagining what might be and stopping ourselves. This means taking local action, though we all resist the step. I know this resistance well: I'm the least political animal imaginable, no more likely than an osprey to carry a picket sign. There's a humorlessness in advocacy, I understand, and if I'm becoming an advocate it's a truly reluctant one. Fanaticism doesn't come naturally.

The letter, the plea, that I wrote to my new neighbor was my own declaration of dependence—dependence on this land. How am I to be a good neighbor? I'd better start by trying to preserve what's best about our common place.

That means that, like the ospreys, I may need to warn off intruders, may need to screech and flap and drive them out of my territory. After all, I'm vocalizing essentially the same things the birds are—*Respect my home and leave me alone*—the only difference being that I can talk. And since ospreys can't write letters, I'd better help defend them while I'm at it. It is, after all, the neighborly thing to do.

A Deeper Vision

In the hawk's eye is an original,
cosmic world we have yet to understand.

—JOHN HAY

My new telescope, a Bushnell 60mm Spacemaster, changes
everything. It arrives via UPS, and the world transforms. A
technophobe, I'm loath to admit that a tool can make such a
difference, but it does. Where I'd feared that adding another lens
would put distance between me and the birds, it has the opposite
effect. Much more than the binoculars, which I'm forever setting
down or adjusting, the scope forces me to leave myself behind. All
that exists is what I see through the viewfinder.

Suddenly there's a whole new level of vision. I'm inside the
nest with the birds. Everything becomes more vivid, colors and
shapes taking on an almost hallucinatory intensity. I see the pink
insides of the nestlings' mouths, the buff streak down the backs of
their necks, the reddish hue in the trout's tail that the Chapin male
devours. The ospreys become individuals; for the first time I really
see their faces. The white tufted crowns above the masks, like pom-
padours, the sharp black overbite hook of the bill, the swirling
chocolate masks around the eyes, and, most of all, the eyes themselves. The eyes shine a fierce yellow, perfectly round, containing
a perfectly round black pupil, the outer eye encircled by another

ring of black, as if painted with savage eyeliner. But that is the wrong image: with the scope anthropomorphism becomes harder. The eyes look predatory, intent, like nothing human. And it's not just the eyes, with their glaring stares and black pupils, but the tongue, too. The nestlings' tongues dart out pink, the color of grade-school erasers, but the older birds' tongues are darker, and now it's not so hard to believe that these birds evolved from reptiles. Sometimes the warning cries and the movements of the bills don't quite match up, like in an old Japanese Godzilla movie, and the tongues stick out when the bills open. *What kind of tongues do ospreys have?* I write in my journal. It seems a new kind of question, better than my old vaguely philosophic ones, reflecting the specificity of my new vision.

Feedings become events. Now I can really see the delicate placement of food in the nestlings' mouths, and it's even more savage and beautiful than I'd thought. I see the ripping of the fish, the mother's head shaking as she pulls off a long strand of skin, the quick pull back when it rips free, a sight so visceral that you're surprised you can't hear an accompanying tear. Then she delicately tilts her head and places the morsel into the gaping mouth of the chick. Her bill is much more hooked and pointed than I'd noticed before, more dangerous and sharp, and her talons, which pin the fish to the nest, much larger, like grappling hooks, which makes the gentleness of the act all the more impressive. She tilts her head like a nervous teenager hesitating before making out for the first time. But as delicate as her act is, there's a jostling among the nestlings that I couldn't see before through the binoculars, an intense yearning and battle for the scraps of fish. The pecking order, formerly a concept I read about in books, becomes real. With the scope I make out four nestlings at Chapin—an exceptional nest!— and while the first chick eats, the second and third battle for position, a battle that number three consistently loses. The mother takes her time, doling out chunks, most to the dominant bird but occasional bites to number two. When they are both full she turns to number three, while the smallest of nestlings, the runt, clearly out of the running, stays on the other side of the nest—*dejectedly*, I can't help but project—moving tiny sticks around and patting them down in miniature imitation of his parents' housekeeping.

More and more, my time centers on Chapin, due in part to the sheer excited activity at that nest. I am specializing, centering in on what I want to see. I often focus the scope on the Chapin female during the feeding, but when I enter the world through the viewfinder there's something particularly fierce about the profile of the male. While she hasn't had a bath in a while, and looks as disheveled as the nest, his feathers still present a sharp contrast of black-brown and clean white. Wind sometimes adds devil's horns to the tufts of white atop his head, and when he returns with a fish, he will *rip* into it, no matter the commotion of begging at the nest. This practical selfishness is particularly necessary now, since he has to spend up to three or four hours a day fishing to support the brood. When he tears at a fish you can really make out the screwdriver twist—he gets his shoulder blades down into it—and if he tears off a particularly long strand he will sometimes throw his head back and catch it in midair. If athleticism is variable in the animal world, I stick to my original contention that the Chapin male is the neighborhood's best fisherman. Were I to choose one bird to support a brood of four, he would be it. Unlike the harbor male, who, despite his new title as father, seems to like to show off the fish he catches, flying by the nest in taunting circles like a football player dancing in the end zone, the Chapin bird works in a direct, no-nonsense fashion. He can't afford the fancy stuff. The harbor pair are a bit like teenage human parents; they don't quite believe parenthood is happening, sooner than they expected, and sometimes seem to half-play at what they are doing. But the Chapin male is deadly serious. When he flies the remains of a trout over to the nest I study his long, vivid white legs, built for reaching down into the water. White feathered knickers grow halfway down, until they are replaced by the scales, the bottoms of the toes studded with spicules. The talons themselves look awkward and oversized, and when he stomps around the nest, he sometimes gets sticks or seaweed caught in them by accident. But if awkward here, how perfect when set to the task they were built for, the catching of fish. Through the scope I can see that the poor fish must not just be speared but also trapped, *enclosed,* when the enormous and deadly cage of the talons descends on it.

The scope makes empathy with the birds more intense, but it also brings me closer to the fishes' plight. It's no longer so easy to haze over the sheer savagery of the ospreys' daily work. One morning, June 13, I watch the Chapin male fly back to the nest with a still-wriggling trout. The fish must weigh two pounds, more than half as much as the bird does, and its gills still open and close, struggling for breath. As usual, on the nest the male ignores his prey. He stares off in the distance with an impassive deadly gaze, his head held up, proud and still, wind ruffling his feathers. There is nothing extraneous to the Chapin male's body, or to his attitude. Certainly he has no time to waste on pity. He holds the fish in one foot, not even in all the talons but between two, as if pinned there by calipers. He opens and flaps his wings once or twice, adjusting his stance, but is generally content to let the fish die on its own. I study the yellow and black stripes of the scales, watch the fish flop again, and then I'm surprised, caught off guard, when the osprey jabs its bill violently down into the still-living trout's head. Meanwhile, the female tries to feed the nestlings the remains of an earlier catch, but they're not interested. They know fresh fish when they see it, and they crowd around the male, their oversized wings flopping, staring up at the pink-red meat of the trout. He ignores them and rips the fish apart, taking particular pleasure when he gets to the intestines, slurping them up like long spaghetti strands. Finally, over half the fish eaten, he pauses and weighs his decision, balancing the tastiness of the trout against the needs of his family. The trout wins. I know exactly how he feels when he turns more slowly back to his meal. He bends down, looking almost reluctant, tired, staring at his food just the way I do when Hones cooks dry-rub ribs—bloated but not quite ready to quit.

The telescope makes me feel part of the family scene, and it's revolutionary in another way, too. When I focus in on the nest itself, the background trees, another hundred yards off, become hazy and unfocused. The oak trees turn vague and then fluid, a background mosaic of pulsing green, and last year's phragmites shine brown-yellow even as this year's green swallows them. Against this arty backdrop, like an impressionistic stage setting, the actors in the nest gleam even more defined and sharp. Occasionally this presents a contrast of the pastoral and gritty, like when I see the sun glimmer off the male's bill and, focusing in, realize that its sharp black point glistens with fish blood.

In some light the ospreys' eyes have that same gleam, as if the pupils themselves were wet with the insides of fish. Again and again I'm drawn back to the eyes. There are moments when the female will turn her yellow irises right on me, with vision nearly as strong as my scope, and stare until I grow uneasy. There's a cartoon element to the eyes, a perfect circle and black dot, easily drawn, but if you try to stare down an osprey you'll soon find there's nothing funny about it. I wouldn't want to go eye-to-eye with the bird. They bring us directly into our past, when we weren't so firmly ensconced on top of the food chain. They present an aesthetic of savagery, leaving little doubt about what they would do to us if we were small enough and swimming.

AN OSPREY'S VISION is almost eight times greater than a human being's, but that only begins to hint at their acuity. All birds rely heavily on vision, predators in particular. A raptor's eyes are one of nature's great inventions, the most acute in the animal kingdom. Some eagles and hawks have eyes as big as a human's, obviously much larger in proportion to their body size and taking up a good portion of their heads. The section of the eye we can see, the exposed cornea, is only a small part of the eyeball, an eyeball that's virtually jammed in its socket. Because of this ocular tight fit, the eyes themselves don't move much, but this is made up for by the great flexibility of the birds' heads and necks. In *A New Dictionary of Birds,* A. Landsborough Thomson writes, "In birds such as hawks or owls which have frontal eyes, and therefore a relatively small visual field, the head can turn well over 180 degrees."

Like all diurnal birds, ospreys see the world in living color. Having never quite recovered from reading as a child that dogs viewed life in black and white—like a grainy 1950s TV, I imagined —I was glad to learn that most birds see the world pretty much as we do, if with far greater accuracy. Raptors, scanning the ground or water from hundreds and sometimes thousands of feet in the air, must be able to focus in on prey as intensely as I focus through my scope. "Birds of prey have rounder or almost tubular eyes," writes Roger Tory Peterson. "These take in less territory than flat ones do, but see farther and in greater detail, pinpointing living targets with the precision of a bombsight." A falcon, for instance, can recognize a dove from three thousand feet—or ten football fields—away and can pick out a waving handkerchief from fifty-one hundred feet. Peterson continues: "A bird has more sensory cells in its eyes than other animals have, particularly in the area of the fovea, a small depression in the retina at the point of acutest vision. The fovea's convex sides help magnify part of the image—as much as 30 per cent in some bird species. The retinas of hawks are from four to eight times more sensitive as those of humans, making these birds the keenest-sighted of all living things." Birds, then, see not only farther but more clearly than we do.

An osprey is a hawk adapted for fishing, the variations most obvious when looking at the size, the scaliness (the gripping spicules, for instance), and the flexibility of the legs and talons. But evolution has also fine-tuned osprey vision for peering into sun-spangled waters, even down to the smallest details. An eye structure called the nictitating membrane allows birds to focus while diving, and some biologists believe that genetic specialization even accounts for the bandit masks they wear, dark eyebands that reduce glare, like the eye-black that pro football players smear on during games.

At Chapin I'm given daily demonstrations of the birds' ocular superiority and my own inferiority. If there is a visual pecking order, I know who the runt is. The mother and nestlings start their begging calls, a chorus of high-pitched pleas, well before the one they beg for becomes even a dot on my horizon. Sure enough, soon enough, the male will appear, gradually coming into weak human sight, carrying a fish.

A NEW CLARITY illuminates the days. Honeysuckle sweetens the air and the post oak's leaves wave big and waxy, no longer mere drooping half leaves. We approach the solstice, the annual climax of light, the days when we see longest and clearest. The other night a luminescent apple core, cleanly split in half, stood in for the moon, and later fireflies sparkled. I sleep rocked by a larger rhythm, the ocean breathing in and out. It doesn't take much imagination to understand why ospreys choose to live near water. On some nights I walk down to watch the world's eye sink: the sun drops into the water of the bay, staining the sky with pinks, yellows, and oranges.

On June 14 the air swirls with pollen like snow, covering windshields. That night, over drinks, I set up the scope for Nina and my mother, who ooh and ahh as the ospreys feed at the harbor nest. Never before—at least not in the last fifty years, and probably a good deal longer—has the town of Dennis witnessed such a profusion of young ospreys. With three nestlings at

Simpkins Neck, three across the harbor, and four at Chapin, our town is doing its part in the New England osprey comeback. These are fecund days, with three of the four nests succeeding, and I haven't entirely given up on the fourth. I now have a crazy hunch, with everything going so well, that the Quivett nest will be successful, too. Why not? I feel the luck of a gambler on a roll and the next morning, June 15, I'm there early. I clean bird droppings off my father's grave and throw out the old geraniums. The marsh bristles with a rainy, lush green, nothing like the marsh I first came to back in March. Two young white-tailed deer, their coats brownish-red, graze right in front of me, not fifteen feet away. When they notice me they run off like stray dogs, only transforming back into deer to hop over the creek. Once they've run a hundred feet, they stop and stare back at me. I train the scope on them: their coats shine red-brown and beautiful, their bodies slender, with no fat at all.

The female osprey is off the nest, and there's no indication of nestlings or feedings or even eggs. Maybe the second batch, if there was ever a second batch, has failed, too. I feel a pang of sympathy for this early-bird pair, having seemingly floundered despite their conscientiousness. They are the neighborhood nerds, shining an apple for the teacher and stacking their papers neatly, doing everything right but felled by that uncontrollable variable: bad luck. It isn't something you want to think about too long: how preparation and hard work sometimes don't mean a thing. I still don't know what did them in. Likely the thief was a raccoon shimmying up the pole—but how did he get past the mother? Or maybe it wasn't a predator at all, but bad weather or wind. I don't know. The demise of the Quivett nest will remain a mystery, open for speculation. But whatever the reason, it appears to have failed.

Even this fact can't depress me for long; June isn't the time for depression. On the drive home I'm granted a lifting vision. The sun sets behind Bridge Street, the road that leads into Sesuit Neck like a bridge over a moat. The tidal creek tints rose-colored, and I stop and watch a great blue heron fish in the shadowy light. The heron itself presents just a knife-thin silhouette, the silhouette reflected in a bluish-rose circle of water that it now spears. Ripples spread where the heron jabs, but it comes up empty-billed. The bird begins to stalk again, *waiting,* rising up taller, as if on tiptoes, to get a better look from high up, its reflection stretching farther down into the water. I turn my scope on it just in time to see the second plunge, its bill violently jabbing into the water, destroying a painting of rose hues while spreading a circle of blue outward like an aureole. This time the bird emerges with a fish.

Sights like this one convince me that I'm beginning to see better, to notice more. Or maybe I'm just getting luckier. The telescope brings me closer to the nest, while my white journal pages fill with black marks: drawings of hawk eyes, bills, and talons.

THE TELESCOPE also brings the Barbie on the side of the Chapin nest into greater focus. Her long plastic legs are open in a particularly unladylike fashion. But she has the good sense to wear more clothing than I'd given her credit for. Extensive observation reveals that she is decked out in a skimpy green-and-yellow striped leotard. And that's not the only difference I notice: I'm even beginning to question my initial hypothesis that she is indeed a Barbie. "Maybe it's a Spice Girl," I note in my journal.

Of course, as always, I have my doubts about what I'm doing out here. I've been calling this an "experiment," but an experiment in what? Neighborliness? I'm not so sure a good neighbor is one who points a telescope into your bedroom. What's undeniable is that I'm seeing new things. The other day I walked down to the beach and surprised the Chapin female, who was making a rare trip off the nest and seemed to be bathing in a foot of water, cleaning off the season's grime. Another too hot morning I swear I saw her shading the nestlings with her wing, like a parasol, and when I got home my books confirmed what my eyes had witnessed.

Maybe then, if forced into a corner, I'd call what I'm doing an experiment in seeing—in *vision*. More and more I doubt that things are all in my mind. A better bet would be that they're all in my eyes—if, that is, I can manage to keep my mind out of the way. To see, to look for long moments without preconception, to watch without judgment, that may be the beginning of deeper understanding. If we can quiet thought and see, then, our minds refreshed, better thought will come to us, and this must hold true for both scientist and artist. The osprey's dive is blunt, to the point, aggressive, but, I remind myself, the seeing before is as important as the dive itself, the direct act preceded by a vision of what will come. The best hunters spend energy frugally. Before ospreys dive, they look long and carefully.

The telescope allows me to focus. Strangely enough this odd (and expensive) tool with the stork legs performs the function of the best sort of teacher, facilitating, pointing beyond itself. With the binoculars I spent too much time fumbling with the tool, but now, on my best days, I focus beyond the lens, to the nest, like a Zen archer seeing the target. The other complicated tool I need to get beyond is my mind. I know that when an osprey catches a fish it isn't worrying about how it compares with other birds, how foolish it will look if it misses and "fails," or whether that failure will reflect poorly on its birdhood. Rather, it focuses on the fish alone, intensely, brilliantly, seeing beyond itself—seeing the fish so clearly, so accurately, that even the water's refraction is naturally taken into account—seeing and spearing down through the surface into the thing itself.

That would be a good way to see.

. . .

SEEING OSPREYS up close, I'm constantly reminded just how perfectly built they are for what they do. This isn't accident but evolution; like humans they become what they do all day. In fact, they've become what they've been doing for millions of years. They fish, they focus on fish, and so they become, more and more with each evolving minute, fishermen.

It's easy to forget that people are always evolving, too, constantly becoming what we see. To turn to a less learned source, consider the words of Flip Wilson's Geraldine: "What you see is what you get." There is more than comedy here; like the chameleon, we're colored by the leaf we rest on, and, since we're colored by it, we'd better watch where we land. I look at my friends as they get deeper and deeper into their given professions—lawyers, movie producers, carpenters—and see how, with each passing day, they turn into what they do. But even more than what we do it's what we focus on. What—and *how*—we see.

I wouldn't want to be restricted to just one way of seeing the world, but if I were somehow bullied into choosing only one mode, I think I would see the world as a painter. I would see shades pulsing and dashes of silver, the red shine of bittersweet on a gray December day, the long blue shadows on snow, the midfall silver shining at the edges of leaves. I would see the cranberry bog flooded blood-red during its wet harvest and whitecaps crashing in at dawn while the morning slant of light rides their back. I wouldn't see essays or theories but russet, scarlet, raw umber, geranium, salmon, fawn, spectrum blue, and olive-brown.

During my twenties, working at various jobs, I also tried to paint for a while. Of course, like everything else, it happened on Cape Cod. Though I hadn't planned on painting, one particular October overwhelmed me. October was a month when bayberries turned a chalky blue, tree swallows spotted our roads with shadows, and the marsh blazed like a green-gold fire. It was a month when the full moon rose over the pink-blue pastel of the harbor sunset and the blue-gray juniper berries shone iridescent at dusk, and when masses of speckle-bellied starlings filled the trees (and the air with their squeaky-wheeled sounds); a month when the ocean vacillated between the foreboding slate gray of November and a summery, almost tropical blue (while occasionally hinting at its darker winter shades). Most of all, it was a month of color, a month when the entire neck caught fire in a hundred shades of red.

That year I painted not out of any desire to create great works of art or out of a belief that I'd actually become a painter, but from a simple need to react to the swirl of color around me. I drove to Orleans to buy tubes of oil. My motives, I suppose, were super-ficial—superficial as in *surface, surface* as in *color.* If I may be for-given my romanticizing of a time that was romantic to begin with, I think it's fair to say that for a while I became drunk on color (and on the notion of being drunk on color). I wanted not just to ooh and aah like the Sunday foliage viewer, or even to hoard color, but to live steeped in it. I stood and watched as the bluff burned red: the brilliant scarlet of Virginia creeper, the husky maroon of poi-son ivy, the peach color of sumac, and, in the lower pasture, the oddly patriotic red of the few cranberries left after the harvest. Be-low the bluff, more red: the ever-bleeding tips of the olive eelgrass. Thoreau called himself the "inspector of snowstorms," and for that short while I became the examiner of eelgrass. Eelgrass was the bluff's calendar, how I told seasonal time, and I recorded the changes day to day.

Maybe the word *visionary* means nothing more than seeing well, and ospreys, therefore, fit the visionary bill. You could argue that van Gogh simply saw better than other people. Sometimes I think that Emerson was right, that to see is everything. For hu-mans, as for ospreys, vision comes first, affecting all else. "I be-come a transparent eyeball; I am nothing; I see all," wrote Emerson. If this image of the eyeball sometimes seems awkward and goofy, it is nonetheless vital. Before we smirk at the notion of a giant, well-groomed eye, or consign transcendental ideas to the history books, we might remember that "it" can still happen to us at any minute. Who hasn't had brief moments when we've seen better and so glimpsed a better way of seeing, when we were part of the world, not lost in our own world, when, as Emerson says, "all mean egotism vanishes"? It's simple: when thought stills, we see. Referring to the moment of transcendence, Emerson's biographer Robert Richardson writes: "Its point is exactly the opposite of narcissistic self-absorption."

Empathy for the nonhuman is not achieved through proper language or scientific objectivity. No shaman ever became an animal through logic; and only through very human moments can we glimpse a nonhuman world. First we must see.

NOT LONG AGO I had a run-in with Emerson. I teach a class in Boston once a week, and in late May I stopped in at Harvard's rare book collection in Houghton Library. At first I wasn't quite sure what was leading me, but after applying for admission, putting my bag and coat in a locker, and entering the inner sanctum, I heard myself asking the librarian if they had the original copies of Emerson's journals. They did, and so I sat at the long oak table and waited for the books to be brought up from wherever they were stored. Pens weren't allowed in that silent, churchlike room, only pencils, and the etiquette sheet informed me that pages should be turned from the corners, one at a time. Four of the journals were brought to me and placed on a large black foam reading stand, and I paused for a minute, staring, before opening the first. I felt some of the scholar's excitement, and some of the detective's, the excitement of tracing things back to their root causes. The first journal I opened was about seven inches by nine, and wore a semi-psychedelic cover more fitting the 1960s than 1830s, though that might have been due to the wear of age. I carefully lifted the cover and stared down at the yellow-white pages and sepia handwriting. The journal, still bound fairly well, was from 1838, when Emerson was thirty-five years old. The epigraph he'd written on the front page was from Donne: "For virtue's whole sum is to know and dare." As I carefully turned the pages, one at a time, Emerson became more and more real. Despite the aphorisms—"the Poet is a namer," "There is no history only biography"—there was a distinct humanness to the whole enterprise, like the way the writing became less legible when he grew excited or rushed. It wasn't impossible to see Emerson as a young, if not particularly meek, man in a library. One especially poignant entry came in the next journal, beginning in 1841, when Emerson was my age, thirty-eight. It was written on the night his son died of fever. It read: "28 January 1842—Yesterday night at 15 minutes after eight my little Waldo ended his life." Four blank pages followed.

Reading the books it occurred to me that Emerson has suffered a horribly ironic fate for a determined iconoclast; he has been turned into a statue. The lover of fluidity and flux has been settled, frozen, and while Thoreau remains alive for so many of us, Emerson has, to use his own words against him, been "turned to stone." In fact, not a hundred yards from where I read there was a statue of the man, sitting leisurely and Lincoln-like, inside a building called Emerson Hall (with tall windows, out of which bored students stare). He's become the stodgy Concord sage, unable to get his hands dirty trundling that wheelbarrow with Thoreau, a dispenser of epigrams that at their worst read like self-help affirmations. Richardson's biography has revivified Emerson for me, shattering the plaster and revealing the man as human, passionate even. I'd accepted the cliché of the man and forgotten the Emerson who woke me up when I was young, shaking me alive. The real Emerson would have liked our local salt marshes— they have the right instability, change, daily chaos. Richardson makes clear that those ecstatic experiences, those times when he felt like the famous "transparent eyeball," were the foundation on which Emerson built his life. This is not quite as mystical as it sounds. Emerson was convinced that these moments were "natural, not supernatural," and as they spilled over "exhilaration became a habit" and his life, as Richardson notes, took on that "workaday exaltation" I've mentioned before. Of course we're made uneasy by the suggestion that we may still be able to experience the world as intensely as Emerson once did.

I READ EMERSON'S journals for a little while longer, engrossed, and then took a break. From the library's foyer I called Nina back on the Cape, babbling excitedly about my discovery. Then a strange thing happened. A tall, silver-haired man in a yellow rain slicker was struggling to get in the door while carrying two large boxes in his arms. I naturally pushed the door open and, once he was through, grabbed the top box without thinking. Somewhere between when I took the box and when I set it down on a desk inside, I realized that the man was John Updike. The box I carried contained his papers, brought to Harvard so that maybe they could someday make a statue of him, too.

The only person I've ever known who responded cleverly during an encounter with the famous was my friend Dave, who, upon seeing Eddie Van Halen on the other side of a small tidal creek in Malibu, said: "Go ahead, jump." I wasn't as quick-witted. Instead I muttered "your welcome"s to his gracious "Thank you"s, then retreated to my locker and grabbed a copy of one of my own books, which I proceeded to crassly jam into his hand. Emerson would have no doubt counseled that no man should be intimidated by the past, and would have had me toss a playful punch at the Updikian shoulder. I retreated back to the inner sanctum and back to the journals. "With the past as past I have nothing to do, nor with the future as future," I read soon after. "I live now, I will verify all past history in my own moments."

I browsed haphazardly for a while, even more excited after my encounter in the foyer. Then I remembered something from the Richardson biography. Emerson had been a fanatic organizer, indexing each journal extensively. I turned to the end of the journal I was reading, and sure enough, subjects and page numbers marched down the inside back cover. A half dozen listings fell under *Eyes*. "He that hath rich eyes, everywhere falls into true relations with his fellow man. . . . I think sometimes that my lack of musical ear is made good to me through my eye. What others hear, I see." I couldn't read all the words in one entry, written in his rushed, excited hand, but made out enough to get the meaning: "Go out and walk with a painter and you shall see for the first time groups colors clouds . . . and still have the pleasure of discovering in a hitherto barren ground . . . as good as a new sense in such skill to use an old one. When the telescope turns on our own barn and chimney we like this new sight better than the finest foreign. . . ." I noted the date so I could fill in the blanks from the collected, edited journals.

Before I left I found one last sentence about vision, which I thought the day's finest. On page 263 of his journal of 1838, Emerson wrote: "Painting seems to be to the eye what dancing is to the body."

ON JUNE 24 I make a different sort of pilgrimage, heading down to Alan Poole's Westport cottage again, this time a little more confident in my osprey knowledge. Since I last visited in March the year has filled in its green blanks, and, after parking in the crushed-shell driveway, I walk through an overhanging tunnel of leaves and brambles. There's an Edenic quality to this little house, with its gray shingles, red door, and wild roses climbing the side, and I emerge from the path in time to see a newborn tree swallow pop its head out of a birdhouse. When I climb up on the porch and look through the sliding glass door, I'm not particularly shocked to see Alan down on the floor, stretching in a yoga posture. The truth is that, so perfect is this day and setting, I wouldn't be surprised to hear Disney music playing or to see a little band of wood elves dancing around the gnarled tree that grows up through the deck.

In the absence of elves, Alan will do. He greets me with a calm smile; we're more familiar now since we've spoken and e-mailed several times. Even more than I remember, his eyes are clear, blue, intense, looking directly at me. When we walk to the beach he points out birds and I happily play the acolyte. We watch a kingbird demonstrate territoriality, chasing off a willet; a beautiful orchard oriole, burnished a darker red than the Baltimore oriole; and a bobolink—"A skunkbird, some call it" says Alan—which sings ecstatically, looking distinct in its black and white plumage. When we get close to the ocean, in an open meadow, Alan stops and has me listen as a grasshopper sparrow snips out its ticking then trilling song.

At the beach we spot a mother eider and her ducklings, just two days old, bobbing in the surf. "At the utmost south of their range," says Alan, with the authority only someone editing and writing the definitive guide to North American birds could muster. When the ducks paddle away we watch terns dive—avian arrows *thwuck*ing into the water—leaving little or no splash, like Olympic divers. Soon enough we join the eiders and terns, plunging into the surf. "Even the seaside goldenrod is shriveling because of the drought," Alan says as we wade in, and it's true, we haven't had rain for weeks. Now we rid ourselves of the day's heat, diving down deep to the bottom, where it's coldest. A small but strong man, Alan has something of the sparsity of the Chapin male about him. While we dry off I ask him about the books I've been reading, particularly the ones that suggest birds may have a more complex emotional life than previously thought.

"Could ospreys feel joy?" I ask tentatively.

He towels off his hair and takes a second to answer.

"Joy?" he says. "Who knows? Maybe. But I suppose I'm too much of a sociobioligist to believe it."

When we get back to the house, he takes a tin pot down to his backyard sandbar and forages for our lunch. He walks the short path, through the phragmites that he's fought back with a machete, and digs up some clams. There's something happily ospreylike in this direct link between the getting and eating of lunch. We slurp down littlenecks, cool and raw, along with goat cheese, bread, and strawberries. He tells me about his new diet, a Thoreauvian attempt to eliminate sugar, meat, booze, and caffeine, and I nod, admiring from a distance. It's natural enough for Alan to be studying Buddhist thought; he seems calm, predisposed to it.

For dessert I eat enough jam and bread to bloat myself, and when Alan retires to meditate, I indulge in my own less-conscious form of mediation, napping on the lawn. I know it would be pushing it to ask him to fire up the wood-burning hot tub, so I take the mat he gives me and roll it out on one of the sun-dappled paths by the water. When I wake, groggy, I walk down to the water's edge and notice that Alan's osprey platform on the marsh remains empty, the pair not returning this year. It makes me appreciate my own nests back home: full, loud, crowded with young.

Later, close to six, Alan takes me down to the marsh at the edge of the Westport colony, the place where he did much of the fieldwork for his book. In March the platforms were unpopulated, a ghost town, but now they surge with life. I've never seen so many ospreys in one place before. A dozen or more active nests stand within my sight, and by aiming the telescope from one to the next, I can check in on pairs at all different stages, as if moving instantly forward and back through time. One brood is far more developed than even the Chapin family, and I watch a youngster make its first tentative efforts at flight, flapping and jumping from one side of the platform to the next. "They're only a few days away," Alan says before he leaves.

After we say good-bye, I stay for another hour, excited by this virtual osprey city. This is the place where the ospreys held out in Massachusetts, their last foothold, during the bad times of DDT in the '60s and '70s. Most of the ten nests that remained during the historic low were right here along the Westport River, many on platforms built by Gil and Joe Fernandez, which earned them the title of "Mother and Father of the Massachusetts Osprey." It wasn't an official title, of course, and I doubt they were often addressed that way, but they have merited some recognition. All of us who've come later owe them something.

At dark I finally pack up my scope and cross the highway to where Alan had me park my car, near a bar called The Back Eddy. It's a long drive back, so I stop in, drink a Tremont Ale, then decide to make it an all-clam day, ordering a bucket of steamers. The sun has stained my face red, but driving home, beer and clams in my belly, I sink into a kind of sated animal satisfaction. Once again I can't help but think that sitting out watching birds all day is a good human activity, one I'm lucky to have stumbled on. If we become what we do, then I wouldn't mind becoming what I do here, that is, wouldn't mind becoming better adapted to watching, to seeing. I envy Alan Poole his years on the marsh. It's worthwhile, if somewhat quirky, work. The fact is, I think as I start the drive home, I've begun to love it.

I point the car north and it occurs to me that a bird or person's angle of vision may be as important as vision itself. Alan and I began our hunts with different "search images," to use his terminology, and to a certain extent, despite attempts at openness, each of our minds predetermines what we will see.

I stare at the glowing embers of taillights. As much as I love theorizing, I'll admit that maybe a grand synthesis of science and art is a little ambitious for a two-hour car ride home. Enough philosophy for today. My eyes are tired, bleary and red, by the time I cross over the silver hump of the Sagamore Bridge back onto the Cape. I need some sleep. For one day at least, I've seen enough.

Respecting Our Elders

There is nothing new under the sun.

—ECCLESIASTES

Thus Ospreys quite similar to the ones
we know today were well established in much of their
current breeding range at about the same time
our earliest ape-like ancestors left forests
and began to walk upright across the plains of Africa.

—ALAN POOLE, *Ospreys*

Ospreys, as best I can tell, don't have much use for the idea of "originality." While my morning rounds reveal that to a certain extent the birds are individuals with distinct personalties, none vary much from the general game plan. Having found a good way to live, a way that works, they stick to it. And why not? They have nested and caught fish as they do now from the Ice Age on and have been peers of mammoths and saber-toothed tigers. Scientists have found an ospreylike fossil from thirteen million years ago, in the mid-Miocene era, and some evidence suggests the birds were common in North America as far back as fifteen million years ago. Just as I stare up at their beautiful white breasts and wings and feel my mind take wing, so likely did Cro-Magnon man look up to the birds. The ospreys were good role models, embodying the patience and aggressive directness of the hunt, but it was more than that. The evidence on cave walls is clear. "Since the earliest of times, predatory birds have figured prominently in the art, ceremonies, and legends of human societies," write Noel and Helen Synder in *Raptors*. "Fierce images of raptors abound in cave paintings of primitive peoples around the world." Gazing at wings beating out a code of the sun's silver, man felt one of his oldest urges, the instinct to *re-create,* to make the creation again. The birds did then what they still do: stir the impulse to make art.

Since the harbor chicks have entered their reptilian stage — dark, scaly crouching creatures, hardly birds at all — it isn't hard to let my mind wander back in time. I pick up a copy of Björn Kurtén's *Dance of the Tiger,* a novelistic account of the meeting of Neandertal and Cro-Magnon man. The book, written by the man who was Europe's most respected evolutionary paleontologist, quickly shatters the stereotypes I hold about early humans. I learn that far from being grunting, simian troglodytes, Neandertal people — as well Cro-Magnon — were large-brained creatures who likely spoke an elaborate language, built tools and weapons, traded, worshiped, lived in crude homes — not caves — and created art. In short, man thirty-five thousand years ago was a lot like man today. Kurtén writes of the primitive artist-hunter:

They strove to catch and render in undying images those transient shapes that burn into the retina and are seen again in exquisite detail and precision when the eyes are closed: animals in repose, in action; the sights before the hunter in that fleeting moment at the point of the kill, when endurance, skill, and cunning are to be rewarded. In that moment, javelin poised, muscles and sinews already exploding into the throw, the strength and beauty of the beast are forever impressed upon the hunter.

Neandertal man's life intertwined with the life of his place. Food, art, building materials — all came directly from the land.

And magic, too, of course. While hunters portrayed and sought absolution from the animals they ate, shamans went further, taking on animal shapes, *becoming* animals. As Gary Synder writes in *The Old Ways:* "The shaman speaks for wild animals, the spirits of plants, the spirits of mountains, of watersheds. He or she sings for them. They sing through him. . . . In the shaman's world, wilderness and the unconscious become analogous: he who knows and is at ease in one, will be at home in the other." This isn't as distant from us as it may sound at first, just the act of empathy taken to its extreme, and I'm not surprised to read that Shamans were considered protopoets. How different is their transformation from the ones described by Keats? "If a sparrow comes before my window I take part in its existence and pick about the gravel." Or "the man who with a bird, / Wren or Eagle, finds his way to / All his instincts."

For me the most exciting moment of Kurtén's book comes when he briefly mentions "the Land of the Osprey." In the hill country of the West, from which the Great River flows, lives a small band of men who hold the osprey sacred. A story is told of a man named Cornel, whose life is saved when his brother comes back as an osprey. Cornel was out hunting caribou in a gorge when "the hunter became the hunted," and he found himself being stalked by a black tiger. Chased by the tiger, he has no hope; then "suddenly the clouds part, and a single shaft of sunlight falls on the wall of the Gorge. At the same time Cornel sees a great Osprey swoop up the Gorge." The bird leads him to a rowan, the ospreys' sacred tree, and Cornel climbs to safety.

Though this is the only mention of the Osprey People in Kurten's book, it's enough to fire my imagination. In my mind's eye I see a water people, a fishing people, living close to the edge of sea and land, bedecked in feathers during their ceremonies, shamans becoming ospreys and learning the birds' high-pitched language, artists carving and painting images of the great hawk with wings spread, then tucked; I see a people who discover everything they need to learn about life — from patience to directness, from persistence to commitment — in the spirit of this one bird; and I see a people who find mystery and then faith in the bird's annual disappearance in the fall and reappearance each spring, who in this way look to the bird not just as mystical totem but as practical calendar. Finally, I see a tribe that must respond to the first begging cries of spring with a deep welling of hope and joy, who must look at the birds' return each year as a kind of pagan resurrection, the bird itself as an avian Christ figure long before Christ, a bringer of the news that the world will soon warm.

If I'm getting carried away it's only because I wish I could be. Reading Kurtén's book makes me dream of being lifted up, not just in flight but into a culture so thoroughly permeated by the sacred and the animal. Maybe it's time to slip that osprey bone under my skin. Having created my own little subculture of the osprey, I feel the urge to proselytize. I'm happy these days when Nina ushers our evening guests toward the telescope, and happier still when they respond, as they invariably do, with the proper enthusiasm. *Look how big they are! They're like eagles! The mother is so beautiful. God . . . look at the way she feeds the babies!* Unless our guests are simply placating me, which is possible —"There, there, *of course* we understand why you carry on about your birds"— I suspect that it would be easier to convert people to ospreyism than to Christianity.

Why not? There's just as much ritual in the former, and far more concrete evidence of the miraculous. One day a local minister who does "minisermons" on the radio calls me up to ask about the birds. The people at the natural history museum have directed him to me, telling him I can help prepare the sermon he wants to give about ospreys. I keep it conventional: much talk about the birds' annual resurrection, their rebirth from DDT, their "family values" in committing to spouse and nest and brood. I decide against confessing my more sacrilegious notions. I don't tell him that I prefer the vividness of the osprey Eucharist: a tilt-headed sacrament fed from a black-masked priest to a yearning reptilian flock. I say nothing about true communion achieved over the consecrated, all-giving flesh of fish.

ANOTHER DAY in late June I set up my chair and scope at Chapin before sunset. It's a cool, almost fall-like evening, and long shadows stretch from where I sit toward the nest. Though the tide is low, the shadows fill the creek bed dark blue like water. Even Barbie glows radiant; she has somehow turned a half cartwheel in the nest, so that for the first time I notice she wears sunglasses. While I watch the nestlings they watch the sky; flying isn't too far off and they are ready, primed and poised. In this light the new golden markings on the backs of their necks shine full orange — a pumpkin orange. Despite a deep sense of satisfaction, something makes me glance up from my journal, a half thought: he should be back with a fish soon. On impulse I look to my right, and for the first time all year, maybe because of the dying light, I notice the speck that is the male before the nestlings do. This is a triumph. Sure enough, he flies past me to his post, with a fish whose flatness says "flounder" until I see the spiked demon tale and recognize it as a skate, its white belly lit up red. I again feel a connection with this, my favorite bird, though I remind myself again that the connection is only one-way. As the male starts tearing at his chewy meal, I sit back and, for a brief moment, feel entirely at home. For once the prospect of what I have to do tomorrow, the almost constant nagging and niggling of the future — of the imagined time when things will be better — subsides. I listen to the pulse of the ocean, slight but steady, and that same sound pulses through the golden sand, the olive spartina, the blazing nest.

I walk back to the parking lot just in time to see the sun drop, the last fast-motion descent, down to an orange-blue sliver, and then gone, fizzing in the ocean. I'm in a place that is very much my own when another human being intrudes. A big guy in a cutoff sweatshirt pauses from loading up his jeep to point at my telescope and ask what I'm up to. When I explain, he smiles.

"We got them over in Centerville, too," he says, "We call them sea eagles."

I smile back and for a second imagine I see a glint in the big man's eye. *Are you a fellow true believer?* I want to ask him. *Have you found Osprey, too?*

BY LATE JUNE the young birds are finding their voices, filling the air with echoes of their mother's stronger cries. Osprey language is fairly simple, direct, and not too hard to understand if you give it some time. (It's harder to speak, of course.) Vocalizations are used to assert ownership, to warn off, to attract mates, to alert chicks or mates of danger, and to beg for fish. Alan Poole makes out three distinct calls: the standard early-warning calls, the more agitated alarm calls, and the begging calls. All the experts seem to agree on these general categories, though they quibble when it comes to matching letters to the sounds. Clinton G. Abbott writes:

I have often stood, pencil in hand, and tried to put upon paper the remarkable variety of screams to which nervous Ospreys give voice. The commonest note is a shrill whistle, with a rising inflection: "Whew, whew, whew, whew,whew, whew, whew." This is the sound usually heard during migration; and when the bird is only slightly alarmed. When she becomes thoroughly aroused it will be: "Chick, chick, chick, cheek, cheek, ch-cheek, ch-cheeek, cheereek, chezeek, chezeek," gradually increasing to a frenzy of excitement at the last.

Abbott also claims that he hears a specific cry at the moment when the osprey seems "to pause in flight, extend her legs downward to their fullest extent, hover on rapidly-flapping wings and

call out—very appropriately—'Feesh, feesh, feesh, feesh.'" Though
this may be a fairly wishful spelling of the noise ospreys make during their fish display, I don't think it's too far-fetched. The fact is
that the letters which different writers ascribe to avian vocalizations often seem quite random, as do many of our own human
words. The other night when I told a friend I was studying ospreys, she said that *osprey* had been her childhood word for the
phosphorescence that sparkles in the night surf. *Os-spray* didn't
seem such a bad way to describe the fizz of the luminescence in
splashed water, and might well have been our English word for it
if we hadn't randomly pinned those syllables on a bird.

Some other human vocalizations we've stuck on the bird are
visarend (Dutch), *fiskgjuse* (Swedish), *fischadler* (German), *balbuzard
pêcheur* (French), *gavião pescador* (Portuguese), and *kalakotkas*
(Estonian). The full scientific name—*Pandion haliaetus*—comes
from the bungling marriage of the name of a mythical Greek
called Pandion with *haliaetus,* which, translated from the Greek,
means "sea eagle." According to Stephen Carpenteri, the Latin
name roughly translates to "bone-breaking sea eagle." Whatever
the exact meaning, the history of the osprey's name is spotted with
error. For one, *haliaetus* is a misspelling of the Greek *haliaeetus,* a
mistake that has been allowed to stand after years of repetition
(the correct spelling, with two e's, is used in the bald eagle's scientific name). And, according to Anders Price, the creator of a
wonderful osprey Web site, the whole Greek mythic name is off
the mark:

Pandion was the king of Athens in Greek mythology and was
poorly chosen as a scientific name for the osprey. Pandion had two
daughters, Procne and Philomel. They became caught in an illicit love
triangle with Tereus, son of the king of Thrace. This angered the gods
and Procne was changed into a swallow, Philomel into a nightingale,
and Tereus a hawk. Tereus was sentenced to forever chase Procne and

Philomel. The scientist who gave the osprey its scientific name, Marie-Jules-Cesar Lelorgne de Savigny, somehow associated this story with the osprey simply because it had a hawk in it. The osprey should have been named Tereus, since Pandion was only marginally involved in the story and Tereus was the one transformed into a raptor. But even that would be stretching things since ospreys usually eat fish, not swallows or nightingales.

If that isn't enough, for years there was squabbling among taxonomists about the osprey's mistaken inclusion in the order Falconiformes, along with other hawks and falcons. By the early twentieth century, taxonomists had begun to reconsider this grouping. Recently ospreys have been considered sufficiently unique to be the only raptor to merit a taxonomic family all their own: Pandionidae.

Since we are unable to get our own languages straight, it's no real surprise that humans disagree on what they hear when listening to the birds. What Abbott calls a "chick" noise, Poole hears as *ick-ick-ick;* and I find myself dying to put a *k* in the *whew* noise that others hear, turning it into *kew, kew, kew.* I've always had a tin ear, but one thing I do know is that the standard high-pitched cry, often described as "musical," is anything but, unless the music these scientists like to listen to is made up of piercing whistles. But I do agree with Bent and Prevost that there are times when the slurred end of the standard call sounds a little like the whimpering of a tea kettle right after being taken off a stove.

Frankly, if I were a better mimic, it wouldn't be that hard to speak osprey—much easier than, say, mockingbird, with its two hundred or so songs. Most of what the female says to the male is easily enough translated as *More fish, you idiot, more fish!* In a like manner, a lot of birdsong is decipherable, largely dependent on the needs of the season. Stand outside in early spring and the bird chatter has a male, locker-room feel: *Look at me! I've got big balls!*

I'm full of testosterone! This is my turf! On the other hand, there are levels of bird communication far more complex than once imagined. After a territorial dispute has been settled, northern harriers bow gently to each other to acknowledge new borders. (If only my neighbor on the bluff and I could reconcile our differences so gracefully.) Even crows, whose *caw* the most inattentive of us can imitate, manage to put enough inflection in their voices to get their different points across: their mobbing cry, for instance, can rally the troops, bringing dozens of their brethren out of the woods to attack an owl.

"All over the world learning the language of animals, especially of birds, is equivalent to knowing the secrets of nature," wrote Mercia Eliade in his classic work on shamanism. "Becoming a bird oneself or being accompanied by a bird indicates the capacity, while still alive, to undertake the ecstatic journey to the sky and beyond." I've tried several times to talk back to the ospreys, and on more occasions imitated their cry for Nina, but I'm no shaman. For now I'll content myself with having picked up some of their language, a kind of pidgin Osprey. If not able to speak it well, then at least I'm able to recognize, with eyes closed, most of what's being communicated. One of the more pleasing parts of my day is having the first thing I hear in the morning be ospreys. Several times I've wakened to the cries of the punk-rock harbor birds, their calls prying into the edge between my unconscious and conscious mind.

NOW THAT MY WIFE and I are jammed into a single upstairs room, however, I feel occasional spasms of inadequacy. In bad moments I can see my life in a scary light: a bird-obsessed, nearly middle-aged man living in his mommy's house. But if I shake and tilt the facts just slightly, they rearrange themselves in a more hopeful fashion. I am part of a heritage, a family, a place. It wasn't long ago historically, I remind myself, that adult children often lived in homes with their parents. Anyway, whichever angle I choose to look at it from, my mother lives with us for only two and a half months. I'm lucky that Nina and my mother get along well.

At night, after we have supper together, I retreat upstairs to my books. Near the end of June my reading shifts from bird language to bird learning. I wonder: how is it possible that the osprey nestlings, barely able to walk across the nest, will be able to dive for fish on their own in less than two months? Biology provides the tools—the powerful, water-resistant wings, the cagelike talons—but who provides the operating manual? Instinct prods and parents act as examples, but so much will come from trial and error. Repeated error will prove fatal. Starvation is always a threat for young birds. They will need to begin to master an incredibly complex task—fishing—in an absurdly short span of time. Only half of the nestlings that I watch will survive their first year; only a third will find their way back here two springs from now. Learning —and learning *fast*—is vital.

My books remind me of something that most of us already know: birds do much of what they do out of what we choose to call instinct. Instinctive behavior predominates in the avian world, birds occasionally killing each other not out of some smoldering hate but because of the color of another bird's breast. Flash the color red before a male robin and you're waving a matador's cape, filling him with territorial fury and the urge to attack. But put another robin nearby, a competitor, minus its red breast, and the fury dies. Even feeding, including the gaping of nestlings, is guided by the strict hand of instinct. For the most part, birds do what birds do.

But birds learn, too. They learn from each other and from their parents, a process we've labeled associative learning. In this manner a crow, to take a particularly bright bird, can watch another crow and pick up on something. More generally, as Short explains, a chick may be born with the instinct to peck but must be taught *what* to peck by its mother, so that it just doesn't end up with an instinctive mouthful of thorns. In general, larger, long-living birds are "smarter," as are birds that need to adapt to varying environments and diets.

Habituation is the most simple form of bird learning. Habituation means, simply, getting used to something, and the harbor ospreys present a good example. They have learned not to be startled by trucks, tractors, and cranes, enormous and enormously loud machines that would terrify the more isolated and shy Simpkins Neck ospreys. Birds can also learn through conditioning and, of course, trial and error. But most exciting, and much more rare, is *insight learning,* when "a creature, presented with a problem, suddenly spies a solution, and does whatever it takes to resolve the problem." In *The Lives of Birds,* Lester Short cites examples of cedar waxwings passing fruit to each other, and woodpecker finches using cactus spines to dig out insects. These behaviors require an "insight," followed by a dramatic alteration of behavior. In the *The Wind Masters,* Pete Dunne writes speculatively about the insight learning of a common black-hawk. This bird has learned to lift its wing over the water, understanding that fish will seek out the shade, while also "waving the tip of her wing in the water, troubling the surface" knowing that to a fish it will look like "some small creature were struggling." Then, after waiting patiently for several fish to move below the wing, the hawk will "thrust out a net of talons, closing a fish in her grasp."

The capacity for insight makes me reconsider the expression *bird brain.* I also read in Short about how a green heron steals bread and tears it into crumbs, dropping them in the water to lure fish. And about the male mockingbird, who sings the two hundred or so songs in his repertoire not just to protect his territory but to impress females with the *complexity* of his song. Short writes, "Springtime in Norway and Sweden finds some Hooded Crows pulling up lines that fisherman have poked through holes in the ice. A crow will grip the line in its beak, walk slowly backward as far as it can, and then walk toward the hole on top of the line. This prevents the line from slipping back into the water, and is thought to be an example of insight learning."

But before we get too excited about bird intelligence, it's best to circle back to instinct, and to remember that immutable genetic laws govern most of a bird's behavior. You can sit around a long time waiting for insights and, generally, you'll be disappointed. Even flight is ruled by instinct, although, Short explains, the subtleties of flight—landing, banking, and so on—are likely learned.

Watching the Chapin nest, already worried for the nestlings' futures, I consider all they will have to learn over the next two months. It is considerable and intimidating, a crash course. I vaguely understand that their ability to catch fish, for instance, will spring from a mixed soup of instinct and learning. But I don't know the half of it. There will be many near misses and miscalculations, much fumbling despite all the tools that nature has provided them with. I've read some accounts of parents weaning the young off their feedings and even dropping fish from the air for the young to "catch," bolstering their confidence, perhaps. But contradictory studies show that fledglings raised alone can learn to fish quickly, sometimes within just a few days. Of course, experience is what sharpens instinct, and experienced fishermen are better fishermen. Instinct drives the ospreys to hunt, but technique must be learned—from trial and error, from their parents, possibly even from watching other birds. The trick is to live long enough to become experienced.

FOR HUMAN BEINGS the equation is more complicated, though possibly more heavily weighted toward instinct than we'd care to admit. In some ways I'm no more an original than the fledglings. If words come to me when I walk to the bluff, don't they come out of an *instinct* to make language? How is my response to a beautiful place any different than that of my Cro-Magnon ancestors, a sort of scrawling on cave walls?

Human language owes more to the land, to the old ways, than we sometimes care to admit. Recently I read that the ancient Greeks wrote one sentence from left to right and the next back from right to left, mimicking the way they plowed their fields. We are not so different from the Greeks, or from Cro-Magnon man, for that matter, and language and earth can't be peeled apart, no matter how hard we try. Since Nina and I moved back here it sometimes seems as if all I've been doing is simply harvesting words, plucking things that have grown of themselves. My chief tool for this harvesting has been my journal. While I work on other projects, the journal has been my real book of the year: of spring's infatuated return, summer's booze-and-pork-filled complacency, the ecstasy of fall, the melancholy of November, and the final wedging downward of deep winter. From our very first spring back, the drama of the ospreys' precarious nesting at the jetty nest made my fictional world look dull in comparison. The journal reminds me of my neighbor J.C.'s front yard. In that yard he collects items scavenged from the beach: lobster pots for tables and buoys hanging like Christmas bulbs from the juniper tree; shells pave his driveway. The sentences in my journal are just like that: things I'd found thrown up on the beach.

On the other hand, members of *Homo sapiens* more clearly (or at least more obviously) are constant practitioners of associative learning. Like our fellow primates we're great mimics. The instinct to make stories may be encoded in us, but my experience teaches me that human language often comes directly not from one but two places: the world and words about the world. Or put another way: if one source for our own words is the land, the other is the words of those who came before us.

For instance, as I write about ospreys I would be helpless if I merely depended on my "original" insights. Fortunately, I have an entire library to lean on. Most obviously, Alan Poole's research has helped me make my way through the maze of the bird's behavior. But, because we are the one animal that has managed to record our vocalizations with some permanence, I can access human writing about ospreys dating back to 410 B.C., in the work of Athenian playwright Aristophanes. Or if I choose I can sample Aristotle's writing on the birds in his *Natural History*, or dip into Shakespeare's words in *Coriolanus*:

> I think he'll be to Rome
> As is the osprey to the fish, who takes it
> By sovereignty of nature.

What are books if not the result of our instinct to communicate — and to make things *stay?* We report what we have seen, but to whom are we reporting? Our future selves? If I were so inclined I could read an account even older than Aristophanes's, traveling to the very caves on whose walls our Cro-Magnon ancestors scrawled hawklike forms.

TODAY, JUNE 27, I put my books aside and plan a long bike ride, hoping to take a survey of all the nests. My first stop is an easy one. While eating a roast beef and horseradish sandwich I check in with the harbor nest, which, as best I can make out, supports three nestlings. I've been quick to attribute "personality" to the harbor adults — loose, late, disheveled, hardly workaholics — but this may be more fancy than fact. The truth is that most of their originality and individualism, their behavioral differences from the other nests, is attributable to youth. I'm almost certain that this is their first brood and they haven't yet learned to conserve energy at all costs. They will learn. There are times when the harbor male seems run ragged in his efforts to feed himself and four others, as if not quite sure what he's gotten himself into. He looks ready to chuck it all and go raise hell with his mates, but he won't, instinct prodding him toward continued matrimony and fatherhood.

After throwing my binoculars and journal in my backpack, I jump on my bike and head over to the Chapin nest. It is a perfect June day, the world wide awake, full and open. On my way to Chapin I pedal up to Scargo Tower, the Cape's highest point. I get off my bike and climb the circular stairs to the top of the tower, staring out at the fish-shaped pond and ocean beyond. While most Cape Cod osprey live by the ocean, they do a good deal of their fishing in our many inland lakes and ponds, particularly the ones, like Scargo, that we've stocked with fish. A week ago I witnessed several osprey dives and near dives from this stone perch, one from at least ninety feet up. From this height, I could stare eye-level to where the birds began their dive, giving me an even better idea of the penetration of vision required; it was like watching an arrow being shot into the depths of the lake.

I descend the tower and glide down the hill on my bike, cutting across 6A and back into the sandy streets that lead to Chapin. I pedal faster as I get closer, ready for new sights. The Chapin nestlings are ahead of the curve and always seem to be up to something new. About two weeks ago, around June 10, they stopped looking like exaggerated embryos and started becoming more like real birds, miniature versions of their parents, though still awkward and reptilian. Then, when gulls rose and swirled behind the nest, joined by terns flashing like slivers of light, the nestlings would flop over to watch, and poke their heads in the air, mouths open, curious. Their great downy wings flapped up uncontrollably, like the necks of spastic emus.

Soon after that, the first feathers replaced down: orangish, rusty pinfeathers on the head, a black-and-white pattern emerging on the bodies. It was around June 15 that I became certain that the

Chapin pair were one of those rare parents who were raising a brood of four nestlings. Today I toss my bike down on the marsh and pull my binoculars out of the pack. The afternoon grows dry and hot, the slather of sweat from my ride soon splotched with bugs. I train my binoculars on the nestlings: beautiful black-and-tan feathers pattern their wings, black and gold along the backs. The birds have transformed into little masked raccoons, and golden tan feathers run like racing stripes down the back of their heads. They jostle about the nest, jockeying for position as the father prepares to relinquish what remains of a flounder.

I watch the Chapin birds for an hour before riding over to Simpkins Neck. There I ditch my bike behind a patch of catbrier and make my way in through the woods. Though just a mile farther inland along the same tidal creek that the Chapin ospreys live on, this family remains the most unknown to me, protected as it is by bugs, thorns, briers, and a longer walk. I check in here only once, maybe twice, a week, and I can't quite get a grip on what's going on. For one thing, they are the most private of the birds I watch, unaccustomed to the presence of humans, and I'm careful to observe them from much farther back. They remain shy, quick to leave the nest, and seem to have a running feud with a northern harrier who lives nearby. The harrier, apparently unaware that he is half their size, has never gotten used to having such ungainly, such *obvious* birds on his little section of marsh.

I emerge from the briers onto the salt marsh, only a few houses visible through the thick summer leaves. I point the binoculars and confirm what I thought to be the case: three nestlings huddle at the nest. I ease closer, missing my boots, my sneakers soaking as the tide rises through caked mud, hoping not to agitate this overprotective mother. To my eye, there's not much individuality or personality among the nestlings; like their down-creek neighbors they are gaping, begging, eating machines. They wear the same black-and-tan feathers, and their young eyes shine the same strange, bloody orange. Awkward-looking tongues stab out from open bills. Though there's much learning ahead, for now raw instinct and hunger guide them.

This family of birds is the least consistent of the variables in my osprey experiment. Though both clutches are between three and four weeks old, the truth is that I don't know which of the broods along the tidal creek was born first. I've just assumed that the Chapin birds are older because they have monopolized my interest, but these youngsters could easily have been born during one of the periods I didn't visit.

I watch through the late afternoon, then make my way out of Simpkins Neck, slapping away mosquitoes and flies and wishing I had a machete. God knows how many deer ticks I've collected over the course of the summer, only luck keeping Lyme disease at bay. But I'm not worried, at least at the moment. Adding up the totals of my survey—four nestlings at Chapin, three at the harbor, three at Simpkins Neck—I come up with ten new birds, the most this area has seen in half a century at least (and, likely, because of deforestation, a full century or more). Even if less than half of the nestlings never make it back to Cape Cod as adults, that number still bodes well for the future.

Once I reach the end of the path I pull my bike out of the briers, brush off the seat, and climb back on. The sun is sinking toward the bay, but, feeling upbeat, I decide to push it, pedaling up to the bike path. Out of a sense of duty I'll include the Quivett nest in my survey, though I know that I won't find any young there. I rarely visit Quivett these days. But the least I can do is be conscientious toward this most conscientious pair.

To avoid riding along 6A, I climb up Old Bass River Road to the Rail Trail, cutting through Harwich and Brewster, ending up at the Stony Brook Herring Run, the spot that Hones and I paddled and then trekked up to in May. I feel tired but happy, and stop at the run to look around. I know this place both through experience and words. Those words belonged to the great Cape writer John Hay, and, a mile after I bike by the run, I ride down a dirt road to a sign at the bottom of a long wooded driveway that reads J. HAY. That sign, simple and hand-painted, surrounded by trees, seems the perfect fit for Mr. Hay.

I stare at the sign. Cape Cod is crisscrossed with sentences, crowded with the words of others. Growing up, it seemed the worst sort of luck to have fallen in love with a place that had already been so thoroughly settled and developed, literarily as well as architecturally. But today, maybe relaxed by the endorphins pumping through my system, I feel blessed rather than cursed to have predecessors nearby. Montaigne wrote, "Still I am pleased at this, that my opinions have the honor of coinciding with theirs, and at least I go the same way, though far behind them, saying 'How true!'" Maybe I've finally begun to understand that I'd better try to respect my elders. Last March I finally met John Hay. I rode my bike up the long hill to his house and talked with him for half an hour. It was Mr. Hay who first gave me Alan Poole's number and suggested I call him. I'm pleased to be relying on Alan, just as Hay did for his beautiful book on terns.

We need to imitate the spirit, not the letter, of the writers we admire. I don't want to steal words, but I'm happy to plagiarize actions or, rather, a manner of being. If our human learning is associative, then I would like to learn from how earlier writers have lived. Japanese landscape artists could serve as corrective examples to our current craze for originality: their goal was not to do something radically different than what had been done, something that no one had ever seen before. The goal instead was to approach the work of the masters.

What better way to learn to do something well than to steep

yourself in the work of those you admire? What could be more direct and simple? This doesn't mean we mimic them; it means we learn a way of being, of looking. We grow so that the older voices no longer intimidate us, or come at us in a furious babble. Eventually, if we're lucky, we feel on equal ground with the voices. We feel that we can, with gradually building confidence, talk back.

"HOW'S IT GOING, DAD?"

It always amazes me that I, a firm discounter of an afterlife, often talk directly to this gray slate stone. The last leg of my bike ride brings me from John Hay's sign to the Quivett marsh, but before checking in with the ospreys, I pay my respects at my father's grave. How this piece of rock embodies my dead father I have no idea, but it somehow does, at least to a part of my brain. Maybe it's the manifestation of words in the landscape again, like Hay's sign. In this case: DAVID MARSHALL GESSNER. In early spring I passed this gravestone every morning, on my way down to watch the Quivett birds. Many times, more than I'd like to admit, I stopped to chat with my father.

Some days I'd just tell him how the Red Sox were doing, or news about my mother. It's a silly ritual, primitive, I know, to give this lump of stone such import, but it's also reassuring to have something to talk to. If a little odd, it's at least harmless. Today I relate the news of my osprey survey, my thoughts on John Hay. Literary forefathers have nothing on the man buried here, at least in terms of intimidation. His voice may be silenced now, but it still resonates in my head and will continue to until I join him in the ground. More and more I like what I hear when my father's voice speaks to me. As sad as it is that it took death to get the proper distance, I now appreciate my father in ways I didn't when he was alive. And as I speak out loud to the rock that represents him I think I recognize in my own voice some of his directness, bluntness, strength. A part of him that—in a concrete, not spiritual way —has carried on.

I walk away from the gravestone, down the path through the greenbriers and phragmites to the marsh. I've been riding most of the afternoon, and now, as the sun drops, I stare quietly at pink clouds bulking up behind the osprey platform. The male is nowhere in sight, the female on the nest. After a while she slowly flaps toward the water, perhaps to clean herself, perhaps to fish. Whatever the reason for her departure, when she lifts off she leaves behind any illusion that she will produce young this year. Certainly she deserves the marathon award for nesting: she has been a paragon of patience—a restless patience, but patience nonetheless. The fact that instinct compelled her makes her endurance no less impressive. But while she was a marathon sitter, a brilliant sitter, her persistence couldn't change the way of things. She will add no numbers to my survey's total. But next year she and her mate will return, the tragedy forgotten, driven to reenact the drama once again.

As twilight settles, the songs of day birds give way to an owl's hooting. I would hazard to guess that neither owl nor osprey spends a whole lot of time wondering about where their voices come from. Thoughts of that sort are left to the perpetually self-conscious species of which I'm a member. My brain, trained by writing, likes to wrap things up, draw conclusions, make sense of things, but that, as I'm learning again and again, won't do on the marsh.

My time with the birds does reinforce one human conclusion, however. We are all a lot less original than we like to believe. While not as strictly hemmed in by instinct as an osprey's vocalizations, my own voice is more a product of others than I might want to admit. "It is not from ourselves that we will learn to be better than we are," wrote Wendell Berry. If the bluff sometimes speaks through me, then on a simpler, genetic level so does my father. At the same time I rely on the work of those who have given words to the Cape. In all these ways I am the very much the result of my place and those who came before. To thrash rebelliously against this fact may give the momentary illusion of independence, but it is not honest. To admit debt, to honor it and respect it, is the beginning a larger, greater freedom.

Growth and Death

A s June ends there's no time to waste. Life blooms at the nests, change occurring at a preposterous rate. Before I know it the nestlings have gone from being scaly little black reptiles to majestic, nearly full-fledged birds. Every twenty-four hours brings dramatic change, as if a human baby were to grow six months older with each passing day. And yet, in ornithological terms, this is a relatively sprawling and leisurely development. The ospreys' downstairs neighbors, the house sparrows, take just seven days to grow to their full stature.

While the birds grow, parts of the marsh have taken the turn toward death. The year has no sooner climbed to its apex then it starts sliding down the other side, some plants already beginning to retreat, to brown and curl, and the plushness, the fullness, shriveling. But while drought withers the green, Hones reports that the fish are still jumping, and the combination of fish and steady sun make it an ideal season for osprey growth.

Excited about seeing the changes, I begin to wake earlier and earlier — at five, then four — getting out on the Chapin marsh before dawn. It's the time of year when light crowds out darkness, and the nestlings look enormous, fuller, stronger, with more clearly checkered black-and-white backs. In fact, they're too big to call nestlings. The young are now larger than jays, and they put their whole bodies into their warning and begging cries. But while the wings have grown, they remain unwieldy. These are wings that, for all their size, have outpaced the birds themselves. When one of the Chapin young tries to stretch out her wings all the way, she falls face forward in the nest. (I assume the two larger birds are female, and the two smaller are males, since females are generally larger than males. But this is admittedly guesswork. For instance, a female born last might well be smaller than a male born first.) "Awkward adolescents," Alan Poole calls them, though these birds are luckier than humans, in that their early adolescence lasts only about twenty days. I'm witness to all of it, to a change that seems almost miraculous in speed. As the nestlings grow their young eyes blaze orange through bandit masks, and the patch on the back of their neck shines orange, too. As the primary and secondary feathers fill out, the black-and-gold pattern grows more vivid, as if coming into focus in the telescope.

AT THE END of a buggy June I watch the ospreys change daily, too transfixed to leave my post now that the plot is thickening along with the air. There's a new excitement to making my rounds, to checking in on each nest, an excitement only partly dulled by the constellation of gnats, flies, and mosquitoes that hover over my hands and face. Mosquitoes pierce the open flesh on the back of my hand. It would be a gross exaggeration to say I've begun to like the feeling of bugs crawling all over me, but it's true that I've at least started to enjoy what I associate with this feeling: it lets me know I'm out on the marsh, looking through my scope, living on osprey time.

While I wear a halo of bugs, a thousand more insects buzz around the nest itself, drawn by fish and fish guts. Ticks, mites, larvae, and God knows what other microscopic creatures swarm in the interstices of the nest. For the nestlings, it's an intensely itchy life, bugs combining with the uncomfortable sensation of feathers growing in. One of their dominant sensations of being alive must be the need to scratch. Not surprisingly, they spend a lot of their time doing just that, pecking at their feathers with their bills when not sleeping or feeding.

Of course, much of what they do is feed. All this wild growth requires fish, and it's a good thing that the Chapin male is a great hunter. With four young, and six total mouths to feed, this is a family that requires more and more fish. In *The Lives of Birds* I read of the "wear and tear" on pairs of bird parents with large clutch sizes, but, other than the female's ragged appearance, I haven't noticed anything amiss. The male's life simplifies to the point of obsessiveness. Other than resting and eating, he spends almost all of his time hunting, and when he delivers the fish to the nest, usually after he's taken his share, the nestlings break into a cacophony of begging. They waddle and sprawl around the nest, their mouths open and their awkward-looking tongues jutting out demonically. As the mother begins to tear off a strand of silver skin, taking a gulp or two for herself before doling out the food, the nestlings aggressively jockey for position. For these young birds fish isn't just fish but a substance to be converted. This is true transubstantiation: fish is energy, fish is growth, fish is size and strength. Flounder and trout are the object of intense yearning, begging, jostling, and fighting, for, though only a few weeks old, these growing birds already know that, on the most basic level, fish means life.

Even young ospreys eat with gusto and savagery. You wouldn't want to get in the way of their meal. I have a running argument with my wife about the relationship she has with her cats. It's my contention that if she were mouse-sized, her cats would torture and then kill her, but Nina claims that they would recognize her voice and face, and wouldn't hurt her. For the sake of nonargument I usually concede this point. But even if her house cats are potentially benevolent, then you would be hard-pressed to say that of ospreys. I have no illusions as to the results if I were fish-sized and swimming.

Ospreys kill to live. Daily murder of other animals is central to their survival, and they take pride in their work. In *The Wind Masters,* Pete Dunne writes of a northern goshawk: "The truth, I believe, is that the bird *liked* to kill. It was something projected by the bird's stance; it was something that could be seen, by things that hunt and things that are hunted, in the bird's eyes."

ONE DAY DURING the last week of June a stranger visits me at my Chapin watch. At first I'm wary, worried that he is horning in on my osprey turf. He walks up from behind and puts his hands casually on the back of my lawn chair. I stand up quickly and try to instill a look of territoriality into my eyes, but he ignores the warning.

"How many of them out there now?" he asks, as if it were *his* nest.

I resentfully admit to four fledglings but loosen up when he explains the reason for his visit. He introduces himself as Ralph Holmberg and says he was friends with "Scotty." All spring long I've wondered about the little plaque on the pole of the lopsided nest, a tribute to Clinton Scott, "dedicated falconer."

"He took that falcon everywhere," Ralph says. He tells me the story of Scott's somewhat eccentric life, a life centered on birds.

"His house was a mess. It had a picnic table in the kitchen. He lived frugally because what he cared most about was raising young birds."

I like the sound of that. A simplified life, as pared down as the Chapin male's. Ralph explains that Scotty took him out in the bogs and swamps, teaching him about plants and birds. I ask how Scott died. He says that they discovered him on the beach in Nantucket, where he'd fallen down from a heart attack.

"They found him there with his falcon perched nearby," he says. "The falcon had a rabbit."

Dying outside on the beach with his bird next to him seems a fitting end, and I say so. He agrees. My irritation at Ralph's intrusion turns to gratitude. He has brought me a gift: a birder's fable to attach to the lopsided nest.

ON JUNE 30 I head up to our local fish market, Northside Seafood, and talk with the owner, Peter Thombly. Not long ago I'd explained my osprey project to him and he'd said he was interested in helping. Today he lays out a variety of fish on the cutting board and has me run my fingertips along the scales of a flounder. Going against the scales, it feels like a cat's grainy tongue. "The scales are bigger than you'd think for a small fish," he says, sifting the flounder skin through his fingers as if testing fabric. He slices the skin off a salmon and shows me the white hairlike fibers that span the skin and pink membrane. I ask him what the toughest skin of any fish is, and he says that, after shark, he'd pick striped bass. "They've got a coat of armor," he says. Since he doesn't have any stripers today, he sends me home with a garbage bag filled with chunks of bluefish, salmon, and cod, and one entire flounder.

Armed with these goodies, my mission is to get a little sense of how it must feel to rip a fish apart. I resolve to make something of a ceremony out of it, and, to get in a more animal mind, I take a long run. I come back covered in sweat. I carry the bag of fish and an assortment of pliers, knives, and hedge clippers out to the back deck. With the house to myself, I decide that I should perform the ritual naked, as the ospreys do, but soon this feels too silly even for me. Wearing gym shorts then, I squat over the various pieces of fish that I've laid out on the lawn. I start with the flounder. It gleams orangish along the edges, the tail, fins, and back ridge; its two dead eyes—just above the small gill with the red innards peeking out—stare up at me. I first try ripping it with my hands. I've seen enough flounders torn apart by ospreys to get the idea, but while my fingernails are long, they only manage to scrape off the bluish scales. If I really had to tear this fish apart with my bare hands, if my life depended on it, could I? Maybe, but right now there seems no way *in,* no way to pull it apart: it's too tough, too slippery. Scales clump brownish under my nails, like peeled skin after a sunburn.

When I give up on bare-handed, I go at it with the biggest set of pliers. Once I manage to pinch a bit of skin, I can tear it back, and for the first time I get a real sense of why the ospreys need to give it such a full twisting motion. To pull the skin back, down to the white meat and bloody middle, takes a good twist and rip. You can see how the birds have to work their heads down into it, down between their shoulder blades. I try the needle-nose pliers, which aren't much better, and then decide on our small hedge clippers, which have a hawk-nose approximating the osprey's bill. That's better, and gives me a feel for just how sharp the actual bills must be. The clippers cut as well as rip, and I quickly get down to the cold cubish white of the flounder, the meat that must be the tastiest to the birds.

The wind comes up and dries the sweat from my skin as I turn my attention to the beautiful blue-and-white pattern of salmon skin, tearing with the clippers down to the familiar pink-orange flesh, orange staining the underside of the white skin. Next it's cod dotted with orange leopard spots and bluefish with classic silvery scales of intertwined diamonds. The bluefish has a more brownish-red meat and is the hardest to cut, making me wonder just how tough stripers must be. An osprey's head will sometimes jerk back when a tough piece of fish finally gives, and my hand mimics this, jerking back quickly when the bluefish skin finally comes ripping up. I find a small bluish-white chunk caught in the clippers, probably just about the amount a female osprey would feed her young.

Tearing fish apart is an intensely smelly procedure, and for the rest of the day I'll reek, despite repeated scrubbings. Osprey nests must stink powerfully of fish, and the females, without the benefit of the males' repeated dunkings, must truly stink. If ospreys become what they see, they also become what they smell, and it's a good thing that their noses, two small slits above their bills, aren't as well developed as their eyes. Or maybe fish, even old fish, smells good to them.

Finally, despite the odor, I turn my thoughts to dinner. I use my brother's old filleting knife on the flounder, which, though dulled from the years, still works pretty well. Later tonight, I'll wish I had my brother's skill as well as his knife. I'll be surprised by all the bones and cartilage that the ospreys relentlessly gnaw through, gulping everything down. Because I've never filleted a flounder before, I'll end up grilling it more or less whole, and will eat it while avoiding looking down at the bulging eyes and the internal organs I've missed. But I'll eat it all—despite any squeamishness—as the final step in this odd little ceremony.

MY YOUNGER BROTHER used the knife I use today to fillet flounder while working on the *Albatross,* the commercial fishing boat that docks in the harbor right across the street from our house. Standing out on the back deck this morning I can see the same fifty-two-foot-long boat loading its morning passengers. During childhood summers my brother helped tourists with their lines, strengthened his arms pulling and dropping anchor, and filleted fish in fast motion back at the docks. Most of the money he made was in tips, which he later pulled out of his pockets and dropped in our room so that the floor was covered with dollar bills that smelled of blood and flounder. Because he was irresponsible enough to leave his money lying around, it wasn't hard for me to rationalize picking up a buck or two whenever I needed it. He was my little brother, I must have thought, and therefore it wasn't really stealing.

Since Nina has known my brother he hasn't been himself, and it's hard for her to believe me when I describe him as a sweet kid with a good sense of humor. The man she's gotten to know has long been at war with himself and others, chemicals inside him creating a world that no one but him sees. Coincidence or not, his breakdown began just after my father died of cancer, five years ago. My father was a strong man with a strong voice, and my brother and I measured and defined ourselves both by and against him. The three of us were deeply linked, and are still linked despite anger, death, and mental illness. My father's death at fifty-six was the great cataclysmic event that shook my family, and continues to shake my family today. My coming back to Cape Cod and rooting myself is in large part a reaction to my family's intense uprooting. My brother hasn't had such a lucky or healthy reaction. It's been over two years since he's been back here, to our family home, in large part because the rest of us are afraid of him.

On Thursday, July 1, my brother comes to visit. Nina and I pick him up at the airport, but he won't speak to us. In the two-hour car ride home, through bad Boston traffic, he says almost nothing, glares at us, stares out the window, angry that we won't let him smoke in our car. That night he doesn't sleep, slams doors, takes my mother's car from 2:00 to 5:00 A.M. When he returns at 5:00 he claims that the neighbors are heckling him and calls the police. We wake to hear him yelling at my mother, and I come downstairs to try to calm him. At 5:30 I decide to take him out to the Chapin nest with me, and he comes along reluctantly. Though I suspect it's futile, I attempt to interest him in the birds. But the outside world holds no appeal. He is turned chronically inward, and when I head out to the marsh, he sits with a cigarette in my station wagon and takes notes in his journal, filling the car with words and smoke. At the nest, I feel my own notes taking on an inward-turned intensity, and find it hard to concentrate on the birds.

Over the next few days the mood in the house darkens. This character currently inhabiting my brother's body is angry, loud, sulking, and, seemingly, evil. It isn't him, of course; it's his illness. But like some ancient mythic creature, or the childhood bogeyman, he brings chaos and uncertainty wherever he goes. We have explored every option but there is no way for us to help him until he's ready for help. My mother has spent a good part of the last two years trying to better his situation — worrying and fretting over him around the clock — but he seems to feel nothing but anger. *How can this have happened?* some part of him must still know to ask. When he heads back to Texas after six days it's as if he's been here a year. It will take us weeks to recover and will leave us all feeling dazed and depressed, upset and angry. A less consistent but more poignant sensation is an occasional deep, stabbing sadness for my brother and for what has become of his life.

SOMETIMES LIFE PROVIDES coincidences that art would blanch at. During my brother's stay an event occurs at the nest with symbolic repercussions that for the most part I try to ignore. Before my brother's arrival I began to notice the workings of the pecking order, but the intensity of the competition increased while he was here. Other than jockeying for position, well-fed osprey nestlings don't fight much, and up until recently the Chapin group has seemed remarkably harmonious. Nevertheless, the rule of muscle and size has applied at the nest since the first days I saw the birds. The biggest nestling, the one I now call No. 1, is always first in line and takes her time eating while the others beg. (I assume the nestling is a female since females are generally larger than males, and this one is by far the largest of the clutch.) She eats more aggressively than the others and, like her parents, sometimes lets go with a good canine head shake when downing a scrag of fish. While No. 1 eats, No. 2 will sometimes sidle up and manage to sneak a few bites, maybe one bite to every four the bigger bird gets. The size drop-off from No. 2 to No. 3 is fairly dramatic, and even greater between No. 3 and the runt. The gap between the largest and smallest birds is truly remarkable: while No. 1's head now looks almost like her mother's, the last bird is clearly less developed, half her sister's size. The runt appears almost a full stage of growth behind, its goofy reptilian head still wobbling. Often the runt sleeps or lies low while the others eat, holding little hope that he'll ever get his share. This is the same bird that I saw housekeeping as if to keep his mind off the rumblings of his stomach.

"Nature isn't Disney," my friend Reg Saner said the last time we talked, and all it takes to understand this is to watch a single feeding. One day I see the female osprey hop-fly across the nest with half a trout in her talon, briefly putting the runt in the best position to eat. I'm hoping to witness an act of benevolence, but this hope ends when No. 1 barges back across the nest and knocks the runt over, essentially sitting on the smaller bird's head while she starts to eat. Reminded of junior high school indignities at the hands of bullies, I root hard for the runt to break free. When he finally crawls out from under and actually gets a bite I let go a little cheer, but the victory is short-lived. Soon No. 2 and No. 3 have pushed ahead of him, No. 3 delivering a vicious stab in the process. Other than shoulder-to-shoulder tussling, this is the first truly violent act I've seen between the siblings, putting the *peck* in *pecking order*. As with humans, those with little tend to turn on those with less, and over the next days No. 3 grows more and more violent toward the runt. As the birds become bigger they need more fish, and while the runt seems resigned to getting less, the second-smallest bird becomes increasingly frustrated in his efforts to eat enough.

I remind myself that the nestlings aren't really any more heartless than human children. Childhood is war, after all, though it's easy to let memory glaze over this fact. On a walk recorded by James Boswell in *Journal of a Tour to the Hebrides,* Lady McLeod asked Samuel Johnson if he believed there was an inherent benevolence in human feelings, to which Johnson replied, "No madam, no more than a wolf." Or, he might have said, had he seen one diving in a nearby loch, no more — or less — than an osprey.

It doesn't do to get too excited about a bird's "humanity." My reading confirms that life at the nest can be quite gruesome and un-Disney-like. My books teach me about birds called brood parasites who lay eggs in the nests of other birds and whose offspring, once hatched, go about the quick work of killing their stepsiblings. Some brood parasites, like the freshly hatched cuckoo, follow an instinct to push the other eggs from the nest; others, like the honeyguide, take things to an even more murderous extreme, briefly developing a special needlelike point on their bills, made especially for killing birds that hatch at the same time as they do.

ON JULY 2, my brother's second full day here, the world blows sideways, then leaps ahead to fall. I'm out at the Chapin nest early. It's the sort of day you wait all summer for, reminding you just how still, dry, and stultifying the season has been. My constant companions, the insects, are now swept off across the marsh. Pewter-gray clouds shift in front of a smudge of sun while beach grass blows and my journal pages flap. The light shifts low and jagged, the beach grass cutting more cleanly through the charged air. The Cape I love is back, even if I'd never realized it was gone. As I set up my chair and scope, it feels good to shiver with cold.

This has to be a strange day for the young birds, who up to this point have known mostly stillness, heat, and sunlight. Their new feathers blow, the gusts teasing out cockatoo hairstyles, and it must feel good to be cleansed by the wind. The string and rope that usually hang down from their nest now trails westward as if dragged behind a boat, while the nestlings stare up at clouds the color of healing bruises, clouds that stream westward with the string. The female, harried and windblown, hunkers down, protective of her brood. At first the nestlings refuse to follow the leader, standing straight up and facing into the wind, seemingly enjoying the way it cools their feathers and drives off bugs. After a while, though, they hunch down almost out of sight, at least until one large black-and-white wing flops up and over the nest edge like something unattached to a body. Though the birds have grown to two-thirds of their full size, their wings still remain things they have little clue how to operate. But at least they're exercising now, and two of them, No. 2 and No. 3, stand up to give it a try. This, of course, could be a dangerous day to practice flapping. They don't know much about wind, there's been so little of it in their short lifetimes, and I worry that a powerful gust might sweep them out of the nest. As if hearing my thought or, more likely, the same worry communicated by their mother, the two nestlings settle back down.

They're all up again five minutes later when the male returns with the usual slimy, glittering prize, the headless reward—this one a trout, I think. I hadn't noticed the runt until this minute and I'm reassured to see his head pop up, though he barely stirs, looking dazed and tired. What must it be like to be perpetually hungry? Now his head flops to one side, almost entirely lifeless, and I worry that this may be the moment I've feared. Is he dying? Have the days of hunger and abuse finally taken their toll?

If so, the mother seems pointedly unconcerned. I'm struck by this seeming lack of caring, this sheer brutality of nature, as she tears apart the fish. The others muscle in, three tails in the air, while their tiny sibling lies sick or dying in a clump on the other side of the nest. Though I know I'm anthropomorphizing again, the mother's lack of concern, her attention to feeding the other birds, seems particularly cruel. The only life that stirs in the runt occurs when the wind ruffs up his black-and-gold feathers, or when he gives his neck a halfhearted flop.

Meanwhile, the female doles out food in her usual inequitable fashion: three bites for No. 1, a bite for No. 2, no bites for the others. Furtively, No. 3 tries to work his way in around his siblings' tails, but they have him pretty well blocked off from any possible approach. He turns around and stalks off to the other side of the nest, as if giving up, but then he sees the runt. It's as if he's just looked into a mirror at his own potential fate, and he charges back into the scrum. His begging cries grow intense and agitated, but No. 1 is in a particularly hoggish mood today and, despite the high-pitched complaints, won't relinquish her spot. Finally, No. 3 gives up, retreating again to the far side of the nest.

It's then that I witness something I'll never forget. No. 3, banished to the nest's other side, kept away from the food, turns on the runt. He pecks viciously into the side of the tiny, already dying nestling, tearing out feathers with his bill. The runt recoils in a manner that lets me know he's indeed still alive, though not for long. No. 3 grabs the runt's neck between the mandibles of his bill, closing on either side, and begins to savagely twist the neck this way and that, displaying the same sort of wild energy usually reserved for eating. He lets go after a few moments but then immediately stabs at the runt's neck, tearing off more feathers. Then No. 3 again grabs the now-limp neck and twists and turns it until the runt is clearly dead. The fury of this action, which continues well after the runt is motionless, is nearly indescribable, the second-smallest bird working a ferocious figure eight with the smallest bird's neck.

While the murder occurs, life on the other side of the nest goes on as usual. The mother ignores the fratricide and continues feeding No. 1 and No. 2, until finally, much too late, she seems to take interest in the deadly spectacle across the nest. The remains of the fish still in her single talon, she flies across the nest and sounds an alarm over the runt's body. But this is blowing the calvary call after the slaughter. No. 3 has finished his work, and the runt lies dead, balled in a lifeless clump. Seeing there's really nothing to be done, the mother hops back across the nest and resumes feeding the other two birds.

When the two largest nestlings, apparently sated, go back to practicing flapping, No. 3 finally gets his chance at the fish. I stare down the heartless little bastard while he eats. To look into his little orange eyes is to see something not just wild but purely *savage* — and not savage in any romantic sense. The fish finally devoured, the nestlings all hunker back down, casually sharing their bed with a corpse. The mother flaps over and stands directly above the runt's body, but decidedly *not* standing guard. It's far too late for guarding.

I lean back in my chair, away from the scope, taking a break from the intense, violent world of the nest. The wind blows across my face as I try to make sense of what I've seen. For me the phrase *pecking order* has long since passed from the conceptual to the concrete, but today it's changed into something even more dramatic, something blazingly, achingly corporeal. I think of how hard the runt struggled up until now, how it pecked its way out of the egg and how hard it fought just to live this long. Its one month of life was nothing but struggle, a losing battle to get food, the one thing, the only thing, that might help it live long enough to fly and escape a nest where its position was firmly entrenched and unalterable.

THE NEXT MORNING the clump of the runt's body is no longer visible through the scope. Among some birds of prey the body would be cannibalized, precious nutrients not to be wasted, but not among these fish eaters. I assume the body's been thrown over the edge of the nest in the night, but by whom I don't know — mother or sibling? I rule out the father as a suspect on the grounds of his general distance from the nest's inner workings. I consider walking right up to the platform to hunt for the corpse, but I don't want to spook the other nestlings, especially now that they've begun to practice flying. Likely the evidence has already been disposed of, dragged off by a delighted raccoon or fox.

Over the next couple of days coming to the nest fills me with anger. And superiority. "Savages," I call the birds in my journal. Of

No. 3, whom I refer to as "white trash," I write poetically: "I'd like to see that fucker blown right off the nest."

On a more intellectual level I understand that no one is to blame, that this all makes perfect evolutionary sense. The fact is No. 3 has done everyone a favor—now no precious food will be wasted on the futile act of keeping the runt alive. And, according to the strict laws of instinct, the mother is also blameless. Her job isn't to be a referee. She doesn't want her kids to play fair; she wants one or two of them to remain alive. It's logical to keep feeding the ones who are already strongest first, even if it rankles our human sense of fair play.

But it's one thing to discuss or write about the remorseless mechanism of the world, another to see it in action. I can't get the murder out of my mind. The nestlings will never again be quite so adorable. I feel an as yet unclear change in attitude: a less romantic view of the nest? An acceptance of cruelty? A more honest relationship with the birds as what they are? I'm not sure. Certainly it gives me pause, making me reconsider all the wonderful qualities I've been attributing to the ospreys. Maybe the best thing, the only thing, that can be said for the murder is that it keeps me from attributing at all for a few days.

I know one of my faults is that I'm overly quick to read meaning into things, to regard events as if they were so many tea leaves. Taken to an ugly extreme, symbol making defines the sick human mind. My brother is a case in point, reading portents in everything. I'm human, too, and can't resist stewing over what things mean. For instance, if I were just a little crazier, I might see the events at the nest as a sign about how I should deal with my brother. Not that I should kill him, of course, but that I should harden my mind. The fact that this happens while he's here is almost too much. But I'm clearheaded enough to realize that the events I witnessed have nothing to do with how I should handle my own sibling relationship.

What I saw was not a symbol of anything, and certainly not of that. We are human, and we — or most of us — do not remorselessly kill our brothers, no matter how much harm they cause the brood. I'm not claiming that humans are above this sort of behavior — we kill each other every day — or that our motives are all that different from those of No. 3. As a species we kill for the same reasons: jealousy, frustration, bitterness at our mistreatment, hunger, desire for more. For me it isn't the murder itself that defines this event as below, or maybe more accurately, *beyond* human. What made it so foreign was not the murder but the reaction to it by the fellow members of the nest, by the bird's family. The complete impassivity, barely a glance from even the mother, whose yellow eyes had never looked colder or further away. If in the past I've been surprised by this impassivity, during the murder I am shocked. "I hate those birds," Nina says after I come home and tell her what has occurred. Despite myself, I briefly share her reaction.

But for the birds it isn't a question of hate, or love, or judgment. Certainly it isn't a question of any imposed human morality. This death springs from a yearning for life, a yearning that occurs at the most basic, savage level. What I take away from this event, in the end, is nothing, no meaning, or at least no human meaning. The murder is a more savagely distilled example of what Thoreau found nearing the summit of Mount Katahdin, a vision of nature where the human was foreign: "Man was not to be associated with it. . . . There was clearly a presence of a force not bound to be kind to man."

But it won't do to quote from classic books either. This is least of all about books. It is what it is. The thing itself. Horrible and brutal, it is also life, a thing that even I am incapable of wrapping up in a neat and tidy human package.

Flight

To most of us flight is a miracle.
To primitive man it certainly must have seemed one.
— STEPHEN DALTON, *The Miracle of Flight*

The murder at Chapin occurred at 7:30 on the morning of July 2, and since I watched the whole thing, I feel no need to question anyone for alibis. The next afternoon when I play detective, following up on the case, I find that I've been wrong about the fate of the corpse. It hasn't been tossed overboard, as I assumed in the morning. For the next two days it remains in the nest, a dead clump of occasionally blowing feathers. I wonder if it hasn't begun to reek, though I suppose that eaters of raw fish aren't very picky concerning olfactory matters. By the third day the clump is gone and I feel my anger toward No. 3 (whom I've begun to call "the murderer" as well as "white trash") abating. Soon I'm actually beginning to sympathize with him. Following the relentless way of the world, he now becomes the runt he killed. Though there should be plenty of food to go around, it seems that, more and more often, the now smallest bird is muscled out of feedings entirely. The other two, decidedly larger, have begun to occasionally pull chunks of fish away from their mother and eat them on their own. They peck at the food in a more aggressive, even vicious, manner, their orange eyes shining. While they eat, No. 3 crouches low, submissive.

Just as the murder itself did, the new pecking order reinforces the fact that theirs is a world separate from my own way of being, from my ultimate concerns. And this might be the most vital lesson, or nonlesson, of all — that the birds' usefulness to human beings is, ultimately, irrelevant. That what *is* relevant are *their* concerns and *their* lives. It's hard not to shoehorn those lives into something that fits into mine, but hard is not the same as impossible. Like anything else, resisting this impulse requires discipline. For longer periods now I find myself observing, noting habits, watching the ospreys without my usual rushing back to self. The more time I spend out here the more I understand — and don't just believe intellectually — that there are ways to be other than the human way. When I do turn back to me, my journal scribblings are often cryptic and nearly indecipherable. "Wild is not man," I write. "It's *other*. . . . To be in this is not to think 'I am in this,' but to be."

But if my words aren't particularly coherent, I'm also less suspicious of words themselves than I was when I started this experiment. My sentences will never get at what it feels like to really be here — the thing itself, the ineffable moments — but at the same time I believe that they connect as much as separate me from the birds. What could be more natural than wanting to express how we feel when we become intimate with someone?

IT WOULD BE nice to say I've changed entirely and that, once and for all, my time at the nest has stilled my need for symbols. But it wouldn't be true. Something is beginning to happen at the nest that will not allow for a quiet mind. A palpable excitement builds as the young birds edge toward what will be their greatest and most daring adventure.

For the first month and a half of their lives the nestlings lacked the very thing that will most define them, but now they edge toward flight. In the days following the murder they begin to flap with more and more intensity. As early as July 5, three days after the runt's death, No. 1 has begun to practice hard, but I can't quite bring myself to believe she will take off. She looks too awkward and goofy, barely able to walk well, let alone fly. Despite this she undergoes a strenuous bout of practice, hopping off her long white pantalooned legs and flapping as if she really wants to get into the air, and suddenly, for a split second, the wind lifts her an inch or so off the nest. When she comes down she looks as surprised as I am, neither of us quite ready.

The harbor birds have begun to practice, too, but being at least a week or two behind, they can't match the intensity at Chapin, where wings pulse air in earnest flapping. If two weeks ago the Chapin nest was crowded, it now seems more so, despite the recent cruel subtraction. The nest bulges with birds, particularly when two or more decide to practice flying at the same time. Young wings swat young heads; the father stays on his far perch, unamused and aloof; and even the loyal mother hops up onto the crossbar a foot above the nest, freeing up much-needed space. For the nestlings it must feel good to finally be flapping, using their wings for what they were built for. Not just the sheer joyous movement of it, but the ridding of insects and itchiness, the end of enforced stillness.

I haven't spent nearly as much time on the Simpkins Neck nest, but since my bicycle survey I've started hiking in more often, usually after my visit to Chapin. I throw my scope over my shoulder and endure the half hour of swatting aside catbriers, mosquitoes, and poison ivy, while hoping to avoid the dreaded bite of the deer tick. By the time I arrive at the nest I look like I've been in the jungle for a week. These nestlings, too, are caught up in a commotion of wild flapping. So much so that it sometimes seems as if the nest itself will take off, levitating over the marsh.

JULY 6 PROVES the strangest weather day of the summer. My mother, Nina, and I are stunned by the heat. Oven-hot air renders us listless, and, despite the excitement of flight practice, I watch the Chapin nest for only an hour, rush in and out from Simpkins, and quickly check in with the harbor birds. The nestlings, too, seem more subdued, and I can't imagine them taking off into this oppressive windless air. Nina and I retreat to the beach, preparing lesson plans in beach chairs and spending the afternoon dipping in and out of the bay. While wading I see a silver-and-sand-colored striped bass squiggling a foot or two above its own shadow on the ocean floor. The heat makes work and thought impossible, and in the afternoon we head back home to lie in front of fans and take siestas.

The weather breaks suddenly at seven that night. Black clouds scud toward us and darken the sky, the air cooling thirty degrees in twenty minutes. The sky rumbles as we race around closing windows, energy returned to us by the dropping temperature and the urgency of the storm. We ready for sheets of rain, but they never come, and the thunder and lightning, which seemed ready to burst upon us, remain a distant rumbling and sparking. This faux storm is disappointing, frustrating, after so many days of heat and drought, but the winds rise wildly, coming at us in great blasting waves, pushing out summer, swirling around the house and thrashing the trees and briers.

THE NEXT DAY I learn that, at almost exactly the same moment I began shutting windows, a thirteen-year-old boy on the other side of Cape Cod was experiencing something that the young ospreys have so far only dreamed of. Jeffrey Plumer was sailing his thirteen-foot boat, *Flying Tern,* when he saw the same thing I'd seen—darkening skies and rising winds. Sensibly, he headed for the shore of Oyster Pond. Making it to his mooring, he began to lower his sails. That was when the miracle happened. A funnel cloud approached and a huge gust caught the part of his mainsail that remained up, the gust lifting the whole boat into the sky with Jeffrey still inside the cockpit. Riding the wind, the boat and boy flew from the shore to the center of Oyster Pond, two hundred yards away! In the course of its short journey, the *Flying Tern* rose into the air and flew *over* several other moored boats before landing and capsizing in the pond's middle. The boy's mother, Kristine, who had looked out her window seconds before to see Jeffrey safe by the beach, looked out again to see her son in the water two football fields away. But the boy quickly righted the boat and began to bail, and was soon towed to shore by a neighbor in a Boston Whaler.

The whole experience, from shore and back, lasted less than fifteen minutes. Meteorologists believe that a "gustnado," a small-scale tornado, was responsible for the freak flight. James Lee of the National Weather Service compared that flight to that of a parasailer: "If the wind got under the sail, he became like a human kite."

JEFFREY'S FLIGHT HAS been all over the papers and TV, and I can't help but feel a little jealous. What does it feel like to be part of the wind?

In hopes of getting some answers, I flirt with the idea of trying out hang gliding, even going out to watch a few takeoffs. But the fact of my actually running over the side of a cliff seems far less feasible than a young osprey, equipped with built-in wings, jumping off the nest. On a couple of occasions the hang gliders I watch run toward the cliff edge and then suddenly experience a failure of nerve, backpedaling or crumbling and pulling their sails down desperately toward the safety of earth. No wonder they hesitate. The miracle is that any of them do it. I know deep down that I'll never be able to make that particular leap, and am glad when Nina insists that I cut the nonsense and stop even considering it.

Grounded, I content myself to merely watch, which, it turns out, is exciting enough. In the week after the gustnado, the wind picks up again and spurs the birds to flap harder. Alan Poole has explained to me that often the very first flight is accidental, just like Jeffrey Plumer's, brought on by a particularly strong gust. I root for that gust, hoping to witness the first wild, inadvertent flight — that abrupt metamorphosis of creatures whom I have so far known only as sedentary. It will be an event of more historic importance than Kitty Hawk, at least to me and the nestlings, and I stay at the Chapin nest for hours, wanting to catch the exact moment.

After the Chapin No. 1's early lead, there is a period during the second week of July when No. 3, having benefited from a growth spurt, works hardest at flapping. This seems a classic case of over-compensation. After all, he has the greatest motivation to get the hell out of the nest, away from this place where he is always last. There's evidence that adult ospreys bolster this motivation by beginning to pull back on feedings as fledging approaches, adding the impetus of hunger to the building instinct to leave the nest. The parents are understandably impatient, and not just because their once quiet nest has begun to resemble a helicopter pad. The simple fact is that the young birds need to make the trip to South America in less than two months, and the sooner they learn to fly the better their chances of survival.

Despite the delight of the cool fall-like weather that follows the gustnado, I share the elder ospreys' impatience. Some mornings I come to the nest looking for flight to find only napping or fish begging. When the practice sessions finally begin, I root for the young birds while they dance their step-stomping dances from talon to talon, flapping and hopping up anxiously toward the sky. There are other changes, too — the nestlings more actively follow life outside the nest, whether a plane or bird flying by, and they're beginning to develop a side-to-side head movement, which I call the "pigeon bob." But the real show is flight, or the preparation for it.

• • •

ON JULY 14 I make a quick dawn trip to Quivett. With all the activity at Chapin, I've barely had time for the single "unproductive" nest on my watch. The Quivett birds look truly aimless now, as if they've lost their purpose (which, on the most basic level, they have). The pair just sit next to each other at the nest, wind ruffling their feathers, going through the motions, displaying a distinct lack of urgency during this urgent time of year. When I brought Nina here the other night she agreed that the female looked desolate. Sitting back low on the nest, she conveyed a desperation about her enterprise. "The lost nest," I call Quivett in my journal. Of course, put in perspective, the tragedy of the Quivett nest is no tragedy at all. They are long-lived birds, were successful last year, and likely will be again.

Anyway, I have little time for Quivett. By 9:00 I'm back at Chapin. Over the last few days I've noticed another change: brief hops across the length of the nest, nothing you could really call flying, but hops with greater hang time than before. This morning's high point occurs when No. 1 leaps the full length of the nest and floats in the air for a good two seconds, fluttering her wings, while I feel a corresponding flutter inside. I assure you that when you see this lift, this hover, it's impossible not to feel the quick internal lift of delight. What's more, I find myself caught between excitement and fear: flight can happen at any minute, but, like a father who fears his child will never learn to walk or speak, I don't really believe that my birds will ever learn to fly. Perhaps I'm getting closer to taking that leap of faith, but more often it's a leap that still, at times, strikes me as preposterous. In fact, it's one thing to believe in an extended hop like the one I saw just now, but the next step requires more than a mere leap. That step is simple: these birds will do the nearly impossible. They will peer over the nest's edge, as if it were the end of the world, stare down at the twelve-foot drop to the ground — a drop that would have killed them a few weeks ago — and then they will crouch and leap and suddenly *be in the air.* They will trust that their wings—these things that so far have been only good for flopping around spasmodically—will lift them into the wind. If this is "natural," it's also lunacy, a mad risk, an example of evolution's sense of the absurd. Can there be a crazier gambit, a more wild bid, than this? But apparently these are the sort of gambles you must take to lead a life of flight.

AT NIGHT I steep myself in the literature of flying. Witnessing the murder has made me more hardheaded, and at first I'm temperate, sticking to avian physiology, learning about the remarkable evolutionary adaptations that make flight possible. "The first essential property is lightness," Jean Dorst writes in *The Life of Birds.* I discover how every part of a bird, even its skeleton, is remarkably light, helping explain how the ospreys, which sometimes look as big as small dogs, can weigh only four pounds. To this first property are added two others: streamlining and strength. "Every projection," writes Dorst, "is suppressed. The legs can be retracted into the plumage . . . or stretched out horizontally. The head, neck, and body are shaped to part air and ensure a smooth airflow." In addition, an osprey's heart beats six times faster than ours, and its circulatory, respiratory, and digestive systems are all "remarkably efficient." Anything that doesn't aid flight shrinks (even reproductive organs during the sexual off-season), creating perfect aerial athletes with no wasted motion.

While man has joined them in the air, birds still have one great advantage over man-made wings: feathers. "The feathered wing's aerodynamic form, lightness, and remarkable ability to change shape represent perfection in functional design," writes Stephen Dalton in *The Miracle of Flight.* No plane will ever maneuver like a bird, in large part thanks to a feather's perfect design. There are theories but no one really knows how feathers evolved. However they came into being, the nestlings are now getting their first clues about what they are good for. One of the things the young ospreys are doing, when they aren't practicing, is learning how to care for their feathers, constantly preening. Large birds, like raptors, may have as many as twenty-five thousand feathers.

An osprey's bones, while light, must be rigid and strong enough to absorb the impact of hitting the water at forty miles per hour. In most animals the skeleton is the heaviest part of the body, but in birds the bones are not only hollow but, Dorst says, "full of air which is in communication with the respiratory sacs." I don't quite understand what is meant by "in communication" and scribble down a note to ask Alan Poole about it. I learn that the phenomenon of having air cavities in the bones is called pneumatization.

I'm doing well, keeping my reading disciplined, until my eye happens to glance down a few dictionary entries below *pneumatization* to *pneumatology,* the study of spiritual beings and phenomena. With that stroke of bad luck I leave my science reading behind for the night, my imagination taking off despite my efforts to ground it. I push the ornithology books aside and wonder about human notions of flight. How many of us will ever know anything close to true flight? We glimpse it a little through drink, drugs, the exhilaration of sport, moments of empathy, art, falling in love, lovemaking. But we miss more than we see.

I'm not unique in my failure to stay literal on this particular subject. The human imagination can't seem to leave flight alone. We talk of *flights of the imagination,* for instance. Empathy is flying out of your skin into the skin of another, and ecstasy means flying out of the self all together, though maybe *jump* is a better word than *fly.* Maybe what humans call "flight" is really no more than a hop, and a relatively small hop at that, mere approximations of the real thing.

Take Keats, for example, whose empathic nature made him an ideal candidate for spiritual flight school, and who dreamed of lifting off "on the viewless wings of Poesy." Even he, with his ability to leap into the lives of animals and people (and things) outside of himself, and his constant desire to experience "the greeting of the spirit," could lift off only for precious seconds, as the odes to the nightingale and on the Grecian urn attest. To truly get beyond ourselves is the dream, to lift up and out, but how many of us can sustain lift against the drag and weight of our self-consciousness, even for a short while?

Maybe human beings were built wingless for a reason. To fly means to stay in the air, not just momentarily gaining the sky before dropping back. Of course even avian flight begins with a jump, usually a crouching down and then a springing up. But jumping only approaches flight, is only a momentary suspension. Though we hope for it and dream about it, how many of us will ever know actual soaring? How many of us will ever experience what Jeffrey Plumer did at the edge of the Oyster Pond?

After letting my mind drift with these airy thoughts for a while, I wrestle myself back to fact, picking up my science books again. Enough with humans and human ideas of flight. It's literal, not metaphoric, flight I need to learn about. How does a bird fly? Yes, they are streamlined and have light bones and all that, but that doesn't get at the simpler problem: *how can something move through the air?* This is one of those basic things, like how a car works, that most of us take for granted and don't understand. We get on board a plane, watch the movie, drink, read magazines, all the while blissfully unaware of how the 200-ton contraption we are sitting inside will ever get off the ground. Now I read about drag and thrust, lift and weight. "Think of air as a fluid, which it is," my books counsel me, "then imagine the air, the fluid, moving over a wing." I try to understand, I really do. I read about the fundamentals of aerodynamics once, twice, then a third time, but somehow it doesn't sink in. I assure myself that over the next weeks I'll master the material. But right now that seems about as likely as my jumping off our roof and flying across the harbor.

On July 15 I head out to watch the real thing. The Chapin nestlings seem only a little more confident than I am in the plausibility of flight. While No. 1 puts a mighty effort into flapping and manages to lift above the platform for three seconds, treading air, flying in place, a minute later she attempts to hop-fly up to the crossbar and misses awkwardly. It's amazing that in three weeks these same clumsy birds will be diving for fish on their own; that by early September they will be flying thousands of miles to South America. For now they can't do something that their diminutive downstairs neighbors, the house sparrows, could do after only a single week of life.

I feel a tug of guilt about not having visited Simpkins Neck over the last few days, but decide to stay here, egging on the near fledglings. Understanding that my rooting has no more effect than yelling at the TV during a Patriots game doesn't stop me from raving like a beatnik hepcat. "*Go, go, go, go, go go, go!*" I chant as No. 3 takes over, almost doing it, lifting off with a clump of sticks from the nest caught in his talons, then landing again and trying to clear the clump. Sometimes I can anticipate when they are about to try to lift by their posture and the way they gather themselves in concentration. They now go through at least two good practice sessions a day, facing into the wind and flapping with gusto, consistently hop-flying from one end of the nest to the other. They're getting more real height, too, lifting about two feet above the nest. I count out the time as they fly: "*One Mississippi, two Missi—,*" the record so far being five Mississippis for No. 1. When the wind comes up they're blown backward almost off the nest, and though I'd hate for them to come to harm, I'd like to see how they'd react to suddenly not having the nest below them. Something tells me, though, that this would be tragic; that they wouldn't be quite ready yet to fly back up and reclaim the safety of the nest.

Despite No. 3's great efforts, their flying ability mirrors their places in the pecking order: No. 1 levitating, the closest to real flying; No. 2 hop-flying; and No. 3 merely hopping about with clumps in his feet. The Vegas odds have them fledging in just that order, though I secretly hope for an upset. Somehow the little murderer has not only gotten back into my good graces but become my favorite. If hope is the thing with feathers, here is hope in its purest form: yearning for the sky. It's hard to hold grudges when watching so much earnest effort and excitement.

Meanwhile, the nestlings have begun to resemble their parents more, not just in their size but in their characteristic movements. Sometimes they scratch themselves like cats, holding their talons against their just-developing feather sheaths, called pinfeathers, while moving their heads back and forth vigorously. Before No. 1 takes off she goes into her pigeon bob, moving her head back and forth like a '70s TV pimp. Or maybe to call it a bob is wrong—it's more a curious shifting back and forth, from left to right, like a bad teenage dancer. Whatever it is exactly, it's part of her warm-up, a warm-up that's sometimes as elaborate, and as seemingly doomed to failure, as those of the men in the old-time flying machines.

But while flight is fun, food is still the real game, and when the male returns with a fish, the practice session ends instantly. It's a flounder, sand-colored and small, already streaked red from the talon gash when it was caught. As the male delivers it, the nest goes wild with noise. No. 1 and No. 2 fight for scraps to drag off on their own now, stabbing brutally at the chunks they take, while No. 3, knowing his place, hunches down in his submissive corvid cower. I take conscientious notes on the feeding, but in truth I've begun to resent the times in between the attempts at flight—times of eating, napping, preening, nest building—anything that isn't jumping and flapping.

MEANWHILE, OUR OWN nest grows more crowded. Every year since Nina and I moved to Cape Cod, my sister Heidi and her son Noah have paid an annual visit from North Carolina in mid-July. This year they arrive with a new addition in tow, the three-month-old Adeline Grace.

Heidi, two years younger than me, is my oldest friend. When she was Addy's age I rocked her in the wooden cradle in which we now stack wood. Of course, I wasn't an entirely benevolent brother. Across the room from the cradle hangs a photo of the two of us as children. Though at first glance it looks like we are embracing, on closer examination it appears I'm trying to strangle my sister. Despite this, we have become very close over the years. "You never get angry at her," Nina says, something she couldn't say about almost anyone else. It's true. My relationship with my sister is my least complicated.

As we toast their arrival, three-year-old Noah runs around naked on the back deck, naked being the state he'll stay in for most of the summer. I point the telescope at the harbor nest, adjusting it for Heidi, Nina, and my mother. When I show them how the harbor nestlings have begun to practice flapping, they react with the same excitement I experienced.

After a big welcome dinner, Heidi and the kids turn in early, exhausted from their trip. I climb the stairs and return to my books. In the big hawk book Brown and Amadon suggest that there is something like play in all this practice flapping: "obviously the young birds don't know they are 'practising' flying, but instead are merely indulging in a form of behavior which, at times, at least, they appear to enjoy." I read various ornithology books for a while but then push them aside. I dip into more mystical texts, again leaving behind pneumatization for pneumatology. Despite witnessing the murder and despite vowing to become more scientific, I can't seem to break old habits. I read Meister Eckhart, the German mystic, in hopes of gleaning some secrets of flight, but my energy is mostly concentrated on Mercia Eliade's *Shamanism*. In Eliade's book I learn that stories of flight were common among different peoples, Asian, Siberian, Arctic, and North American, and that they were called myths of ascension. These ascents to the sky were central to the roles of shamans among the Katshina, Winnebago, Beltir, Proto-Turks, Ugrian, Yakuts, Buryats, and a hundred other tribes. According to Eliade, the "shamanic vocation or initiation is directly connected with ascent to the sky"; for instance, the great Basuto prophet "received his vocation after an ecstasy during which he saw the roof of his hut open above his head and felt himself carried off to the sky." Neophytes undertook these ecstatic journeys to the sky through different techniques of ascent: ritual tree climbing, the sacrifice of horses, ascensional trances. They also played the world drum, cut from the world tree, as a means of communication between sky and earth, an aid to ecstasy.

When I first wintered on Cape Cod I often had flying dreams. I couldn't get over the bird life, the millions of seabirds and songbirds migrating overhead, couldn't get over the good luck of being a witness to these mass movements. Now I'm spending more time than ever with birds, but the dreams haven't returned. I'm not sure why. These days I'm healthier, stronger, reading books on flight both ornithological and mystical, while back then I preferred Meister Bräu to Meister Eckhart. It takes a strong ego to leave the ego behind, a strong self for selflessness, and I think I'm better prepared to leave myself for a while, trusting that when I come back I won't be any worse for the wear. John Elder wrote, "Humility, finally, means to value something for its own sake, not for the way it reflects oneself or one's values." I'm an egotist, true, but the discipline of sitting with the ospreys helps me in this regard. With greater frequency I'm able to project myself into their nest, without projecting the grid of my mind, able to just watch and be there with them. I like to think of this as a kind of minor flight.

For the shaman, flight meant nothing less than ecstasy, the joyful leaving of the self behind. These lifting moments are also what Emerson valued most, and it seems he spent his most potent creative years almost constantly flying up toward or dropping back from this heightened state. "This inner wildness, this habit of enthusiasm, this workaday embracing of the Dionysian is quintessential Emerson," Robert Richardson writes. "He is wild or he is nothing."

These are my standards as well, though they are in fact impossible standards as we muddle through our long, ordinary days. Nevertheless, I still find them the best way to judge my life, even if this often sets me up for disappointment. I wait like Jeffrey Plumer on the edge of Oyster Pond, knowing that when the lifting moments do come they will blaze like fireworks. Then my everyday concerns will seem like just what they are — everyday — and I'll get a brief but exhilarating glimpse of the fact that I'm part of something infinitely larger, a life force, if not religious then at least biological.

THE NEXT MORNING, July 16, sure that this will be the first day of true flight, I'm at the Chapin nest by six. The sun is an orange disc, and purple strands of clouds tear across the sky, while high tide glistens the spike grass and glasswort. The nestlings strut bravely along the very edge of the nest, no longer afraid of falling over. Wings beating furiously, No. 3 hover-hops up onto the crossbar, a vast improvement from only twelve hours ago. Then, as if not to be outdone, No. 1 lifts straight up and floats in the air with her long white leg warmers hanging down as I count out an easy six Mississippis. I laugh while I count, so startling is the change from just yesterday — this is very close to real flight! My birds are overnight sensations, hopping and flying all over the nest.

I hear myself curse when the father returns with a fish, knowing that this will ruin the fun for some time. It isn't much of a fish either, just the scraggly scrap of a tail. The female immediately rips it from his talons and flies it to the other side of the nest. He doesn't even bother sticking around, but takes right off. Though the Chapin male is my favorite, he is also the classic aloof father, becoming less and less of a presence at the nest with each passing day. The female stops ripping into the fish for a second to aim a few angry begging cries after his receding form.

Knowing that the Chapin nestlings will be preoccupied fighting for scraps and then, possibly, napping, I decide to head over to Simpkins Neck. I tote my beach chair, using it to knock back the branches and briers, and set up behind the marsh elder bushes at the edge of the marsh. Perhaps it's their different parenting styles — the shy Simpkins pair more quick to leave the nest unguarded — or the different angle of the nest for viewing, or my prejudice toward the Chapin male as a hunter. Whatever the reason, I long ago decided that the Simpkins nest is less "mature."

Today I discover just how wrong I am. As I sit trying to record the complicated interactions of the parents, the male again seemingly taunting the female and then flying off to a tree to eat, a strange thing happens. Suddenly, smoothly, in what is definitely not a beginner's flight, the Simpkin's No. 1 pushes off the nest and flies an easy lap around the marsh. There's nothing tentative about the flight; it's a full-fledged lap and relanding. I'm left flabbergasted. I watch for two more hours, and begin to doubt what I saw. But I did see it, and the sight throws things into chaos. I've been so set on seeing a first awkward flight that this brings with it a sense of anticlimax, as well as another reminder of just how far I really am from being an "expert."

The next morning I make the jungle trek back to Simpkins and discover confirmation of yesterday's sight. When I arrive at Simpkins the No. 1 fledgling is already roosting in a tree a quarter mile from the nest, while No. 2 stands on the ground closer to home, leaving only one bird on the nest. My guess is that they've already been flying for at least a week, and I try to reconstruct why I thought these birds were younger — perhaps the greater bulk of this nest disguised their own bulk. Whatever the reason, I'm now faced with an executive decision: to watch this pair or to retreat, both down the path and in time, back to the Chapin nest. It proves to be no decision at all. Having missed both the buildup to flight and the moment of flight itself, I know I need to get back to the lopsided nest, and to put in even more hours there.

Which I do. Forty-five minutes later I'm back watching the more familiar Chapin birds and, through an effort of willful amnesia, able to imagine I'm still searching for the summer's first flight. It doesn't take long to get wrapped up in the drama; after all, for these birds it *will* be the first time. They peer over the nest's edge, considering the leap, their black-and-white underwings flapping while they hop about in sometimes ridiculous fashion, treading air two, three, five seconds. Soon the time will come when one of them, the biggest, bravest, or just the one who happens to get lifted up by an unexpectedly strong breeze, will flap right over the edge of the nest. Over the next hour I count several straight hovers of five or six seconds, then a hitch, a double pump, and back up again with just a brief landing between the two "flights." I watch for the better part of the morning, but these double-clutch flights remain the day's highlight.

By the morning of July 18 I'm now overly ready to see *the moment*. But the world takes its time. Despite the birds' (and my) urgency, life won't be rushed. Nature is like an old-time storyteller moving the plot along subtly, so that the listener doesn't feel the action is being forced or rushed. The year pulses forward, moving like a good story, gradually, inevitably. With each day the beach plums blue toward purple, separating themselves from the green of their leaves, and the fall fire of the glasswort has just begun to ignite, red spreading up from the base. Life has a way of tricking you if you don't pay close attention. It's easy enough to miss the changes, though when you look back, a few weeks later, everything is different.

Today a lingering haze covers the marsh, the same thick haze that killed John F. Kennedy Jr. earlier in the week. I'm tempted to weave him into my journal notes, as he died while attempting to fly, but for once I manage to be respectful, resisting my imagination.

Instead I watch the birds. The first hour proves disappointing, as the air is still, windless, and they seem to have regressed, no longer achieving yesterday's double-clutch hovers. In fact, what the day consists of mostly is a lot of picking, preening, and lazing about in the heat. Their itchy settled life continues. Escape from itchiness adds a supplementary reason for wanting to get up into the air, as if they needed more motivation. If I'm impatient for flight, the nestlings, I suspect, are more so.

IN THIS TIME of strange coincidences, my nephew Noah provides another. It's during their summer visits that I've become friends with Noah, and we've developed a special connection. It's been fun to help him get to know this neighborhood. When Noah was a toddler he liked to grunt up at the moon, and this paganism continues in his love of sand, grass, and surf. He remains our little nature boy, spending the day naked, except when absolutely forced to wear clothes. This year, however, a change has taken place: he now speaks to us in sentences. How extraordinary to have an actual conversation with my old, mute friend. When he addresses Nina or me he carefully places our names at the end of each phrase. "What are you doing now, David?" "Are you trying to work, Nina?" "Are you ready to go to the beach now, David?"

It's hard to answer no to the last question for long. Eventually, at some point in each day, I give in, spending an hour or two making sand castles, playing with trucks, digging holes, and, when he's feeling brave, swimming. On the second day of their visit, I bring Noah down to the beach by the bluff. We dig a giant hole out on a sandbar and sit inside it and erect sand walls around us to protect from the incoming tide. He giggles as the water floods through our defenses, and we retreat to the next sandbar, scaring off a large herring gull in the process. Noah sees the gull take off and then starts running in its direction, leading with his head, a joyful goofy smile spreading across his face. He starts flapping his arms as he runs.

"Look, David," he yells. "I'm flying! I'm flying!"

From the expression on his face it's hard to doubt him. He keeps flapping and running in circles for a minute, almost tripping over his own feet, and then doubles back toward me. He slows down and comes close to explain, as if I am too dense to understand.

"I was flying, David," he says.

DESPITE HIS INTENSE EFFORTS, Noah couldn't take off. Most humans aren't as lucky as Jeffrey Plumer. During my nephew's first week with us I study hard and begin to get a handle on how flight works. Not Noah's flight, not theoretical flight, not literary flight, not shamanistic flight, but flight itself.

Think of air as a fluid. Yes, do. Then imagine this fluid streaming over aerodynamic wings, exerting pressure both upward and down. When the pressure above the wings is less than that below, the wings are "sucked" upward; when the pressure below is increased, the wings are lifted. Wings work by funneling the air downward. A bird's wings are an almost perfect airfoil, directing the air for maximum "downwash" while creating little drag. As the air is pushed downward the bird lifts up. In *The Miracle of Flight* Stephen Dalton writes, "It is rather like walking up a sandy slope — every step upward pushes the sand downward."

As I read more in Dalton's book I feel a bit like I'm the one on a sandy slope. There is something called Bernoulli's principle, which says, as best I can tell, "the faster the fluid moves the less pressure it exerts." Try placing a spoon face downward below a faucet to get the idea: it will be pulled up toward the flow, much the way wings divert air and create an easy forward pull into the airstream. Then turn the spoon face up and feel the downward pull. Because of the shape of a bird's wing, air takes longer to flow over the top, traveling faster, reducing the pressure from above. The greater pressure from below causes the phenomenon known as lift.

None of this does much good without moving air. Air has to stream over the wings for flight to happen, though it doesn't matter if it's the air or the wings that are doing the moving. That's why birds can be seen lifting straight up when the wind is blowing strong, just as you can let go of a kite in a strong wind without running. When the air flow is absent it must be created by forward movement, like a plane on a runway or flapping bird. This is why, while the osprey nestlings don't yet have the strength or coordination to provide the necessary thrust forward, a strong enough gust could catch them and blow them out of the nest, just as it did Jeffrey Plumer's boat.

It happens at Chapin on July 21. It is No. 1, of course, first in flight, as in everything. She does her pimp head bob facing south, showing me the cinnamon swath on the back of her neck. Other than that, and the black-and-white checkering on her wings, she doesn't look much different than her mother now, and it shouldn't be much of a surprise that she can fly. Still, I don't believe it until I see it.

It begins with another new development. No. 1 is watching a mob of crows stream by, turning her head as they pass, when the mother suddenly flies off the nest — just like that — out toward the water. After months of watching her sitting on the nest, involved in her sedentary marathon, this behavior startles me. It's as if she's saying, *Okay, kids, enough's enough, it's time to stop begging and fly on your own.* And, as if instantly heeding her, No. 1 moves closer to the edge and then peers over — leaning forward — looking down at the house sparrow perched on the commemorative plaque screwed into the pole. I anticipate an elaborate warm-up but she gets right to it. She shakes out and ruffles her feathers, stamps her feet a couple of times, and then, without further ado, pushes off.

A leap of faith is easier when you have wings. Even though I've been expecting it for so long, and even though I'm seeing it with my own eyes, I can barely get my mind around the sight. Suddenly, while the other nestlings look on in seeming admiration, No. 1 flaps straight toward me. The gap between six Mississippis and *this,* from jumping across the nest to full circling flight, is enormous. She flies a big lap of the marsh, looking not like a klutzy nestling but like a real bird — that is, until she attempts to reland on the nest. She misses the crossbar and then circles back and misses again. The second time she buzzes the nest, and the other two nestlings start cheeping wildly. Exhausted, she circles the marsh for another two minutes and then tries to land once more. She comes in too high and awkwardly. Not a pretty landing by any means. But a truimphant one. Her siblings serenade her with high-pitched cries as she slumps in exhaustion. She is down safe.

Learning Our Place

That summer I began to see, however dimly, that
one of my ambitions, perhaps my governing ambition,
was to belong fully to this place, to belong
as the thrushes and the herons and the muskrats
belonged, to be altogether at home here.
—WENDELL BERRY, *The Long-Legged House*

The arrival of Heidi and her family signals true summer. The house is full and bloated, six of us now, reminding me of when Heidi and I spent our fortunate childhood summers roaming around Sesuit Neck. My sister plans on staying only ten days, but it's a sure bet she'll remain longer. It's a game she plays every year, imagining she can just come up for a short trip, but then remembering that this is where she belongs during summer and getting pulled back in. We urge her to change her flight and stay, playing the game, knowing she'll plop down the fifty dollars per ticket to make the changes. We even offer to pay, which seems well worth it. For Nina, my mother, and me, having the children here changes everything. They bring relief like rain, clearing out the dark feeling that has hung in the house since my brother's difficult visit.

As the days enter deepest summer they are also becoming something else. It's a transformation I could sense even as a kid, maybe especially as a kid, with school and September looming. Now, as perfect as late July is, I feel that the weather and light will soon change, seesawing on the fulcrum of August. As with any other time of year, we occasionally daydream of what we don't have. I sometimes long for the cooler days of fall, an empty house, working obsessively on two or three projects at once. But more often I think of what we *do* have. Days of swimming, companionship, sun, evening drinks on the back deck — hot days where the weather tells you not to push it. My mother's lilies are in full bloom, and we take turns cooking dinner. Though I look forward to fall, I know there will be winter days when I look back on my sister's visit as if it were a dream.

And if I'm feeling more relaxed, it's not just due to Heidi and the kids. The pressure is off at both the Chapin and Simpkins Neck nests. By Heidi's second week, the last of July, the remaining Chapin birds are flying. Sadly, No. 3 is last again, still hopping around awkwardly while the other two flap out toward the beach and back. But finally he joins them, and the air fills with young ospreys. For months I've been coming to see them, but now they come to me. They fly right by my chair, wings beating heavily, underbellies a familiar flashing white. Though they fly uncertainly at first, wobbling slightly, soon enough they get the hang of it. Each day brings a new lesson, often a technical addition to their repertoires: banking, skimming over the spartina, hovering. They take turns lapping the marsh, staying within the basic boundaries formed by the telephone wires, creek, and beach.

If instinct gives them the final push over the nest edge and into the sky, now comes the time when learning hones instinct. Each adjustment of their primary feathers, each bank and each glide, is new, and must be mastered. And while they are surprisingly adept at moving through the air for the first time, there are also moments when they look very much like beginners. They practice landing, something that at first proves particularly difficult. One Chapin fledgling, No. 2, I think, glides low over the marsh, flaps hard to gain altitude, and hovers above the nest, the others letting loose a chorus of shrieks, like rehearsal for future territoriality (or maybe more like simple cheering brought on by excitement).

Much of the practice will serve the purpose of teaching the birds to hunt, but I fret that the fledglings will never be able to fish on their own. It's a real worry, as starvation will be a constant possibility once their parents leave at the end of August. Despite the improvement in flying, it still seems highly unlikely that these awkward teenagers will really be able to catch anything anytime soon. I've seen no evidence to make me hopeful in this regard, and they still hurry back to the nest when either parent returns with a fish.

The fish deliveries are becoming less and less frequent, however, another parental prod toward independence. If the fledglings take the hint, if they've begun to feel the imperative to hunt, then No. 3 must feel it most acutely. Age hasn't added manners, and the pecking order remains just as savagely civil as it's always been. Once I watch as No. 3, by sheer good luck alone on the nest when Mother brings home a fish, starts jabbing excitedly at the meal only to be rudely interrupted by No. 1, who flies back, tears the fish away, and then blocks out her smaller sibling with wings and backside. Something in me, some impulse toward fair play and justice, still hopes that No. 3 will fight back, winning in the end. This might happen in a Hollywood movie, but not at the nest. Deference has been encoded in his genes through the generations, and that is not about to change now, suddenly, for my benefit. The pecking order works; therefore the pecking order continues.

Not that it would please me if the birds turned suddenly sweet or saccharine. There's nothing dainty or precious about their lives; that's one of the first things I liked about them, and that's what I still like. Resting, hunting, mating, diving, plunging, building big sloppy nests, tearing into their prey—they live the way they live. For all their tolerance of humans, they are not tame. While people have often used falcons to hunt rabbits, and Japanese fishermen have used cormorants to dive for fish, it pleases me that ospreys were never trained to hunt and do the bidding of humans.

I STILL CHECK in at the other nests. At Simpkins Neck the youngsters now spend the better part of their time roosting on trees by the marsh edge, and often when I emerge from the green-briers I find the nest empty. One day, with no one home, I walk right up to the nest. It's taller than I'd imagined, maybe three and a half to four feet high, though not quite as wide as I'd thought, and it's still a wonder that four or five birds with five-foot wing-spans can live inside. Dung and trash litter a circle below the platform. It feels strange to be here without the birds, as if I'd stumbled on an evacuated town, and it occurs to me that soon all the nests I watch will be as empty as this one. Suddenly one of the fledglings appears, on guard duty, though apparently not adept at it yet, giving me a few warning cries before flying off.

The last to fly, of course, are the harbor birds, the birds I now watch with Noah. Though he doesn't accompany me to Chapin or Simpkins Neck, Noah is right by my side whenever I watch our "home" ospreys. In fact, he is right by my side most of the time I'm home, trailing me everywhere around the house. Though I've never been much of a beachgoer, his visit has changed that. Whether I'm trying to prepare my lesson plans, watch the birds, or scribble notes, he begs me to take him down to the water. In the evenings, after our beach trips, I hold him up to the telescope on the back deck, while he closes his right eye and squints with his left. He claims to see the nestlings, though I am skeptical.

"I can see your birds, David," he insists.

It isn't until the first week of August that we see the harbor birds take the big step. And it *is* a big step, bigger than the ones the young at the other nests have had to take. While the Chapin and Simpkins launching pads were twelve-foot platforms, the harbor platform is over twice as high. Noah and I happen to be watching when the last of the young birds takes the plunge. Talons near the platform's edge, he flaps and flaps, as if buying time, peering down nervously, until suddenly, abruptly, he hops forward. At first it looks like this is a mistake. Unlike the birds at Chapin, he heads down, not out, falling directly toward the ground. But then, after the initial dip, he swoops back up in roller-coaster fashion, taking a quick loop around the harbor before awkwardly regaining the nest.

As well as learning to use their wings and bodies, during these midsummer weeks the young ospreys first begin to get to know their places. The local geography is imprinting itself on the developing osprey mind, and the fledglings spend these first weeks of flight learning the particulars of their home ground.

One way of looking at what is going on out on the marshes is that the young birds are committing their neighborhoods to memory, so much so that when they fly back from South America two springs from now they will know just where to build. Now is the time the attachment grows, an attachment that will lead to an unerring pull to return, an instinct for home that is almost beyond human comprehension.

As they explore, the nest becomes less and less the focal point. Though it is still the literal center of their worlds, they spend less time at that center. In fact, Alan Poole reports a strange phenomenon in birds that live in colonies such as Westport. Often the fledglings, while out exploring, will alight on nests not their own. Neighboring parents allow this, relaxing territorial boundaries during the curious teenage years of the young birds. Knowing this, I can't help but wonder if No. 3 has considered nest-hopping over to a place where he is no longer the low man.

This learning process is not without its dangers, however.

One of these dangers is a relatively new one. As we humans have continued to crisscross our world with wires, as if absorbed in some giant game of cat's cradle, the problem of birds roosting or nesting on power and phone lines has become very real. This is particularly true for the Chapin and harbor birds, who have begun to roost right on the wires. Many ospreys even nest on the poles, which, after all, resemble their ideal search image for a nest — a tall, dead, branchless tree. The problem is that, under the right conditions, these trees can send thousands of volts through bird and nest.

Not long ago I received an e-mail entitled "Osprey Electrocutions." On first glance I took the title as a joke, some crank's argument for an avian death penalty. But then I read the message and later spoke to the letter's writer, Joey Mason, who has dedicated herself to the problem of ospreys and power lines. Working with cranberry growers (who've been extremely helpful) and with power-company workers (who've been a little less so), Joey has tried to set up various buffers and grounding devices to keep the ospreys from getting zapped. (Self-interest at least partly motivates both groups: an electrified bird can short out a neighborhood's power, which, in the cranberry grower's case, could stop their pumps from working and let their crop be destroyed by frost.) Joey hasn't had much luck finding ways to keep ospreys away once they've determined where they want to settle, in this way the birds' commitment to place working against them. Over the last three years, eleven ospreys have been electrocuted in her part of eastern Massachusetts, and Joey has assigned herself the unpleasant task of recovering their bodies. Once she found a bird so badly burned that its skin felt like the plastic bubble wrap used for shipping; another time she tried to help a young bird with burns and broken wings while the mother circled right above, calling in distress.

The problem is that the birds can often perch and even nest on the poles without harm, but if their wings make a connection between two wires the current will run through them, particularly if their wings are wet. Young birds, who are, in Joey's words, "kind of doofy when they first learn to fly," are particularly susceptible to crashing into wires. And there have been times when rain caused the nest itself to make a connection, setting whole nests on fire and burning nestlings alive.

JUST AS IT does for ospreys, the modern world works against the human urge to learn about and commit to a place. But if it is more difficult to closely learn our places, it still isn't impossible. Though his exploration lacks the birds' urgency, I believe that over the last few years Noah has been imprinting the sea and sand during his summer visits. While the red clay of North Carolina will always be home, I hope he will remember his connection to the ocean, to the smells of hot sand, seaweed, and low tide.

Perhaps I'm a little dense, but it seems to have taken me almost forty years to just begin to learn the basics of this one place. We "more often need to be reminded than instructed," said Samuel Johnson. How many times have I looked up the same bird or plant in my field guides, having already forgotten the name from the year before?

While my knowledge of bird life has gradually improved over the years, my plant knowledge remains minimal. In hopes of correcting this I invite Lee Baldwin, a guide for the natural history museum, out to the Chapin nest. Lee led me on a tour out to Monomoy Island last fall, during which I learned almost as much about the Cape's plant life as I had in my previous thirty-seven years. This visit in late July is a little more reciprocal, as I get to show her the ospreys through my scope and catch her up on the plot thus far. But mainly she plays the mentor, I the pupil, which is fine with me. It's always good to find teachers, especially those who can attach names to things you care about.

Some names she merely confirms or reminds me of, but others she teaches me. Not long ago I'd wondered what the grasses were with the tiny pinecone type clusters on top, and now she tells me they're called three-square, a sedge with the Latin name *Scirpus americanus*. She points to the sea lavender and the low clumps of beach heather, or "poverty grass," as Thoreau called it, and has me feel the rubbery salt-marsh spurry. We nibble at the edible landscape, too, the glasswort and beach peas and still unripe beach plums. This vegetable world contains medicine as well as food, including Saint-John's-wort and the tiny pink-and-white yarrow, an astringent that Achilles supposedly brought into battle to stop the bleeding of the troops. As we walk she points — shadbush, *Ammophila,* black cherry, red oak — and it's as if I'm with a mender whose job is to sew words to the world and the world to me. After two hours, Lee says good-bye, leaving me with a whole new vocabulary for my daily landscape.

AS WELL AS collecting the names of things, I've lately begun to collect hopeful examples of human commitment to place and old knowledge. In pursuit of these stories I recently interviewed Briar Cook, the husband of a woman I used to teach with. Briar and I spent an afternoon at his house bordering a salt marsh in Hyannis, while he regaled me with stories on his favorite topic: the heroic life of his father. The spartina and phragmites of the marsh grew not fifty feet from his back door; it was in those reeds and mud that Briar spent much of his childhood, and out of them that his father, Jonah, pulled much of what made up their life. When Briar was young his family owned most of the land surrounding the east side of the marsh and creek, and the stories he told paint a picture of a family living almost entirely off the marsh. Jonah Cook was the best fisherman, trapper, and amateur wrestler on all of the Cape. "He had the strongest hands of any man you knew," Briar said, "from setting traps." To illustrate he pantomimed the motion of pulling a trap apart, like a lion tamer opening a big cat's mouth. He told me how his father worked as a postman but would get up at four to check his trapline for muskrats during the season. After that he paused suddenly and, as if I had objected to the violence (I hadn't), came to his father's defense. "He never trapped a place out, though. And he got out and checked the trapline every day, no matter how sick or tired he was feeling. He didn't let those rats suffer."

They got three dollars each for a pelt, and Briar and his brother would skin up to fifty a night. By the end of the season, the cellar floor was painted red with blood. Upstairs his parents were fleshing the animals, wearing silk stockings on their hands to remove fat from the skin. There wasn't much to eat on the muskrats, of course, except for the legs, which they fried and gave to unsuspecting friends at Christmas.

"They were good, not gamy. The rats are vegetarians. One of the reasons you can catch them relatively easy is that they make a feed bed in the middle of the cattails. So you just find the feed bed and set the trap there." There was plenty else to eat from the marsh and woods and ocean. For their annual feast the Cooks piled up everything they'd shot, dug, or caught: deer, duck, raccoon, pheasant, mushrooms, blueberries, scallops, razorfish, oysters, quahogs, mussels, sea clams, and stripers.

At one point during my visit Briar's mother came out and sat with us. She told me how they collected and canned every plant and berry, how elderberry petals were gathered for wine, "though we didn't drink a lot." Then she showed me a picture of Briar as a sixteen-year-old holding a fifty-five-pound striper, as well as the one of her husband standing in front of a line between two trees, a line that held a few hundred muskrat pelts, pelts that looked as thin and splayed as bat wings. She confirmed the nearly superhuman tales of Jonah Cook: how he invented a special cone-headed wire trap, like a lobster trap, a trap that muskrats could swim into but not out of, and how that way he could catch up to eight rats at once. And she told countless more stories of his prowess and strength as a hunter, trapper, and fisherman.

I learned a lot about Briar, too. For instance, I learned that his name was born of a mistake. Jonah had always greatly admired the local high school principal, an upstanding old Yankee named Briah. Since this was how most Cape Codders pronounced "briar," Jonah first assumed that that was the man's name. By the time he named his son after the man, Jonah was aware of his original mistake, but he liked having that final *r* replace the *h,* it being more reflective of the land and the way of their lives.

On the drive back to Dennis I found myself wondering how many Jonah Cooks the modern land could handle, and realized the honest answer was "not many." Just a half dozen could take care of the entire muskrat population of one marsh, though at the time there weren't a half dozen and Briar's father was careful not to trap out his place, since he depended on the muskrats. What is undeniable is that Jonah Cook and his family lived both on and in their place. Briar, after attempting to retire to Florida, found himself drawn back here, to the place he started from, the place he was still connected to by blood and stories.

CLOSER TO HOME, I think of Norton Nickerson, who I followed on a Chapin beach walk to explore plover nesting sites this past March. Since I probably won't be gearing up to trap muskrats any time soon, Nickerson provides more of a realistic local role model for me than Jonah Cook. The plovers have recently been in direct competition with four-wheel-drive vehicles on the local beaches, and it isn't hard to guess which of these two populations is thriving. Not long ago out on Sandy Neck two chicks were found squashed in the tire tracks of an SUV, but despite the bird's endangered status, even this hasn't convinced the town to ban four-wheelers from our beaches. The battle for the plovers was just one that Nickerson, a tenth-generation Cape Codder and Tufts environmental studies professor, undertook until he died, at seventy-three, this past June. Nickerson helped write the Massachusetts Wetlands Protection Act, and, according to our town's natural resources officer, George Macdonald, "If there was an obscure plant no one in the office could identify, there was just one answer: call Nickerson."

What most interests me at the moment is the prospect of trying to follow, however timidly, in Norton Nickerson's large footsteps. It was through leading the Dennis Conservation Commission that he managed to save hundreds of acres of land in our town, and his death has opened up a seat on that commission. I've been told that much of the work for the commission is dull, such as consideration of septic tanks and sewage, and my natural instincts are apolitical, if not anti. But when I recently attended one of the commission's meetings, it rankled me how, without Nickerson, there seemed to be a wink-wink quality between the board and the developers, which prompted Nina to say, "They seem more like the anticonservation commission." I know at this point it's time to put up or shut up, but still I resist, not quite ready to throw my hat into the ring.

THE OTHER AFTERNOON, a few days after Noah's arrival, I watched as one of the ospreys' downstairs neighbors, decked out in his usual chestnut cap and black bib, stole some twig and string from the osprey nest to use in repairing his own. The larger birds, mother and nestlings, just stared, impassive and curious, at this act of larceny. That same night I stumbled upon the fact that a house sparrow isn't really a sparrow at all, but, according to our local authority Peter Trull, is "actually a European weaver finch introduced to the United States in the late nineteenth century." Part of my new education has been to differentiate between the native and the introduced, and I confess that this prejudices me slightly against the generally likable sparrow. It may be the naturalist's equivalent of xenophobia, but I find myself resenting the outside invasion of species, like the phragmites that threaten to take over our marshes and destroy their variety, as well as the phragmites' ornithological equivalent, the mute swans, the great bullies of our creeks and lakes.

I take more than a little pride in my growing knowledge of the local bird life. The other night at the Barnstable Courthouse I gave my first public talk as an "osprey expert." Since I didn't have slides I demonstrated the birds' behavior by pantomime, acting out the feeding of nestlings by tilting my head to the side and opening my mouth. One of the people in the audience that night asked me if it wasn't boring sitting out there watching birds all day. I was flummoxed for a minute, but then replied passionately. It was hard to communicate how what I've been experiencing this summer has been the opposite of boring, and how the more I learn, the more absorbing it gets. I don't know if I convinced my interrogator with my stories of birth, murder, love, and intrigue at the nest, but I'm beginning to believe in what I once thought impossible: that settling can be *exciting*.

The more I live steeped in all things osprey, and on osprey time, the more each day brings something different, often dramatically different, than the last. Not just differences in the young ospreys' size — they now look like young eagles skimming above the marsh! — but differences in weather, light, and animal visitors near the nest. One day I might see a muskrat trundling across the Quivett path, on another the Chapin male might fly so close I can hear his feathers' whisper, and yet another a platoon of ducks might riffle by, beating their wings in a motion that is the antithesis of gliding, as if expending their last possible ounce of energy. Just as important as sightings like these are the daily changes in the tides: the high-tide creek lapping against the spartina with a delicate music like rainfall, or the low tide sliding lower with the trickle of a mountain creek. I suspect I sounded like a lunatic preacher when I responded to the audience member's sensible question, but I do feel something of the proselytizer's zeal. My interrogator was actually lucky I didn't jump down off from the podium and lay hands on him. What I really wanted to say was: *You don't understand! If I can do this, if I can learn these secrets, then anyone can! You can learn Osprey, too!* Fortunately, I restrained myself.

NOW THE CHAPIN NO. 1 is dipping down over the tidal creeks, flying out toward the bay, buzzing me at my chair, and spending more and more time off the nest. Some days she and No. 2 practice aerial maneuvers like fighter pilots, dipping and flying after each other, banking and turning over the marsh. Once they even engage in a World War I–style dogfight, screeching and interweaving. This is play with serious results.

The fledglings have begun to look even more like their parents, though they are still easy enough to distinguish by their pale tail bands and more dramatic checkering. But while they *look* more grown up, they still have a ways to go. Alan Poole writes that some birds catch fish two or three days after fledging, but most are still fed by the adults for ten to twenty days. Despite the fact that they are flying with more grace, I strongly suspect that the Chapin fledglings aren't yet catching any fish.

Their relative independence has freed up the mother, however, and she now heads off to hunt on her own. The Chapin male has faded deeper into the background, spending a lot of time at his auxiliary guard post or entirely away from the nest, out of sight, apparently losing interest in the proceedings now that his offspring can fly. More and more often it is the female who returns to the nest with dinner.

When she does it's like a cry of "Ollie-Ollie-in-come-free." The fledglings return from their explorations like metal scraps to a magnet. Though they are now almost the size of their parents, the pecking order still holds. No. 1 or No. 2 will rip the fish from the mother and begin a vicious tug-of-war. Whichever bird wins no longer needs to be fed small scraps. Those days are gone. Now they tear into scales and skin with a savagery rivaling the adults'. Using their feet to pin the fish, they employ their bills as I did the pliers, pulling back with rips that should be accompanied by the sound effect of separating Velcro. Their now developed bills are one of the main ways the young birds encounter the world. I'm fascinated by the strength and versatility of the bill. Despite their hardness, the mandibles, like our fingernails, are made of keratin, a tougher sort of skin that constantly replaces itself.

YOUNG HUMANS ALSO like to explore their world by putting things in their mouths. This I learn from watching Noah. Noah was born two years and a week after my father died, my mother's first grandchild. Everyone said he looked just like my father during that first year, and it wasn't just wishful thinking (though, honestly, he also looked a lot like Winston Churchill). Now Noah and Addy help fill up this house, turning it back into what it once was, a family place. These midsummer visits are important to me, in part because they confirm something I sometimes forget: we are still a family, if a reduced one, and we still have our place and our stories.

Over the last half dozen years my family has been shaken by tragedy. This is not melodrama, just facts. After sailing along for decades as a kind of over-the-top embodiment of the American dream, we have been rocked by cancer, bereavement, mental illness, deep depression. These are not particularly unique to my family, true; they're the sorts of things we all run into once we've been alive for a while. But, unique or not, they have left me questioning, wondering just what I should do with my time left in this world. Heidi, too, has found herself asking questions in the wake of all that has happened. This coming year she will return to school, attending Duke University's Divinity School for a graduate degree in religion.

My own response to our familial chaos has been to think long and hard about how to live, searching for clues in books, in nature, and in the lives of people I admire. I haven't reached any earthshaking conclusions, but I have made a choice. While my brother remains homeless, I will make a home. I have decided that, in the face of uprootedness, I will send forth roots; that, in the face of a radically unsettled life, I will attempt to do something radical—that is, I will attempt to settle.

One of my human role models in this attempt at placing myself has been Scott Russell Sanders, who I met two years ago. In his writing Sanders offers an alternative to the two traditional psychological reactions of flight or fight, "a third instinct, that of staying put." It is that muscle—the *settling* muscle—that I've tried to develop since returning to Cape Cod with Nina.

Some might suggest that by *retiring* to Cape Cod and dwelling on these things I'm digging myself an early grave. Maybe, but then maybe that isn't such bad work for the second half of a person's life. If death is the ultimate settling, then I'm getting a jump on it. My father, it seems to me, had the right idea, asking that his ashes be spread both below the ground and on the waters of Cape Cod Bay. I'd like to be dispersed in a similar fashion (though I hope one of my braver friends will sneak some of my dust up to my neighbor's land above the bluff).

Finding a place is no laughing matter, but rather, as the ospreys know, a life-or-death proposition. I don't want "sense of place" as some fancy concept, a kind of modern pastoralism. What I'm after is an embracing of place in *all* its details, gory or not. Not a pastoral commitment but a savage one.

It has meant everything to me that Nina is getting more and more attached to living by the ocean, that the salt air has seeped into her life, too. Like the ospreys, we will ideally nest in two places, spending some of our time in the mountains of Colorado. But while I once feared being a polygamist of place — charging from coast to coast like an adulterous husband in a madcap '60s movie, passionately declaring my love for one place before hurriedly packing my suitcase to rush back and proclaim my love for the other — I now know that, to paraphrase Wendell Berry, I'm wed to both my wife and to this place by the sea. I remember what Alan Poole said about the ospreys, that their commitment to the nest might be what secures their monogamy, even more than their commitment to each other: "It seems most likely, therefore, that pairs continue together year after year because both members of the pair have a strong attachment to the same site." While I suspect this isn't true in my marriage, it doesn't hurt to love your place as well as each other. Nina shares with me a kind of tenacious pastoralism, not a quaint love of "nature" but an aggressive need to dig into the places she cares about.

I'm convinced that, no less than the ospreys, we need to stake our lives on place, even if they have to shoot us to get us out of their chimneys. If there is a degree of mindlessness on the ospreys' part, sometimes committing even though it gets them killed, we could stand to emulate some of that mindlessness. Whether we admit it or not, similar instincts operate within us: we have an instinct to build, of course, but we also have an instinct for the land, a drive to find a place and love it that is encoded in our genes. By neglecting this instinct, we banish ourselves. By living as if it doesn't exist, we kill ourselves. That we don't die immediately shouldn't reassure us. It's a gradual, long-term suicide.

Returning from his Florida exile, Briar Cook must have been relieved to be back in a landscape that had old stories attached to it. So am I. Familiar lands are storied lands. Each day when I drive to the Chapin nest, I pass the stone wall my brother and I built, bordering Willie Nick Road. I can't look at that wall the way I might any other — one in Illinois, for instance, or even Colorado —

for the simple reason that I built it with my own hands. Working for a local contractor, my brother and I lifted those stones into place, and if the wall isn't particularly artful, it's significant, at least to me. To look at it is to retrieve that sweaty August day when we hauled rocks for twelve hours, which, at ten dollars an hour, meant the most I'd ever earned in a day. If the money is long since spent, the memory is still there, available each time I drive or walk by the wall.

Here is a sad but common practice on Cape Cod: a parent dies and the children cash in, selling the family land to a developer who then tears down the house and builds another, often one that bulges to the edge of both borders and regulations. We blindly accept money as a true gauge of value, but if we stopped to think about it for even a minute, I doubt we'd be so quick to sell our heritages down the river. The ospreys have been living the way they live a while longer than we have and, I think, are a little wiser, or, at least, a little more in touch with the old ways, ways that have worked for millennia. They become part of a place as the place becomes part of them, an image resonating in their minds when they see their home again. Though their brains are much smaller than ours, they have held on to something that we, in our rush, have carelessly misplaced. On some level the birds understand that their first places are, practically speaking, places that served their parents well and will likely serve them well, too. While our images of place dim, theirs remain vivid. And following this burning picture, honed by instincts that have withered in us through neglect, they are able to find their way home.

Saving the World

For again, this old world's end is the gate of a world fire
new, of your wild future, wild as a hawk's dream
—ROBINSON JEFFERS, "The Torch-Bearers' Race"

We do not inherit the earth from our parents,
we borrow it from our children.
— Native American saying

July becomes August. Heidi, as usual, decides to stay one extra week, then two, but there is no postponing the sense that things will end soon. One day on my way to the beach to see Noah, Addy, and Heidi, I hear a familiar cry, close and loud. I look up over my shoulder and right there, twenty feet above me, just as I climb the hump of Highland Road, one of the harbor fledglings flies over my shoulder.

On the marsh, summer streams by. If you look closely enough at the plant life you can see the future, and the future is desiccation and decay. Green reddens, or withers to brown-yellow. The heads of the grasses give parts of the marsh the look of a wheat field, while the poison ivy gets an early jump on the season, edging toward a flashy red. But what really signals the change is the glasswort. These rubbery little plants rise like fuses from the marsh, and fuses they prove to be. At the moment they've just been lit at the bottom, climbing the green with early blazes of red and orange, but soon their tips will spark red, as if momentarily both match and fuse, igniting the entire marsh. In September, when the ospreys leave for their trip back south, the glasswort will explode in an assortment of blazing pink, orange, red, and the pink-purple of Western wildflowers. Sea lavender, now just beginning to bloom, demurring from the spotlight, will add more subtly to the conflagration, flaming at a lesser heat with a subtle blue-purple.

Meanwhile the beach plum, which by late August will be a deep, almost blue, purple, is still a week or two from being edible. Some are slashed with red, others the color of peach, and a precious few close to the bruised-thumb purple that signals their tart ripeness. By August's end the bayberries will have changed from green BBs into a waxy gray; and we can soon expect chittering masses of immature starlings roosting on the wires and the annual staging of thousands of tree swallows. Though nature's story is a gradual one, there are certain times of year when the plot speeds up, and this is one of those times.

I know that I won't be coming out to the nests for too much longer. As always, the end of something fills me like nothing else with appreciation. I've seen just what I'd hoped to see this spring and summer — hunting, birth, death, first flight — and while I can't complain, I still feel sadness that my osprey time is ending. I've become connected to these birds, enough so that the coming break in this connection will cause some pain or, at least, discomfort. "I have now had a love affair with terns for many years," wrote John Hay in *The Bird of Light*. It's taken me longer to use the L-word, but now that my time is ending I can't avoid it.

ON AUGUST 12 I travel to Long Island to visit Art Cooley, one of the founders of the Environmental Defense Fund. I have some questions to ask, but nothing substantial, and I'm not really sure why I make the trip. Maybe it's because I feel a debt of gratitude to him. He and his partners, after all, are almost directly responsible for the fact that I have ospreys to watch on Cape Cod. The phrase "saving the world" has become at best a kind of hip, ironic joke, a derogatory description for those who indulge in quixotic causes. But this man took the joke seriously, and, among his tangible results, he can point to the birds that once again crowd Long Island.

As the ferry pulls into Orient Point, Gardiners Island rises out of the haze. Gardiners is the place where great colonies of ospreys once nested on the ground, unthreatened by predators; the place, too, where the greatest predator of all almost wiped them out entirely, and where the birds were saved by the same species when, over thirty years ago, Dennis Puleston collected egg samples and brought them back to Charles Wurster's lab for testing. For a while the Gardiners colony was back and strong after DDT was banned, but lately there is cause for worry, as the numbers have begun to drop again. A reduced supply of fish is one suspect.

But if the numbers have fallen slightly on Gardiners, there's no question that the birds are back on Long Island. As I drive in from the eastern tip of the north fork, through a moraine landscape formed by the same glacier that scraped Cape Cod, the birds form a virtual greeting committee. Within the first few miles I spot three active nests above the marshes, and then a fourth, on a forty-foot-high platform right near the road, with three large fledglings flapping around—on and off—the nest. At one point, as the road opens up after a corridor through some apple trees, a large osprey flies not forty feet above my car with a fish, torpedo-turned, heading to his roost to eat.

The local human animals are obviously well aware of their feathered neighbors' revival. I pull into a store called Osprey Gifts, with the bird's Latin name—*Pandion haliaetus*—stenciled on the window, and then pass a vineyard called Osprey's Dominion. It's a good name, since I do feel as if I've stumbled into the bird's very dominion. I find it powerfully reassuring that the birds have managed to reclaim this particular island, sprayed in its entirety with DDT on at least four occasions. True, Gardiners, where three hundred pairs nested on the ground at the beginning of the century, could more truly be called the bird's dominion, but how hopeful that they have a foothold here, on this crowded extension of New York City.

I find Art Cooley bodysurfing at the Surf Club in Quogue. He invites me for a swim and I join him, and for ten minutes we let ourselves get tossed around by waves rolling in across the Atlantic. Considering my subject matter, it seems appropriate that I have now dived into the surf with both Alan Poole and Art Cooley. Though Art must be in his sixties, I'm struck immediately by his immense vitality. With slate-blue eyes and curly white hair, he reminds me of a larger, more fit Norman Mailer. I remember the description of him in *Acorn Days,* the memoir by Marion Lane Rogers, the secretary for the Environmental Defense Fund. "I always felt that, like LBJ's, his physical vitality helped subdue many a dissident whose point of view had been thoroughly aired," Rogers wrote. "You suspected that Art could easily pick up any offender and toss him out of the meeting bodily and this generally held perception helped keep the meetings moving briskly along."

Since I haven't offended him, Art doesn't toss me farther out into the ocean, and after we dry off, we retire to the club's deck to eat fried chicken nuggets and talk about the old days. Between bites he describes the EDF's origins.

"The founders were all scientists, but we wanted to be scientists against something," he says. "And *for* something." He talks about those days with justifiable pride while I try to imagine the excitement of the early meetings, when they moved from house to house, stayed up late into the night ignited by their ideas. When did it first begin to dawn on them that they might actually be able to *do* something about the problems they were discussing? During the late '60s and early '70s everyone was talking about changing the planet, but they set up an organization and went about doing it. I don't ask, but I secretly wonder if that phrase —"saving the world"— ever came up. Probably not. They were scientists, after all, and the emphasis was on saving a part of Long Island or a part of Michigan. But there must have been a great sense of passion and excitement when they began to discover that impotent frustration and rage could be turned into potent action, that mere enthusiasm could be alchemized into solid, effective law.

"We didn't understand the real world at first," Art says between bites of chicken. "We were more mad than bright. But we slowly started to figure some things out."

I know the story of those first lawsuits by heart, of the halting of DDT use, but I listen closely as he retells it, like a child hearing a favorite bedtime story.

"At first we never knew if we would survive from year to year, from week to week. We were a national organization to save the environment but we had no staff, no money, no officers. And the forces against us were formidable. They called us 'sexual perverts' because we were against DDT."

"But we had a lot of fight in us. Our unofficial motto was 'Sue the Bastards.' The thing is, when you're used to fighting you keep fighting. Some of us like the fight more than the victory. Once one fight is over you go looking for the next one."

He explains how, as the EDF grew, they would pull in the some of best young lawyers, recruits choosing meaning over money, content over cash. I feel like shouting "Hallelujah!" Fortunately, I manage to bite my tongue, and, at that point, one of Art's former students interrupts us. I'm reminded that the whole time he was working for the EDF he was also a full-time high school science teacher, a position he held for thirty-three years, and that within the school he founded an organization called Students for Environmental Quality, his students passing five pieces of local legislation. In fact, the Brookhaven Town Natural Resources Committee, the organization that would later morph into the Environmental Defense Fund, was founded after Cooley described a local environmental problem to one of his students. The student responded by asking, "Well, what are you going to do about it?" The BTRNC, Cooley's answer, fought local environmental battles, at first operating within more or less conventional means — letter writing, phone calls, and one-person campaigns — before discovering the effectiveness of the law.

After receiving a hearty pat on the back, the former student goes on his way. We return to our talk and the chicken nuggets.

"One of the great ideas that came out of that time was the NGOs, nongovernment organizations. These organizations have expanded the notion of democracy to a much larger group of folks. By now they've become like a shadow government that keeps lobbing in new ideas. If you're worried about your land on Cape Cod, that's what you've got to do. Get together with like-minded people and form an organization."

It all sounds so simple, maybe because it is — or at least it was for Art and his cofounders. He keeps mentioning the importance of the *idea*, the *seed*, that first led to action. He has stressed this before during our phone calls, the fact that the EDF's victories aren't as important as the idea itself. Likewise I realize that it isn't the EDF that I'm interested in — though I find what they've done fascinating — so much as the notion that Art describes, that an idea can end up having such a huge effect. Think of it: in our complicated world, a *thought* led to the physical fact that there are now ospreys flying all over the north fork of Long Island. It isn't that simple, of course. But it starts that simple. And that's what is most encouraging, as hopeful in some ways as the osprey's return. That a creative idea, followed by extensive action, could have actual worldly results.

I run out of questions fairly quickly. The truth is, he's already answered most of them over the phone or through e-mail. This trip wasn't so much about questions anyway, as it was about being in Art's presence, trying to get a little feel for the mood of those early, heady days. After lunch he walks me back to my car, still wearing just his bathing suit, and as I drive off he stands there, hands on hips, Charles Atlas–style, burly chested, smiling an even-toothed smile.

ON THE FERRY back I stare out through the haze but can't find Gardiners Island. My time with Art affects me like two cups of coffee, setting my head spinning with thoughts of my own involvement, and noninvolvement, in local politics. In the fall of 1997, half a year after Nina and I returned, a referendum called the Land Bank was defeated on Cape Cod. The Land Bank, which marked my first minor foray into volunteer politics, was a modest and sensible proposal for putting aside some money to spare the remaining undeveloped land on the Cape, to stop it from going the way of the Jersey Shore. But because that money would come from the profits of the sellers of real estate (1 percent on sales over $100,000), local conservatives decided the time was ripe for another Boston Tea Party. The real issue was that developers and real estate agents and builders wanted to keep on developing and selling and building, but of course they couldn't come right out and say that. So they pooled a pile of money and called in a big telemarketing firm from Washington that proceeded to reframe the debate entirely in terms of that highly original catchphrase "No new taxes."

In the wake of this loss I found myself feeling particularly pessimistic about the possibility of effecting change. But then a year later an altered bill that took the onus off the sellers of real estate passed, and hope returned. I do believe that deep down there is a desire, however it may conflict with the monied interests, to save at least some of the great natural bounty we've been blessed with. The question is whether or not this desire will prevail.

Like most people, I resist the dogmatic aspects of environmentalism. Other than *essayist* I don't like anyone pinning any *-ist* tails on me. But despite bristling at doctrine, I'm beginning to feel I don't have any choice except to take action. That action, political action, must soon follow the course of my newly political thought. Circumstances have forced my hand. Unless I want to turn into an embittered old man, grumbling about the big house up on the bluff, I need to do something.

As we dock in New London I make a decision. When I get back to the Cape I will fill in the card at the town office, applying for a spot on the conservation commission, the spot vacated when Norton Nickerson died. I know I can't do much, certainly nowhere near what Art Cooley did in his lifetime. But if I can't save the world, I can at least try and save a small part of Sesuit Neck.

ENOUGH STUMP SPEECHES. Time to climb off the soapbox. My real work is with ospreys, not politics. What I see at the nest during mid-August amounts to a great preparation. I have yet to witness a single fledgling coming back to the nest with a fish in its talons, but they are becoming increasingly comfortable in flight, and I'm beginning to accept that it's only a matter of time until they make their first catch. As for taking a four-thousand-mile journey to the Amazon, that's another story. Who thought up this plan? How can they possibly pull it off? To make matters worse, I know that the fledglings will be flying south unchaperoned. Through some not-so-brilliant stroke of evolution, the parent birds will leave a couple of weeks before their offspring, abdicating responsibility right before their work is done. This means that the fledglings will make their trip aided only by some mysterious inner compass, an instinct that even scientists don't pretend to understand.

Still, when I manage to quiet my worries and keep my mind from jumping ahead to migration, I find my time at the nest more fulfilling than ever. There's something purely joyful about watching the young birds improve in flight, an emotion that I sense in the birds as well. It may be wildly anthropocentric to suggest that they take joy in the movement of flying, but perhaps it isn't as preposterous as it first sounds. "Joy is the symptom by means of which right conduct can be measured," Joseph Wood Krutch said of Thoreau. We get a physiological lift from using more of ourselves, from being fully functioning, so why shouldn't the birds? In *When Elephants Weep,* Jeffrey Masson speculates that animals feel *funktionslust,* the "pleasure taken in what one can do best." I see that pleasure in the fledglings as they swoop and quarter the marsh. Or do I just imagine that I see it?

When I e-mail Alan, asking again about the possibility of the birds feeling joy, he writes back: "Who knows? Your guess is as good as mine. Maybe new fledglings do feel joy, maybe terror. Seems an easy trap for humans to ascribe our own emotions to other species, however. What does seem clear to me is that to wonder about this is distinctly human, and part of the delight of it. I strongly suspect ospreys aren't wondering about what brings us pleasure."

Cautioned, I press ahead. I think of how for us, for humans, that is, it's the times of change that give us the most animal pleasure — the change from hot to cold, cold to hot, stillness to movement, hunger to satiation. Growth excites us at a level below our brains — and can any human growth compare to the changes the birds are currently experiencing? I think of Noah, and the fact that he now speaks, and admit that the beginnings of language are an enormous leap. But flight is as dramatic. A couple of weeks ago all the young ospreys were good for was sitting on the nest and staring up at the sky. Now they soar, bank with the wind, adjust their feather fingers, glide up toward the sun. They play with each other, and while it's play with a purpose — they are, after all, learning the osprey rules — it certainly looks like fun. Though they retain the black-and-white checkering that makes them easily distinguishable from their parents, with each passing day their skill as fliers grows closer to that of the older birds.

Soon they will be developing yet another part of themselves, finally finding out what those sharp toes are for as they learn to plunge for food. With all this sudden growth, is it too much to suggest that it registers as pleasure or excitement somewhere in their avian brains? Doesn't it make simple sense, even evolutionary sense, that they should be pleased? Before they were sitters; now they are fliers. Unless we accept the notion that these magnificent animals are completely without sense, then how can they *not* feel this?

LOVE BRINGS A terrible vulnerability.

I think this every time I visit the nests, imagining the coming days when the ospreys will be gone. I think it, too, this morning as I watch Nina sleeping, curled around our two cats. And I think it again later when, out for my morning walk, I see Sukie, our Maine coon cat, dash across the road by the harbor, too far from home.

If I sometimes have doubts about the risks of love being worth it, days like today convince me differently. Because on this day in August the coyote's return to Cape Cod changes from a quick glimpse and something I have read about in books into something real. She is a husky, strong, young coyote, entirely brazen, who hunts not twenty yards from me in the big field in front of the enormous house on the bluff. In an effort to further tame our neighborhood, our new neighbor recently mowed down the wild grasses in this field, but he's brought about the opposite of his intended result. The field has inadvertently invited the wild in, the cut grass revealing a virtual smorgasbord of voles, moles, and mice. Apparently emboldened by the plentiful food and late-summer sun, the coyote isn't about to wait for nightfall to dine. After our run together, my friend Brad spots him and we watch as the coyote, ignoring us, trots, waits, and then pounces in what Brad accurately calls a "half canine, half feline" manner. After watching for a while we head home for showers, but as soon as I get home I find myself jumping on my bike and hurrying back up to the fields. The coyote is still there. While she hunts I study her varied coloring, which changes abruptly at different parts of her coat, as if by whim. Gray on the face, she is fox red behind the ears until her shoulders. Then the coloring shifts from red to gray to brown, with a strange circling marking on the saddle of her back that looks like the charred gray-white remains of a just-extinguished campfire. I stand here close to a major predator, blessed to be in her company, and when a flock of two hundred or so tree swallows flies overhead, leaving both of us, canine and human, momentarily speckled with shade, I feel doubly blessed.

Of course, the inevitable worries rush in. Be careful what you wish for, they say. A few months ago I claimed I wanted to be skinless, to experience the world more directly. Well, my skin has grown thinner through the summer. Now at times I feel like I'm virtually tingling with this place, a tuning fork of love and anger, which isn't always such a pleasant experience. Vulnerability again. Will the new owner allow a wild creature to roam on his property? How soon until he decides the wild has to be eliminated and repeats, on his small scale, our familiar national tragedy of domination and death?

"Do *wild* coyotes in the suburbs threaten your pets and children?" This was the inane teaser for the Channel 5 news the other night. But while I rush to mock that sort of alarmism, I must admit that the same question worries me. What if this coyote killed

Sukie or Tabernash? A coworker of Nina's recently saw a coyote dash across her driveway and scoop her cat up in its jaws (only to cough the pet up unharmed when the woman took chase). I'd feel a tear in my heart if anything happened to either of our pets, but not near the tear I would feel for my wife, who is more emotionally entangled with the cats. To a non–pet owner or, more accurately, a non–pet lover, this may sound like overstatement, but Nina's investment of love, both human and animal, is of the deepest sort, which opens her up to the possibility of the deepest sort of loss.

For all the possibility of that loss, I can't help but be happy, thrilled even, to be close to my predatory neighbor. Having the trickster dancing and pouncing for all to see in the newly mown front yard puts the lie to my neighbor's attempts to control the bluff. Of course, this won't stop him from trying. The other day I rode my bike up to the town office to study the plans of his attempt to "build a beach" by clearing rocks, laying down an undersurface of coconut fiber roles, and dumping in imported sand. We can only hope that, just as cutting the grass produced an opposite result, this plan, too, will backfire. Certainly the town's environmental officer thought it would. When I spoke to him about it he shook his head skeptically, certain that the winds and sea would not stand for a beach where one shouldn't be.

"It will be a nice beach for someone," he said. "For someone down in Barnstable."

BY THE THIRD week of August I notice that the wings of the Chapin fledglings are sometimes wet, sunlight tinting their soaked feathers with silver. For a week or so now they've begun to dive down into the creek between the spartina, making not full adult hovering dives but more of an insect dip and cut, as if they were giant swallows. Flight is contagious, even No. 3 getting up to speed. They try everything — gliding low right over the spartina, hovering over the nest, quick downward plunges and rises—though I've yet to see a full-fledged dive. They screech at each other as they weave back and forth, building up a good shrillness. It's a more vocal nest, though sometimes quieter in terms of actual activity. Encouraging self-reliance, the parents are bringing even less food. When they do return with a fish the nest becomes a great swirl of high-pitched begging and aggression.

For the first weeks of flight the fledglings restricted themselves to the immediate marsh area, as if respecting the boundaries of the pines to the south and the phone wires to the north. But now they flap directly out to the sea, and to the east, in the direction of Scargo Lake. More and more their primaries look frazzled, roughed up, as if wet, but I still haven't seen one return with a fish. This could be for the simple reason that many of their early dives have been unsuccessful or because if they were to catch a fish the nest would be the last place they'd go. Rather than head back to this hotbed of competition where food would have to be shared or, possibly, even torn away, they'd likely roost at a far-off tree, gorging on their own. Sometimes when I come up on the nest they're already eating, with the mother nowhere in sight, but I suspect that this is still "delivered" fish.

Eventually No. 1 gets the bright idea to simply fly off with the fought-over fish. It happens one day when No. 1 and No. 2 are battling over a flounder that, from my angle, looks first like a slice of watermelon and then like a dinner plate. Tired of having to block her sibling out, No. 1 picks up what's left of the fish in her talons and flies off for a roost in a nearby pine. While this isn't catching fish, it's edging closer.

One of the best things about this new development is that, after months of my coming out to visit the birds' homes, they now visit mine. On August 20 I have my first real evidence that the young harbor birds may actually have learned how to dive into the water and come up with fish. It is 6:45 P.M. and I'm on the back deck with Noah. The weather has cooled enough so that we both wear coats. When the light dies we begin to head inside, but my nephew stops and points to the sky.

"Is that one of your birds, David?" he asks.

I look up and see an osprey flying right over the deck with a fish turned forward, as usual, in its talons. It's hard to be positive in the dying light, but its coat looks checkered, marking it as a fledgling. I can't be sure, of course, but we could be witnessing the young bird's fist successful catch.

THOUGH ADDY is too young, I'm glad Noah gets to see the harbor fledglings fly before he goes back home. Maybe next summer we'll hike out to Simpkins Neck. Noah's dad, Mike, has a deep attachment to the mountains of North Carolina, and has already carried Noah into the woods. It pleases me that my nephew will be close to both mountains and sea, north and south.

On his last day I take Noah down to visit a friend of mine who is living temporarily on a huge boat at the harbor. I lift my nephew up over the side of the boat to hand him to my friend, but as I do I knock my sunglasses off and look quickly down. At the same moment Noah squirms and I lose my grip. He falls toward the water between dock and boat. By sheer luck I catch him right before he hits the water, but his arm knocks into the boat and he starts to cry. He is fine and stops after a short while. Still, for the rest of the day I can't stop shaking.

THE NEXT MORNING Heidi, Addy, and Noah are gone. Immediately, I miss being nagged to go to the beach. That end-of-summer, school's-coming feeling pervades the house. During my morning watch two of the harbor fledglings sit on the crossbar above the nest, looking like twins, exactly the same size, occasionally tilting their heads toward each other. Having witnessed a murder I have no illusions about brotherly love among ospreys, but still there's something companionable about their postures. I think of my easy relationship with my sister, how even when we don't say much, we are comfortable living side by side.

As September closes in, the fledglings spend less time on the nest, entering the final preparations before beginning a brutal journey from which fewer than half of them will return. The Quivett nest cleared out first, which was no surprise. In mid-August they flew off ignominiously, tails between their legs. Next come the Simpkins adults, soon to be followed by their young. I'm not so worried for the older birds, but more and more my mind jumps ahead to the fledglings' migration. I don't like to think of them making this trip; there is too much at stake, the odds too long. I can't picture them flying over the Caribbean, particularly with hurricane season coming on. They will also face an enemy as fierce, quiet, and relentless as a great horned owl: starvation. They will need to learn on the job, their fishing apprenticeships cut short. Some won't be ready.

Since the Chapin fledglings are often away from the nest—preparing for that dangerous journey, out exploring and even fishing, for all I know—I spend a lot of time at home, watching the harbor young, which is a little like watching reruns of Chapin. In fact, I've begun to spend fewer mornings "in the field," more time up in my study. I know I'm not-so-secretly preparing for the coming separation, for the distance that will soon enough be between me and the birds. My new friends will be wintering in the Amazon, and there will be no long-distance phone calls. I won't see them till next spring, and, defensively, I retreat to old habits, to writing about life, not being out in it. I'm not completely turned inward, however. The clatter of my typing is occasionally punctuated by a sound made sweet by repetition—high-pitched and pleading. Then I stop working and lean back and close my eyes and listen.

When I do get back out to the marsh I catalog the many

changes. Starlings, while not particularly beautiful, impress with sheer numbers as they belly up to the phone wires. They gather in a great squeaking mass on the sand shelf behind the osprey nest. For all our wonder at the ability of animals to "live in the present," they are always looking ahead, anticipating the next season, the next step. Now, as the world prepares for movement, the tree swallows begin to stage. By mid-August they were already practicing, sky-skimming the marsh. With their darting flights and boomerang wings it's as if they were carving the air into sections, and by month's end hundreds of them fill the air, spilling across the sky. From a distance they look almost exactly like the swarms of insects that they feed on.

The vegetable world continues its changes, too. The sea lavender begins to show its colors, spouting tiny purple buds, miniature bouquets that look like red paintbrushes that have been briefly dipped in white. Meanwhile the beach plums play out their increasingly edible story of daily change. In late July I was first willing to call them blue, though on closer inspection, the blue proved a chalky mirage, easily rubbed off with my thumb, leaving them green as peas. But more and more the blue stuck, then purpled, until finally, by August's end, they were the deep purple of Concord grapes and I was regularly popping them into my mouth, savoring their tart sweetness.

The seedy head of the three-square, the sedge that Lee Baldwin first identified for me, moves from green to a lighter green to yellow, giving the fields a wheatish complexion. The marsh is slowly cycling back to where it was when I first came to it in February. Then I watched the land move from brown to green, and so now I witness the change from green to red-yellow and back to brown. While I'm not coming out here as much, I appreciate just what a fine thing it was to be outside through the spring and summer. Alan Poole was right: sitting and watching the birds is a discipline, a practice. Like all acts requiring patience, it isn't easy. But it can become habitual, and many mornings I went automatically through my routine: making my tea, stretching my back, driving out to the beach, pulling on my ridiculous knee-high rubber boots, hiking across the marsh with my telescope over my shoulders, unpacking my backpack, unfolding my chair. I know I'll miss the ospreys when they leave. I miss the routine already.

I've been absurdly lucky to see all I've seen. Maybe it's as simple as this: when you expect the miraculous, the miraculous occurs with regularity. Or maybe it's a cycle. Having witnessed the miraculous again and again, I come to expect it. If grace is an unexpected blessing conferred, then there is also a sort of moment of wonder that you earn by putting yourself in the right place. By coming out here every day I've seen more than merely being lucky would have ever gotten me. One evening in August I stood up from my chair at Simpkins, ready to pack it in, when behind me, in the marsh elder bushes, I saw a large buck, the biggest I've seen on the Cape. It noticed me and vaulted into the bushes, then hard into the pines. I was left standing there, listening to the electric pulse of crickets stopping and starting, thinking how that sight had returned me to a better, older place.

If you listen to the world long enough you will hear what it asks for, and it turns out to ask for quite a lot. It calls for nothing less than a new way of looking, a new way of being. I need to continue to find a new way to be in this world, to develop what Jack Turner calls a "sacred rage." In the spirit of Art Cooley, I need to learn to love the fight.

But at the moment I don't feel like much of a crusader. The first hints of fall cool the summer nights. There are still days when you feel the full summer heat, but there's no kidding ourselves. We are at the end of something.

Living by Water

Yes, as every one knows, meditation
and water are wedded forever.

—MELVILLE, *Moby-Dick*

On Labor Day Nina and I go to the beach. Not for the day, or for a week even, but for the coming year. It is the time of migration, after all, and I, like the fledglings, am belatedly leaving my parent nest. It isn't much of a move really: just down the street and still smack in the middle of Sesuit Neck. But it is a change. For the next eight months we will be house-sitting for a neighbor, settling less than a hundred feet from the water. In doing so we'll be leaving my family house behind and actually wintering in a winterized house.

We lived close to the ocean for the last two years, able to see the harbor and part of the bay; now we will live *on* it. By doing so, we have traded sunrise for sunset. In our old house I could watch the red ball rise over the harbor each morning. While we've lost the morning's rebirth, we gain a new ritual, witnessing the daily sinking of the sun behind the bluff, sizzling into the ocean.

For Nina living on the shore makes all the difference. No longer does she talk about longing for the mountains. Though not usually given to mystical assertions, she can't help herself after several days and nights of falling asleep and waking to the lapping and crashing of waves. "There's something religious about it," she says. "I think I'd always like to live near the ocean." With the buoys ringing like church bells and the staging swallows spiraling upward from the lawn, it's hard to disagree.

Even our cat Sukie takes to the ocean, placing her forepaws up on the window sill and staring out at the watery horizon for hours, like a sea captain's widow. We stare, too. "You never get bored when you have the ocean as your backyard," says Joe Buscone, the owner of Northside Marina. "It changes all the time, like staring at a fire." From my study window, I watch the sea in all its moods —heaving and crashing, pond calm, lit up fiery at night, sacred yellow at dawn. I look forward to the violent, white breakers of winter.

When I look out the west windows I see a different sight. The new house on the bluff rises right above us now; we live in its shadow, like the quarters of a serf. The owners have begun building a second house, a five-thousand-square-foot "guest house," the construction starting just in time to ruin autumn. Despite this, I like being next door to the new building, and not just because it means that a five-minute walk brings me to the base of the bluff. By moving here I have dramatically simplified my life. Everything I love and everything I hate is close at hand. It's as if I've strolled inside of a myth, or a comic book, complete with a blessed land and an archenemy. I now reside within a vastly simplified cosmology.

IT'S BEEN A great summer for comebacks, and not just that of the ospreys filling our neighborhood as they never have in my lifetime. As I write this the Red Sox are nipping at the heels of the Yankees, and seem a lock for the wild card (though you never know with the Sox). Better yet, earlier this summer Lance Armstrong won the Tour de France, in doing so fulfilling the classic hero's journey of returning from the underworld. Near death from

cancer that began in one of his testicles and wracked by chemotherapy, he returned not just to health but to victory in one of the
world's great tests of endurance and power. He exemplifies the
thrill of the comeback: hope renewed improbably after it has been
seemingly, finally, extinguished. We rejoice when the near dead
live again.

With the season over, I read about another osprey comeback,
this one in the Scottish Highlands. Ospreys once built their nests
atop ruined castles and towers throughout Scotland—where,
according to George Waterson, they were known in Gaelic as
"*Iolair-uisig* or 'water eagle,' or often just as *Iasgair,* meaning 'the
fisherman.'" But by the end of the nineteenth century the bird was
in serious trouble. Philip Brown, who played Boswell to the osprey's Johnson, writes, "The story of its extermination is particularly sordid, often characterized by an almost satanic malevolence."
The culprits were egg collectors, poachers, and gamekeepers,
(who saw the birds as competition for their master's fishing interests and had free range to shoot a bird they considered "vermin").
The exploits of the egg collectors, in particular, were the stuff of
vicious myth. They roamed the countryside like sadistic children,
and there are great tales of poachers, like the Scot Lewis Dunbar,
(a kind of real-life Groundskeeper Willie), who swam across
frozen lochs in winter and shimmied up trees to claim the eggs.
Then there were the more highbrow murderers, like Dunbar's
companion and sometime employer Charles St. John, who fancied
himself a "great lover of nature" and often expressed remorse after
killing birds or stealing their eggs, as he does here after shooting a
female bird: "As we came away, we still observed the male bird
unceasingly calling and searching for his hen. I was really sorry I
shot her."

Despite their occasional pangs of conscience, the collectors
managed to all but wipe out the bird by the beginning of the
twentieth century. Ospreys still passed through Scotland, however,

and there were even some attempts at reintroduction (notably by our old friend Captain C. W. R. Knight in Inverness-shire in the early 1930s). Then, in the early 1950s, unconfirmed reports began to trickle in that ospreys were nesting by the lochs in Spreyside. Of course the egg collectors caught wind of the reports and were soon up to their old tricks. But in a effort to thwart the poachers, and to ensure the reintroduction of the species, a small band of naturalists, bird-watchers, scientists, and enthusiastic amateurs, led by George Waterson and the Royal Society for the Protection of Birds, set out to protect a pair that had built a nest at Loch Garten. For three years in the mid-1950s these efforts failed; one of those years the clutch was destroyed by crows, another by poachers. Describing the crow-robbed nest, Philip Brown writes, "For a few days the birds went on building the new aerie in a more and more desultory way until they finally abandoned it." *Desultory,* it occurs to me now, was the perfect word for the Quivett pair.

And *desultory* would describe the Loch Garten nest the next year, too. That year Waterson and company built blinds near the nest of the single pair that had returned, and they manned the blinds round the clock. Despite this, one night a poacher managed to sneak in, grab the osprey eggs, replace them with painted hen eggs, and make a run for it. After the chase, during which the poacher dropped one of the eggs, Brown writes, "I spotted a patch of white amongst the moss and stooping down, picked up the smashed egg of an osprey. . . . It contained a partially developed embryo."

The next winter, according to Brown, "George Waterson never got ospreys out of his mind." Obsessed with playing midwife to the birds' return to Scotland, he prepared for the spring breeding season as never before. Citing the Protection of Birds Act, Waterson helped push a measure through St. Andrew's House that made the area surrounding the failed nest into a bird sanctuary. But more had to be done; this was war. He sawed branches off the tree that held the aerie in a hopes of defending it from both predators and collectors, and ran barbed wire around the tree's base. Then he laid wood planks called "duckboards" over the boggy ground below the nest so he could better give chase to poachers, built a base camp, and, finally, drummed up volunteers who would stage the round-the-clock vigils necessary to protect the birds. "All these preparations took up much time and energy," writes Brown, "but by early April all was readiness." The ospreys, however, didn't cooperate, deciding to rebuild at an earlier site. And so the whole operation was disassembled, moved, and rebuilt. Then Waterson, Brown, and others settled down to living on osprey time, watching and waiting.

That year, 1959, all their work finally paid off. Somewhere during the first or second week of June, three young osprey nestlings hatched in the Loch Garten nest. I have at least some inkling of the joy and pride the watchers must have felt. Soon these feelings were shared by hundreds, then thousands of others. Waterson, figuring that the ospreys would draw curious and potentially threatening sightseers, decided to make the whole affair public, setting up a special blind through which those interested could see the birds. Fourteen thousand people took him up on the offer during the remaining weeks of that first breeding season. Ospreys were suddenly stars, not just as tourist attractions but as the subject of magazine articles and newspaper editorials. One result of the Loch Garten story, according to Brown, was that "it exposed the egg-collectors in their true colors," and, "Public opinion came out strongly in favour of the osprey and those who were striving to keep it on the Scottish map." The next two summers saw successful nests, as well as forty-one thousand visitors, Art Cooley among them. By the early 1980s, there had been over a million visitors to Loch Garten, and close to a hundred osprey pairs now nest in the Scottish Highlands.

• • •

THERE IS SOMETHING doubly hopeful about the ospreys' comeback. It assures us not only that we can change but that, even more importantly, we *have* changed before, giving us confidence in our future adaptation. For, if we're honest, we must admit that it isn't just their comeback that concerns us but our own. We are currently deep in a hole, a hole of our own making. If we are to climb out of this hole, a radical transformation will need to take place, a transformation that allows us to save other species as well as ourselves. Some scoff at the possibility of that transformation. But the proof is in the past. We need only look at the last hundred years for evidence of similar changes. While I hardly believe in the perfectibility of human nature, I do believe that its possibilities stretch a little further than we suspect at our most cynical. I believe, in other words, that we can aim our natures in different directions, that we can put our natural traits—our curiosity, our nosiness, our intelligence, our intrusiveness, our industriousness, our fidgety restlessness—to different, dare I say, *better* uses.

I need to believe this. Threats to the ospreys change with the times. It used to be nest robbing, then DDT, and now (while DDT still threatens) destruction of habitat. Though we have learned to frown on the practice of stealing eggs, we still smile at the prospect of building our dream house, regardless of how many other nonhuman dream homes we destroy in the process. While there aren't as many egg poachers around, there remains a basic human type—acquisitive, meddlesome, destructive, greed-driven—a type we all at least partly recognize when we look in the mirror. As an antidote to high-mindedness, I remind myself that some of the culprits of years past were the naturalists. Guns, not binoculars, were once the tools of natural history. The old motto for those who studied birds was "A hit is history / a miss is mystery," a "hit" meaning a shot bird. Audubon, after all, didn't paint those beautiful birds while they sat posing for him. Had I written this book a century or two ago, I might have included a chapter on what it felt like to shoot an osprey. The trick, of course, is to anticipate what we will find barbaric two hundred years from now. It's easy to frown on the past, easy to judge what is gone; its harder to look toward the future.

There is, in the end, something reassuring in the fact that the Scottish ospreys, once something to be shot and exterminated as vermin, are now looked upon with awe and reverence. And this change occurred in only a hundred or so years. This adaptability on the part of human beings suggests that future adaptability is possible, that we may be able to even more radically adjust our thinking. And this, to me, seems the single most hopeful thing about *Homo sapiens*. We can *change our minds*.

BY EARLY SEPTEMBER the fledgling ospreys are rarely at the nest. In hopes of seeing the young birds dive, I've abandoned the nests, too, spending more time up at Scargo Tower, the stone castle that locals (falsely) claim is the Cape's highest point. The landscape below takes on the clarity of a map: the fish-shaped lake, the trees, and, beyond, the shore and bay, our house, the bluff. Last spring I biked up here and witnessed a spectacular dive: tucked wings, a rocket plunge from a hundred feet up, though the splash was blocked by the shore trees. On that day the oak leaves were just beginning to fill, creating small islands of green, and the air sweetened with honeysuckle, lilacs, and autumn olive. Now full leaves sough in the fall wind, a green island around the tower, their sharp edges outlined in silver. I climb up to the top, armed with binoculars and scope, and I'm greeted immediately by two young red-tailed hawks involved in a serious game of tag. One dives straight down into a stoop at what looks like terminal velocity, then pulls up and easily glides back into a loop-the-loop, flashing breast and belly that shine as white as a gull's. The other follows, just as bold, just as artful. I wonder if this is the same pair that my friend Billy, who lives nearby, saw not a month ago. Then they were just learning to fly, putting everything into flapping from one tree to the next, while their mother led them, coaching and cajoling. Now they can do anything they want in the air, being the only raptor in the East that manages to stay "still" in the wind, not hovering but, to the eye, motionless. When one weaves through the tree line, the other follows effortlessly, their colors rapidly alternating from the brown of their tails to the whites and marsh reds of their undersides. Later I see two young ospreys at the far end of the lake, but they seem no more interested in hunting than the red-tails do, perhaps for now content just getting to know their fishing grounds. Anyway, for one afternoon at least, the ospreys aren't the main event. It's strange, but after immersing myself in the natural world for the last six months, I'm just beginning to see how little I really understand about the lives of my neighbors. The work of immersing is endless: once you start you may never stop. My osprey year could lead to a red-tail year, which could lead to a great horned owl year, which could lead to a muskrat year. That's the joy of it, too, that the wonders and work are inexhaustible, that there is no chance of ever getting complacent, of ever *being done.*

"The secret of life is to have a task, something you devote your entire life to, something you bring everything to, every minute of the day for your whole life. And the most important thing is—it must be something you cannot possibly do!" So said the sculptor Henry Moore in Donald Hall's *Life Work.* If I start now with ospreys and work my way through a season each with my animal neighbors, I'll still only begin to scratch the surface. But what a satisfying sort of scratching.

As I scribble down notes in my journal I sometimes refer to Scargo as the "hawk tower." It's a romantic, literary name, but Scargo Tower can stand a little of the sheen of romanticism. Local high school kids piss inside the tower, shatter bottles in the parking lot, and scribble graffiti on the inner walls. (My own name,

buried under sedimentary layers of spray paint, links me forever
with Jody Cushman.) Worse still, legions of tourists court heart attacks by huffing up the hundred or so steps each day. But right
now I have the top of the tower to myself as the fall light polishes
the edges of leaves and the summer season comes to an end.
Clouds scumble the blue sky, and waves ripple across the pond,
painting it a deep dark blue that you never see during midsummer,
even on the stormiest days. The wind is from the northwest, perfect for early hawk-watching, and sure enough another large red-
tail soon flies by. He, or she more likely, judging by her size, lifts
straight up in front of the tower, less than a hundred feet in front
of me, wings almost completely still, making only occasional ad-
justments. Her alignment into and with the wind is fascinating:
the way she pulls in her wings, tilts slightly, then glides straight
up—with fingertip control—riding the updraft. She stays perfectly still for a minute, then lifts up and down in yo-yo fashion.
Finally she soars off, dropping from the height of the updraft toward the ocean, her wings held up in the slight V called a dihedral.
I, watching from the top of the hawk tower, have to resist the urge
to hold my arms out in flight. Then, what the hell, I don't resist.
No one is around, after all, so here, on the high point of the Cape,
on the edge of the continent, I hold out my arms as the day blows
south through me.

As I open my arms my jaw slackens and drops in that common, almost cartoony reaction we humans have in the face of the
awe inspiring. A question: why is it that, at times like this, our
bodies quite literally open us up to the world? Is it simply a case of
wanting more of the world inside us or is it just the opposite—an
emptying out of ourselves, our clutter, into something larger and
greater? Both, I'm pretty sure. Whatever the answer, I feel freed,
momentarily, from my own cluttered brain. For that I thank the
hawks.

• • •

"ECOLOGISTS SPEAK of an 'edge effect,' the concentration of animal life that often occurs where two different habitats abut," writes Alan Poole. "Ospreys are part of this phenomenon, a shore and coastal bird, their life woven between land and water." Fred Dunford, the museum archaeologist, visits the beach in front of our house and explains how so many rocks came to be deposited on the sand below the bluff, the point I now walk to every day. Likely the land out our back door was at the very edge of an Ice Age glacier when it began to withdraw north twenty thousand years ago. The rocks fell from glacier's edge or were carried down in rushing snowmelt.

The season, too, is one of edges. As true fall arrives we enter a time in-between, a season that's both the beginning and the end of something. The cranberry harvest approaches and the smaller birds train hard for their coming migrations, putting on fat and practicing formations. We've been blessed by the tree swallows, who stage right in our new front yard. Hundreds of them, sometimes thousands, swirl as if blown by a storm, white stomachs shining, as Nina and I run to the windows, transfixed by the whirlwind of birds. They blaze by the house like something thrown and scattered, readying for their enormous journey. They rise, dart, circle, their shadows spraying over the lawn.

Less dramatic, but perhaps more amazing, are the monarch butterflies we now find along the edge of yard and beach. They will travel, if they are lucky, in a fluttery but more or less straight line, from here to their winter roosts in the mountaintop forests of central Mexico, averaging over a hundred miles on a good day. If we stop to think about it, this is not something we easily believe, like being told a scrap of Kleenex will migrate to Veracruz by December.

In mid-September the migration of the ospreys begins. I've been readying myself for the young ospreys' departure for some time, but it still catches me off guard. It occurs to me that mov-

ing away from the harbor may have been an unconscious pre-
emptive strike, leaving the birds before they could leave me. I still
go to the harbor nest daily, of course, but they are rarely there.
Then one evening during the second week of September, just after sunset, two of the harbor fledglings visit me at the bluff.

Even before I see the ospreys the walk is memorable. For the
last week the waters in front of our new house have been boiling
with small silver slivers of fish, and dozens of terns, in response,
wheel and dart down into the surf, immersed in a great orgy of
feeding and death. As I walk past this tumult, I notice that several
groups of human fishermen have tailed the birds: two boats are
anchored not far from our front yard, and two young kids, brothers it looks like, run along the shore to throw their lines in the
midst of the commotion. The water they dip their lines into, and
into which the terns dive, is the furthest thing from the ordinary
midday blue. It's a blue-and-yellow striped ocean, illuminated
eerily by the molten star that is now dropping toward the bay.
These strange bands of light are not restricted to the water but also
flash across the sky and clouds.

The boys seem to be having some luck, as are the terns, and
soon I do, too. Just after I walk around the corner of the bluff and
the fishermen vanish behind me; just after the sun disappears behind a cloud, then reappears as a thin blazing-red slice before descending into the sea; just then I see the little fawn with the white
spots on its side. White also paints the insides of its ears, its throat,
and the undersides of its legs and tail. It sees me and begins a surprisingly clumsy getaway, almost tripping as it staggers over the
rocks, moving, improbably, not toward the bluff but toward the
water. I sit down on a rock and try to keep quiet. It wades into
the surf, then actually swims a little way, before continuing to
wade another hundred feet west. After a while it stands quietly,
still almost shoulder deep in the water, watching me as if waiting
to see how I will respond. Living on osprey time has its advan-

tages, and I employ my newfound patience, sitting still, not moving a muscle, until the fawn finally pulls itself out of the water, on the other side of the rocks, and hurries for the cover of the bluff.

Once the fawn is safe, I decide to emulate it. Protected from the fisherman by the turn of the bluff, I strip off my clothes and stumble across the wet rocks. Gradually, awkwardly, I make my way out into the ocean, past the black massed clumps of seaweed, and swim in the same water the sun sets into.

I don't last as long as the fawn did. The cold autumn nights have begun to make the bay better suited to quick plunges than long immersion. I climb out and use my clothes to dry myself, then quickly dress. At that moment I receive the summer's last gift. The sun has just slipped under the water, that final dip coming fast the way it always does, as if it were trying to sneak away, when I see the birds flapping strong and steady, traveling east along the coastline. They are large birds and they come right toward me. Their crooked wings beat out that stiff motion that the authors of *Hawks in Flight* call "arthritic," a wing beat that now acts as a signature for me, a signature saying "osprey." Even in the silhouette of dusk, they are unmistakable. Then, as they pass right overhead, I'm almost sure I make out the checkered markings of the immatures, though it's true that I may be seeing things. Anyway, I choose to believe they are the fledglings returning to the harbor nest.

I watch the two birds fly off into the distance, sticking to the coastline, flapping by the little beach then over the jettys, back toward my family's house. Several times they slip in and out of sight, the black lines of their wings slightly raised and kinked against the sky. Then they fade in and out again before disappearing completely.

The Off-Season

Though I've been fortunate enough to witness many miraculous sights, there always remains more unseen than seen. In *Living on the Wind,* Scott Weidensaul writes that on one fall night, some years ago, twenty million songbirds were recorded migrating over Cape Cod. *Twenty million!* And yet, for all I see on these nights, there might be ten birds, or two, or none. For proof of my denseness I need look no further than the fledglings, who have already slipped my field of vision. Though they are surely fishing by now, I still haven't seen a single catch. The nest no longer serves as the magnet it once did, and their lives are scattered, while I, lacking spring's energy, have given up the chase and turned to other work. Alan Poole writes, "Once they are independent and feeding themselves, no one knows exactly where young Ospreys go." I certainly don't. We are falling out of touch, me and the birds, my osprey season ending even before they leave. Much of what they do now, including the four-thousand-mile migration that will begin any day, will be invisible to me, accessible only through books and my imagination.

The trouble is that the books seem even more fanciful than my imaginings. I read all the theories about what prompts their coming journey—instinct, food, the tilt of the earth, fading daylight—and I read about what guides the birds—sun, stars, ancient pathways, earth's magnetic field, and some mysterious inner compass—but the truth is, I can't even begin to understand migration, not just the why of it but the how. I suspect that no one else, no human being, that is, really understands either. That's because it just doesn't make sense, not *human* sense, at least.

John Hay wrote of terns, "They seem to me like explorers from a great outer world from which we have been excluding ourselves." It's a world unknown to us, yes, but just how is it known to the fledglings? How will these birds, which I saw take their first balky flights not more than a month and a half ago, actually fly down to Brazil, *on their own*? How can they fly over a sea, the Caribbean, that they have never seen? It seems not only preposterous but wrong. Wrong to expect this of these still-beginning fliers, asking too much, like forcing a toddler to cross the Mojave.

Yet they will do it. Or some of them will. Though perhaps somewhat "arthritic," and not always aesthetically pleasing, the steady wing beats of the ospreys will serve them well over the next months. They will seek out thermals, those columns of hot air that rise above our unevenly heated earth — above parking lots, for instance — and will lift faster than other raptors, then glide down these hills of air, riding the fall's northwest winds, or they will head inland and soar on the updrafts of inland ridges and mountains. But unlike hawks, they will not be reliant on thermals and will even migrate directly over water, unafraid of offshore routes or long crossings. European ospreys routinely cross the Sahara Desert and the Mediterranean. In these instances their strong steady flapping helps; while most hawks soar, ospreys, with their long, narrow wings, are built for plugging away. And while many birds build up stores of fat to live on during migration, ospreys hunt along the way, fishing as they go, sometimes even carrying a fish snack along with them. Though they tend to migrate alone, they will occasionally pass overhead in pairs and concentrated groups, sometimes dozens of them, not for any social reason as much as the fact that they happen to be riding the same rivers of wind.

The mature birds know the route not just instinctively but by eye; they are aware of landmarks, Alan Poole explained to me last spring, the same way that human beings get to know the routes we travel. The fledglings, on the other hand, will be dealing with winds and crossings and lands that they know only through some ancient internal map. For those of us who refuse to believe what we can't see, here is irrefutable evidence of the invisible: the young birds, the ones who make it, will fly thousands of miles until they somehow recognize a place they have never been to, and something within them will say "home." Then they will settle in this ancient wintering ground that they have never seen, a fact that's surely a hundred times stranger than fiction.

THERE IS NO exact moment when I say good-bye, no long dramatic last wave as they flap into the sunset. The Quivett adults are long gone by late August, and the next to leave are the Simpkins adults. Since I now visit the Simpkins nest only about once a week, I can't put an exact date on the departure of the young. All I know is that each time I return the evidence of their having been there at all grows fainter, except of course for the great shaggy flag that is their nest. The same holds true at Chapin. One day in September the fledglings are here, the next gone. Or that's not it exactly: for many days the Chapin nest stands empty, though I suspect there are fledglings lurking, roosting, in the pines on the edge of the marsh. But then a day comes when the place feels even emptier, and I sense, I *know,* they are truly gone.

At my home nest, over the harbor, the birds hang on until mid-September. They were late fliers and will therefore be late migrators. I bike over from our new home, just down the street, visiting them every day, until one afternoon I find the nest empty. The platform looks strange and, though I know I'm projecting again, *mournful,* the dark green garbage bag billowing and one long piece of rope hanging down below the nest, swaying in the wind. The harbor nest actually appears more deserted than the other nests. These were the lazy, good-for-nothing ospreys, after all, the punk-rock ospreys, and the nest was never very deep or well built, more like a tossed pile of enormous pickup sticks. But if they didn't pass muster as architects, the harbor pair, in the end, surprised me, proving fine parents, raising three fledged young despite my lack of faith.

Though I now try to follow the birds imaginatively, even looking at Internet projections of migratory routes and numbers, the truth is I prefer to avoid the statistics, particularly the ones that tell me that almost two-thirds of the young will never see Cape Cod again. Also, it's best not to think too hard about weather reports. On September 15, a day or so after the harbor birds leave, Hurricane Floyd lands in the Carolinas. My sister and her family, who live in a house in Durham where trees threaten the windows, head to Charlotte to hunker down in my mother's house as the storm lashes the coast. It will be harder for the ospreys to avoid Floyd, which cuts a path four hundred miles wide, unusual for a hurricane. As Alan Poole said to me in the spring, sometimes it's just bad luck that does in the birds. I hate the precariousness of it. After the endless care and feeding and work of the summer, it could all end arbitrarily, thanks to the timing of a storm.

The next morning, September 16, with the hurricane due to hit us that night, I yank on my trusty marsh boots and head out to Chapin. Over the last two days Danny Schadt has been pulling boats round the clock down at the marina, and as I drive along the beach road landlords are nailing plywood over the windows of summer rentals. The leaves have begun to stir, though it isn't just the wind that's in the air but also that communal hurricane excitement, human beings scurrying and preparing. As I walk down the road to the marsh I remember a dream from last night: I was watching a storm from the roof of our house with my father, both of us laughing as huge frothing breakers welled up in a Technicolor green-blue sea.

I climb down into the marsh, goldenrod spraying yellow everywhere and beach plums falling off their branches, the few that hold on colored a deep juicy purple. I hike to the Chapin nest through what are now surreal fields of glasswort, red and orange, and even a pretend purple color like Play-Doh. By contrast the sea lavender, growing near the hump of sand where I parked my chair all summer, is a mature adult shade, subtler. Today I don't stop at the sand but march right up to the nest, something I didn't dare do once this summer.

Twenty feet from the nest I come upon the guard post where the male spent many of his aloof hours. It thrusts up five feet tall just above the tallest spartina. Beyond this outpost rises the platform and nest, sprouting out of another spongy field of blazing red glasswort. The nest looks smaller than I imagined, and again I wonder how the birds dipped and hid down in it. A week ago I took a ladder and tried to climb up inside the Quivett nest but found it surprisingly flimsy and unstable. It barely seemed to have any depression at all. The depth I'd hoped to get to the bottom of was shallower than I ever would have believed. No van Goghs in Snoopy's doghouse, no billiard tables, no heated pool.

Now, staring at the ground below the Chapin platform, a thought comes unbidden: *This is where the body of the runt must have fallen.* Of all the wonderful sights I saw this past summer, it's the one truly savage sight that I won't ever forget. I assume that the corpse has long since been dragged off by a fox or raccoon. But, just in case, I get down on my knees and push aside the thick glasswort, searching, though mostly hoping I don't find it. And I don't, of course, though I do find sections of rope and some bones and enough sticks to build another nest with. Also several pieces of old fish skin looking reptilian and scraggly, hanging from a bush like the clothes of a scarecrow.

On the way home, around 11:00 A.M., I climb up to the hawk tower at Scargo. From up here the whole world is chopped off by fog, and Scargo itself, the fish-shaped lake, seems a a big bowl of gray vapor. The oak leaves stir, whispering of the winds to come. Usually I'm a great fan of storms, secretly wishing they'll blow as strong as they can: I like the group excitement, the way a storm simplifies our focus. But today the hurricane seems a great destroyer of purpose, bringing chaos to plans both avian and human.

I'm pleased when the hurricane proves a false alarm, at least for us. After all the anticipation, the winds that come off the sea blow less strong than those of a dozen winter storms. Nina and I actually sleep with the windows open that night, waking occasionally and staring out at a sea that never comes close to rivaling the one I saw with my father in last night's dream. The next morning, the 17th, the house remains intact, as do my illusions about the safety of the fledglings. The winds that blew over Cape Cod were not much stronger than the winds we watched the jetty ospreys nest through the first spring we were back, and that is encouraging. Nina says, "Since I'll never know what happened, I'll choose to believe that they survived." I nod, choosing to believe the same. Choosing, that is, to be hopeful.

I HAVE A complicated relationship with hope. For one, I believe that hope itself is a more complex emotion than we give it credit for these days. When we speak of *choosing* hope we are in particularly dicey territory, allying ourselves with suspect forces. There is something artificial about the notion, something that reeks of Hallmark cards, positive thinking, and self-help gurus.

My father prided himself on being a realist, on not giving in to the fluffier sentiments, and my father is still very much a part of me. My sister and I sometimes fault my mother for the way she deals with my brother, for her insistence, despite the facts, that he seems to be doing better, and getting healthier. She sends him money and support, while I find myself wishing my father were here, being tough, imposing economic sanctions, cutting him off. But mine is just a fanciful solution to an unsolvable problem, a fantasy much more fanciful than my mother's. The truth is that my mother is the better parent for the job, even if the job is one that drains her beyond exhaustion. When I, assuming my father's voice, play the realist, she pleads with me to stop. "I need to have some hope," she says. "I can't keep doing this without it."

I know what she means. While it's easy, in the abstract, to deride the Disney-like quality of "hopefulness," in reality when we lose hope we lose energy. Look at the Quivett nest for evidence: at the purposelessness and dawdling once hope was quashed. This even my father would have had to agree with, if not in theory then in life. "Without hope there is no endeavor," said that great realist Samuel Johnson. But *with* hope our energy surges, infusing us with verve and the excitement of possibility. Hope is the juice we drink, a juice we need if we are to fight on, to struggle. And hope is a physical trait, found in the body. My mother's great gift is her strength, an almost animal vitality, a force that works particularly well in the morning. No matter how difficult the circumstances, how crushing the news or mood of the night before, she usually rises the next day hopefully. She would agree with Thoreau that "morning is when I am awake and there is dawn in me," and I would, too. For all that my father's voice still rings in my head, when I wake I am my mother's son. If you asked me to create a picture of hope I would take out my brush and paint a freshly wakened man or woman with their first cup of coffee or tea in hand.

Hope can't be falsified. The things we look to for hope had better be as solid, or more solid, than the things that bring us despair. Scott Russell Sanders recently wrote a book called *Hunting for Hope*. His litany of reasons to be hopeful included wildness, craft, family, art, and beauty. To that list I would add "ospreys." My season-long experiment in neighborliness has also been, almost inadvertently, a lesson in hope. I don't mean just theoretical hopefulness, based on the fact that the birds have returned from near extinction, but something more basic. In the wild lives of these birds I have seen a daily reflection of the animal vitality, tenfold, that I describe in my mother. They wake each day eager to live, to grow, eventually to leap off the nest and fly. *Hope* is far too pretty and precious a word for the raw drive for life I witnessed at the nests, the pure vital surge to exist. Maybe with the word *hope* devalued, we need to find another, more savage term. Something that better describes the pure green surge of the thing, like weeds pushing up through concrete or a nestling gaping for fish.

ON OCTOBER 13 I take a long walk with John Hay. Since I stopped by his hand-painted sign on the day of my bike survey, I've spoken to him several times about getting together. In his eighties now, John warns me that he will be able to hike only a couple of miles. He wears baggy khakis, a green wool shirt, and a faded orange baseball cap. Before we walk we visit the natural history museum, where he asks me advice about moving the osprey platform away from the main path, in hopes of finally having a successful nest. I'm flattered by the question, and try to give my voice unfelt authority when I suggest moving it back to near the tree line, forgetting for a moment about the threat of the great horned owls. Our next stop is Paine's Creek, the mouth of the herring run and the source of so much of John's early writing. We sit down in the wrack line and listen to the waves lap, and he tells me how he would sometimes come here with Conrad Aiken at sunset and drink something they called orange blossoms, a mixture of gin and o.j.

"Aiken said it was like a sacrament," he says. "There's something to it. It's like a ritual."

I nod and tell him that I know what he means: I think of

drinking beer and grilling meat with Hones, of our own rites and rituals.

He explains that it was Conrad Aiken who first drew him to Cape Cod. How not long after their first meetings, John bought the land on the hill where he still lives, a small house on eighteen acres of wood.

"When I first came here it was a worthless wood lot," he says. "They measured it wrong and called it ten acres and we got it for twenty-five dollars an acre."

As we watch the gulls, I picture his return after World War II. I find myself wondering, What was it like that first fall when he glimpsed the unimagined richness of the place he'd chosen to settle? It must have entirely caught him off guard, and when the marsh turned gold and the swallows swept overhead, he must have sometimes laughed out loud at his good fortune.

From the creek we drive over to my father's grave. We walk down the path to the spot near the marsh elder bushes where I watched the Quivett nest all spring. Though we both curse the invasive phragmites, today they sough beautifully in the light wind, and the sun tints the canopies of oak silver. Inspired by the weather, we begin to hike down to Crowe's pasture, just planning on going a little ways at first but then making the whole trip to the beach and back. For me, of course, this is much more than a mere walk. My favorite stories are of returning to an older home, of finding a home on earth, and that's the story John Hay has told on this land that I know. While so much of modern literature is about alienation, Hay has stuck to an older theme: that of homecoming.

At the beach we sit on clumps of seaweed and stare out at the sea. He mentions how the eagles near his house in Maine will wait on a branch and watch an osprey fish and then, the fish caught, ambush the smaller bird until it drops its meal, which the eagle scoops up. Unlike ospreys, who eat only what they catch, bald eagles are no better than gulls in this regard, picking at carrion as well as stealing. It was because they often performed acts of piracy on fish hawks, Hay explains to me, that Benjamin Franklin objected to having the bald eagle as our national symbol. "They should have picked the osprey," I suggest, more than half seriously. As I walk I happily picture an osprey flag, symbolizing rebirth and regeneration, as well as commitment to our nests.

We walk for over two hours, until I've broken a sweat and have begun to wonder if I will be held accountable for doing in my literary hero. But he seems strong and in good spirits, better spirits than when we began. Near the end of the walk, when we're almost back to my car, he points up at a mockingbird on a branch.

"Strange to have come through the whole century and find that the most interesting thing is the birds," he says. "Or maybe it's just the human mind is more interesting when focusing on something other than itself."

FOR ALL THE PLEASURE it brought me, our walk was not pure nature rhapsody and profundity. One thing we both did a lot of was grumble. Grumble about the state of the planet, about the almost suicidal human insistence on ignoring other species. For at least part of our walk, aggressive pessimism was the order of the day. The Cape provides a handy microcosm for the crowding of the world, the bullying of the rest of us by the monied, and the destruction of nature. His own eyesight now dimming, John Hay seems frustrated by the lack of vision in most people, a blindness to both natural beauty and to consequences. As Thoreau said at the end of *Walden:* "The light which puts out our eyes is darkness to us." We lack the penetrating vision of birds of prey.

Of course I know the usual reasons for pessimism; at times I'm overwhelmed by them. The list is familiar: thinning ozone, ballooning population, acid rain, species extinction, depleted resources, the death of the wild. Perhaps one of the reasons I've spent so much time focusing on the ospreys is that they give me hope, while so many other things I might focus on would bring despair. Maybe, to paraphrase John Hay, the human mind isn't just more interesting but more hopeful when focusing on something other than itself. Whatever the case, these birds have made it easier to feel hopeful.

On October 15 I make my last pilgrimage of the season, heading down to Cape May, New Jersey, to watch migrating ospreys. This trip, like so many of my excursions, is inspired by Alan Poole. He e-mails me to say I shouldn't miss the chance to see the rivers of hawks flowing overhead, funneled by the winds and the contours of the coast. "One golden day in October, I watched 800 Ospreys flying south along the coastal dunes of Cape May," he wrote in his book.

My friend Brad Watson joins me on the trip. We pile into my station wagon at 5 A.M. and get to Cape May by 1:00. He drives the last hour while I read to him about hawks. The reason the skies are so crowded in certain places during migration, as best I can tell from the reading, is a little like the reason the Garden State Parkway is more crowded than the surrounding woods and marshes — it's where the road is. Certain established routes, routes with a prevalence of updrafts and thermals, create virtual hawk highways through much of the fall. Cape May, jutting south from New Jersey into the ocean, is a turning point for many birds. When the land ends, they must decide whether to proceed directly south over open water or to cut west for a shorter water crossing, toward a more inland route. The ospreys are more likely than the other birds to cross stretches of ocean.

We check in at the hotel and then head directly to the Cape May Observatory hawk-watch platform. A chalkboard below the platform announces the season's highs: one day 16,386 sharp-shinned hawks flew overhead; another, 5,038 kestrels. This year's osprey record is 225 birds on October 2, but once we climb up on the platform we learn that this will not be one of those glorious days. Northwest winds (meaning northwest is the direction the wind comes *out of*) are best for hawk-watching, ushering the birds south, but yet another hurricane brewing off Florida has the winds blowing from the south. The mood on the platform is apathetic. Instead of rivers of birds, there is an occasional trickle. Still, I happily set up my scope with the other watchers, pleased by the dozens of people living on osprey—or at least hawk—time. The low level of activity actually helps me get acclimated. Laura Moeckly, a young guide with a pretty smile, points out the landmarks—the cedar top they call the poodle's head, for instance—and assures me that I'll see some ospreys. Armed with thousand-dollar Russian binoculars, she and the other interns identify birds before I can even see them. They're able to make out small differences between the nearly identical sharp-shinned and Cooper's hawks, for instance, from miles away. While the sky doesn't blacken with birds as I'd hoped, I do learn a lot. Laura points out a great egret roosting in a nearby tree and a Eurasian wigeon with a reddish-pink head, as well as flocks of cormorants and scoters flying low out over the ocean.

Around three o'clock a report comes back that an osprey was seen landing near Lighthouse Pond, just a little ways down the trail into the marsh. Scope over my shoulder, I run out the boardwalk between the phragmites in hopes of spotting my first osprey in over a month. Sure enough, when I get to the little viewing area, the friendly couple who are already there point out the roosting bird. It perches in a dead tree, occasionally stabbing down at the mackerel that it pins between its claws, welcoming me with familiar savagery.

It feels good to be hanging with an osprey again, and just this one view assures me the trip was worth it. Birders have a reputation for being competitive, but Anne and Larry Craig, the couple with whom I watch the osprey, prove anything but. When Brad joins us they point out a merlin as it comes flapping by with its hard angry beats, slamming against the wind; the chunky little bird with the amazing flight abilities lands on a branch forty feet from us. Later the Craigs show us a falcon who slips through the air with easy fluid strokes. In turn, once I have my scope focused, I dispense some osprey wisdom. I point out that it's an immature bird, with the telltale checkered wings, something they haven't been able to see through their binoculars. They leave around dusk, and then Brad heads back to the main deck. I spend a half hour alone with the fledgling, as if reestablishing an old bond. Though it is only a one-way bond, I now realize how much I've missed the birds.

The next morning the wind is southerly again. It would have been nice to see streams of hawks, but that's okay. Leaving Brad at the main platform, I walk back out to Lighthouse Pond early. Alone at the viewing deck I try my hand at telling accipiters apart, relying on yesterday's knowledge. Then I watch another great egret stalk his way across the pond, revealing the water as actually no more than the depth of a puddle. I close my eyes in the sun and listen to the phragmites rustle in the wind. When I open them I scribble down these words in my journal: "My trip to Cape May is proving a bit of a dud." It's right then, of course, predictably, that I hear the noise and turn to my left. It is yesterday's osprey, the immature, flying down above the phragmites, not twenty feet over my shoulder. He swoops over the shallow pond, then loops up into the sunlight, banks right, and begins flapping off toward the ocean.

Back at the platform, Brad and I listen as Glen Davis, another hawk-watcher, tells a story of how a merlin flew below a redstart, turned itself upside down while flying, and came up on the other side of the bird, in position to receive it like a baseball catcher. Glen suggests that the redstart died of fright before the merlin's talons even touched it. Later in the morning we see a sharp-shinned hawk turn a quick pirouette below the platform, and later still we watch another "sharpie" (in birder lingo) being banded, its beautiful striped tail fanned and its yellow eyes shining fierce.

Before we leave that afternoon I'm treated to one final sight. Laura, calling out birds to a large group of Saturday watchers, points to an osprey flapping right toward the platform. Watching the bird, this one an adult, I'm struck by the laboring of its wing beats, in sharp contrast to the falcon's fluidity, the merlins slamming, or the several flaps and then glide of an accipiter. It looks like work; there's no easy gliding as he flies right over us. Once he crosses above, the other bird-watchers turn back to the north, and, following Laura's directions, they see a turkey vulture, with its dihedral V-shaped wings and rocking flight. But I keep my telescope aimed south, trained on the osprey. The bird flies directly out over the ocean. It may not be flying into the sunset, but this will be as close as I get. Which is fine. For the experts here at Cape May, who have seen clouds of hawks, days when they get blisters on their thumbs from clicking their counters, this is a "bad day." But mine is a more modest project, and deserves a more modest end. A bad day for these people is a good day for me. I had to wait a month, but I finally got to say a true good-bye. This will be my last osprey of the season.

I take a swim in the breakers before we head back in midafternoon. Our migration home is made easier by a couple of leftover Sierra Nevadas and the fact that the baseball game crackles through the static of the radio, coming in more clearly as we head north. I drive the whole way, almost straight through, listening as Pedro Martinez shines for the Sox and Clemens is booed out of Fenway. For the moment tomorrow doesn't matter. The ospreys are flying home, and the Sox have finally beaten the Yankees. All is right in the world.

• • •

WE RETURN HOME to a Cape long empty of ospreys.

Though I'm always quick to sing paeans to wildness and wilderness, the truth is that I live in suburbia. It's a strange sort of suburbia, however, a suburbia in which most of the population deserts their houses each fall. These fortunate humans, wealthy enough to migrate, leave their summer homes by the ocean to retreat inland for the winters. Cape Cod has always been a place for migration. Fred Dunford, the archaeologist at the natural history museum, explains that before Europeans came the local native tribes would likely spend from late fall to spring in the wooded uplands of the Cape, then migrate to their summer camps right on the coast, where they could take advantage of the abundant seafood and cooler weather. Like the ospreys', these human migrations were prompted by food and temperature. Whether they know it or not, the crowds that clog our bridges during summer are reenacting an ancient ritual of seasonal movement.

Thanks to the migratory habits of many of my neighbors, Sesuit Neck now takes on a feel that, if not exactly rural, certainly comes close. Houses stand empty, and starlings outnumber humans. Fall is the best time on Cape Cod. To be more exact: October, specifically these last two weeks, are the halcyon days, heralded in this morning by slow-flying kingfisher that rattles up over the bluff. For weeks now cranberries have spotted the wrack line, left over from late September, when off-flow from the bog cut a small canyon through our beach, adding the roar and trickle of a mountain creek to the steady breaking of the waves. This is also the time of year when the sun begins to set behind the bluff. All through the warm months it drops into the bay, but, as the winter solstice approaches, it slides south, its final descent blocked by land.

On the first cold morning I take my tea to the beach, the liquid losing its heat before I'm halfway done. Last night's full moon still shines crisp, its light easily burning through a blue-black cloud. Wind chimes the flagpoles and plays the music of distant harbor masts—and of sheets and tackle and anything else that moves, a clattering symphony. I walk around the house to where I will keep my friend Billy's kayaks this winter. As with a lot of things on Cape Cod, these are seasonal possessions, now up for grabs. We reclaim them just like we reclaim Route 6A, our houses, and the privacy of our walks. The other day I saw J.C., my fellow scavenger, by the ocean. Cold reddened our cheeks and sand stung our eyes, and the lifeguard chair and beachballs were long gone, but he smiled a wide, wild smile. "It's our beach again," he yelled to me over the wind.

Which is exactly how I feel. Cape Codders call this the off-season, and while this label may just be a ruse to scare away the hordes, there is something perfectly askew about the name. It's a time when whole trees squeak with starlings, when swallows mob the beaches, and when the annual miracle occurs: the people leave just as the weather gets most perfect. Days yawn before you as time widens and slows. No wonder I grow anxious each Memorial Day, the crowds signaling that the yawning days will end. For the time being, cold protects us. Nina and I ready ourselves for the adventure of settling. Of slowing down. It isn't only the kayaks we have back but the neighborhood, the beach. We can rest easy, knowing houseguests won't be reappearing for another eight months. Up at the post office, as the marsh decks itself out in the flamboyant colors of decomposition, we humans assume the grubby, drab clothes—the old jeans and sweatshirts—of fall. But we smile at each other more freely now that there are fewer cars in the parking lot, as if all of us were in on a giddy secret.

Of course, I don't want to entirely glorify autumn. The bluff near my house isn't just a great place to collect sentences. It's also a good place to find death. The cliffside dirt slopes down to a point of shoreline that is one of the rockiest along the bay side of Cape Cod, the rocks reaching out into the sea and acting as a giant strainer, catching everything the tides drag in. In addition to the seal and porpoise cadavers last spring, I've found northern gannets with wingspans wider than I am tall, their web feet shriveled, and brants with necks like a skin diver's gloves, and cormorants, and, of course, many gulls. Recently I've also seen my share of injured birds that will not be alive come Christmas, and the other day I found a monarch butterfly with a torn orange wing that won't be making the trip south. I picked it up on my finger and felt a sharp pang, and then, my thoughts turning back to other things, I tried to flick it off. But couldn't. It clung with a remarkable ferocity to my finger.

The few ospreys that remain in the north, most sick or injured, will likely die during the winter. The United States does have a few nonmigratory populations, in southern Florida and along the Gulf Coast, but none anywhere close to this far north. Sometime in November our neighborhood birds, with luck, will settle along rain-forest rivers, in Brazil perhaps. There those that have survived the long trip will spend the winter by the mouths of estuaries, where shallow waters provide an abundant source of food. Or they will settle farther inland, alongside the rivers that twist and turn through the forests. Either way, this will be for them, as for me, the most sedentary and least eventful time of the year. They will stick close to home, roosting, resting, and fishing until February.

Meanwhile I, four thousand miles to the north, prepare to greet winter. As the weather starts to hint at hibernation with more fervency, I think back to a sight I saw one day outside my window this past summer. It was a squirrel asleep in a round hole in the knotty post oak, curled all the way around itself, its head turned inward so that the whole of it formed a letter G. I envied the squirrel, how well it fit into the world around it. My dream would be to spend this coming winter settling into my place just as surely as the squirrel. But I'm not a squirrel, or even an osprey.

I'm a human being, and a particularly self-conscious one to boot, a creature of too much thought and contradiction, who will never fit in place as snugly.

That said, I'll keep trying. After my osprey season, I feel ready for the off-season, ready to settle. I am where I belong, and as I withdraw inside my place, memories of the spring and summer still warm me through winter. And not just memories, of course, but anticipation of spring. I know that gradually the sun will work its way back north, until it once again settles each night into the bay. Then the year's turn, the sun's slant, will spark something in the wintering ospreys, and, prodded by instinct, they will start the long journey to Cape Cod, the cycle of movement and mating beginning again. They will fly north seeking a match for the image that burns in their mind's eye, and I will be here waiting for them, confident that they will be back. I believe in their return.

Bibliographical Note

Before listing the books I read during the composition of this book, I would like to make special mention of two volumes in particular. The first is Alan Poole's *Ospreys: A Natural and Unnatural History*, which was indispensable to me, particularly in the early stages of my becoming acquainted with ospreys. If I have sparked anyone's interest in these magnificent birds, I strongly recommend this comprehensive, well-balanced, and beautiful book. Not only did I lean on Alan's book, but I soon discovered that many of the other contemporary osprey texts did as well.

The other volume is *The Return of the Osprey* by Brown and Waterson. Waterson was the determined midwife of the birds' return to Scotland, and I certainly mean no disrespect in my own choice of title. I had been working on my book for several months and had gotten quite attached to the working title when I discovered his wonderful book.

Most of the other books listed in the following bibliography deal with either birds in general or ospreys in particular, but, obviously, the reading that helped me build a book of this sort was only partly ornithological. As mentioned in the text, my own sentences relied heavily on the sentences of those who have gone before me. First and foremost, I have learned from that great teacher Walter Jackson Bate, who, sadly, died during this book's writing. His books—*Samuel Johnson, John Keats*, and *The Burden of the Past and the English Poet* among them—have been vital to whatever intellectual development I've undergone. Bate's work is particularly brilliant with regard to the use of past models in helping ease the crisis of self-consciousness in the modern artist.

One of Bate's chief lessons is the necessity of moving bravely toward the writers we most admire. For me those writers include John Hay, Scott Sanders, Reg Saner, Terry Tempest Williams, Jack Turner, Wendell Berry, Peter Matthiessen, Gary Synder, Barry Lopez, Annie Dillard, Edward Abbey, Robert Finch, Wallace Stegner, and John Elder. If I have stumbled close to their own themes, it was admiration that drew me near. In my journey to discover my place in the world, their works have been indispensable.

Selected Bibliography

Abbott, Clinton G. *The Home-Life of the Osprey*. London: Witherby & Co., 1911.

Audubon, John James. *The Birds of America*. New York: Macmillan, 1937.

Bent, Arthur Cleveland. *Life Histories of North American Birds of Prey*. New York: Dover, 1937.

Berry, Wendell. *Recollected Essays*. New York: North Point Press, 1981.

Brown, Leslie, and Dean Amadon. *Eagles, Hawks and Falcons of the World*. Vols. I and II. New York: McGraw-Hill, 1968.

Brown, Philip, and George Waterson. *The Return of the Osprey*. London: Collins, 1962.

Burton, Maurice. *The Sixth Sense of Animals*. New York: Taplinger, 1972.

Carpenteri, Stephen D. *Osprey: The Fish Hawk*. Minnetonka, MN: North Word Press, 1997.

Carson, Rachel. *Silent Spring*. Boston: Houghton Mifflin, 1962.

Coon, Carleton. *The Story of Man*. New York: Alfred A. Knopf, 1954.

Dalton, Stephen. *The Miracle of Flight*. Buffalo: Firefly Books, 1999.

Davis, Burke. *Biography of a Fish Hawk*. New York: Putnam, 1977.

Dorst, Jean. *The Life of Birds*. Vol. I. New York: Columbia University Press, 1974.

Dunford, Fred, and Greg O'Brien. *Secrets in the Sand: The Archaeology of Cape Cod.* Hyannis: Parnassus Imprints, 1997.

Dunne, Pete. *The Wind Masters.* Boston: Houghton Mifflin, 1995.

Dunne, Pete, Debbie Keller, and Rene Kochenberger. *Hawk Watch: A Guide for Beginners.* Cape May: Cape May Bird Observatory, 1984.

Dunne, Pete, David Sibley, and Clay Sutton. *Hawks in Flight: The Flight Identification of North American Migrant Raptors.* Boston: Houghton Mifflin, 1988.

Elder, John. *Imagining the Earth: Poetry and the Vision of Nature.* Athens, GA: University of Georgia Press, 1996.

Eliade, Mircea. *Shamanism: Archaic Techniques of Ecstasy.* Princeton: Princeton University Press, 1964.

Forbush, E. H. *Birds of Massachusetts and Other New England States.* Amherst: Massachusetts Department of Agriculture, 1927.

Guss, David M. *The Language of the Birds.* San Francisco: North Point Press, 1985.

Hay, John. *The Bird of Light.* New York: W. W. Norton, 1991.

———. *Nature's Year: The Seasons of Cape Cod.* New York: An Audubon/Ballantine Book, 1961.

Jeffers, Robinson. *Selected Poems.* New York: Random House, 1963.

Knight, C. W. R. "Photographing the Nest Life of the Osprey." *National Geographic,* vol. 62 (1932): pp 247–60.

Kurtén, Björn. *Dance of the Tiger: A Novel of the Ice Age.* Berkeley: University of California Press, 1987.

Lanyon, Wesley E. *Biology of Birds.* Garden City: Natural History Press, 1964.

Leahy, Christopher. *The Birdwatcher's Companion.* New York: Bonanaza Books, 1982.

Lear, Linda. *Rachel Carson: Witness for Nature.* New York: Henry Holt, 1997.

Mercatante, Anthony S. *Zoo of the Gods: Animals in Myth, Legend and Fable.* New York: Harper and Row, 1974.

Nigg, Joe. *Wonder Beasts: Tales and Lore of the Phoenix, the Griffin, the Unicorn, and the Dragon.* Englewood, CO: Libraries Unlimited, 1995.

Pearson, Gilbert, ed. *Birds of America.* Garden City: Garden City Publishers, 1936.

Peterson, Roger Tory. *The Birds.* New York: Time, 1963.

Poole, Alan. *Ospreys: A Natural and Unnatural History.* Cambridge: Cambridge University Press, 1989.

Price, Anders. "The Osprey." Kalakotkas.com. This Web site is particularly helpful regarding the osprey in literature.

Puleston, Dennis. *Blue Water Vagabond.* New York: Doubleday, Doran & Company, 1939.

Richardson, Robert D. *Emerson: The Mind on Fire.* Berkeley: University of California Press, 1995.

Roberts, Mervin F. *The Tidemarsh Guide.* New York: E. P. Dutton, 1979.

Rogers, Marion Lane. *Acorn Days: The Environmental Defense Fund and How It Grew.* New York: Environmnetal Defense Fund, 1990.

Sanders, Scott Russell. *Staying Put: Making a Home in a Restless World.* Boston: Beacon Press, 1993.

Schlaer, Robert. "An Eagle's Eye: Quality of Retinal Image." *Science,* vol. 176 (May 1972).

Short, Lester L. *The Lives of Birds: Birds of the World and Their Behavior.* New York: Henry Holt & Co., 1993.

Skutch, Alexander. *The Minds of Birds.* College Station: Texas A & M University Press, 1996.

Snyder, Gary. *The Old Ways.* San Francisco: City Lights Books, 1977.

Snyder, Helen, and Noel Snyder. *Raptors.* Stillwater, MN: Voyageur Press, 1991.

Teal, John, and Mildred Teal. *Life and Death of a Salt Marsh.* New York: Ballantine, 1969.

Thomson, A. Landsborough. *A New Dictionary of Birds.* New York: McGraw-Hill, 1964.

Thoreau, Henry David. *The Maine Woods.* 1864. New Haven: College and University Press, 1965.

Turner, Jack. *The Abstract Wild.* Tucson: University of Arizona Press, 1996.

Van Tyne, Josselyn, and Andrew Berger. *Fundamentals of Ornithology.* New York: Dover Publications, 1971.

Wilson, E. O. *In Search of Nature.* Washington, DC: Island Press, 1996.

Acknowledgments

For her tireless work on and enthusiasm for both the idea and the manuscript I would like to thank my editor, Antonia Fusco. Thanks to Art Cooley, one of the founders of the Environmental Defense Fund, who gave his time and energy to help me understand the EDF's beginnings and how those beginnings intertwined with ospreys. For their help with my research I would like to thank Mary Sears of the Ernst Mayer Library at the Harvard University Museum of Comparative Zoology, Kathy Tuxbury, Lee Baldwin, Gus Ben David, Joey Mason, Norton Nickerson, Bob Prescott, Dennis Murley, Laurel Duuda, Anders Price, and Pat Pratson. I leaned heavily on my great neighborhood resource, the Cape Cod Museum of Natural History, where my thanks go out to Nancy Church, Fred Dunford, Eric Levy, Deborah Diamond, and, of course, the museum's founder and inspiration, John Hay. Thanks to Peter Thombly for supplying fish, to Laura Moeckly and Glen Davis at the Cape May Observatory for helping me see the birds, to Eileen and Pres Bagley for keeping a roof over our heads. Also thanks to Mark Honerkamp, Don MacKenzie, and Briar Cook for lending me their stories. And to Brad Watson, Dave Rotman, Jon Kenton, Brady Udall, and Pat Bellanca. And many thanks to my agent, Lisa Bankoff.

This book would have been impossible without the help of Alan Poole.

ACKNOWLEDGMENTS

Thanks to Heidi, Noah, and Addy for the summer visits that light up our year. And many thanks for the indispensable love and support of Georges and Carol de Gramont and Barbara Gessner. Finally, as always, a thousand thanks to Nina.